Coping With Information Illiteracy: Bibliographic Instruction For the Information Age

Papers Presented at the Seventeenth
National LOEX Library
Instruction Conference
held in Ann Arbor, Michigan
4 and 5 May 1989

edited by
Glenn E. Mensching, Jr. Instructor
University Library,
Eastern Michigan University
and
Teresa B. Mensching, Director
LOEX Clearinghouse
Eastern Michigan University

Published for Learning Resources and Tehcnologies
Eastern Michigan University
by
Pierian Press
Ann Arbor, Michigan
1989

ISBN 0-87650-267-2

Pierian Press
Box 1808
Ann Arbor, Michigan 48106

Library Orientation Series

(Most volumes are still in print;
the two out-of-print volumes are designated.)

Table of Contents

Articles

Symposium

Instructive Sessions

Poster Session Abstracts   123

Discussion Group Handouts and Sample Materials   155

Bibliography   184

Participants   198

PREFACE

by Glenn E. Mensching, Jr. and
Teresa B. Mensching

The Seventeenth National LOEX Library Instruction Conference, sponsored by the LOEX Clearinghouse at Eastern Michigan University, was held on 4-5 May 1989 at the Ann Arbor Inn, Ann Arbor, Michigan.

The theme for this year, "Coping with Information Illiteracy: Bibliographic Instruction for the Information Age," was chosen in order to explore some of the issues or problems generated by the information explosion of the 1980s and 1990s. Recent advances in technology have allowed for rapid access to information. Yet, for researchers trying to choose from the variety of sources of information, in print or electronic format, this can be a great source of frustration. Discussion about information literacy has been appearing more frequently in library literature. Throughout the conference, speakers offered various definitions of this term, providing librarians with an opportunity to formulate their own ideas for programs to battle the problem of information illiteracy in their libraries. We identified the theoretical underpinnings of information literacy, methods of instruction for teaching students to choose the appropriate source(s) or reference tool(s), the role of microcomputer instruction to allow access to various indexes in electronic format, and how to evaluate sources of information. Evaluation was only briefly discussed in this conference--the 1990 LOEX Conference will be a full workshop on this topic.

The speakers who were asked to give papers at the conference brought with them years of experience and knowledge about bibliographic instruction. Patricia Senn Breivik gave the keynote address and has written extensively on the subject of information literacy and gaining the support of academic administrators for programs. Breivik recently served as chair of the American Library Association's Presidential Committee on Information Literacy.

The conference program was comprised of speakers on specific issues in information literacy. Jan Kennedy Olsen and Bill Coons described Cornell University's information literacy program, a prototype of integrating information literacy into department curriculums. Harold Tuckett is an expert in microcomputer literacy and learning theory.

Trish Ridgeway has had many years of experience using active learning techniques with undergraduates. Sandra Yee has led and developed a program at Eastern Michigan University to encourage minority student retention. Rebecca Jackson is the BI coordinator at one of the first large academic institutions to redesign their library instruction program based on the revised ACRL Model Statement of Objectives.

The conference ended with a symposium on the controversy surrounding instruction programs that focus on short-term or long-term goals and how this question relates to information literacy. Richard Feinberg is a proponent of manageable, short-term instruction for library use; Carolyn Dusenbury, active in bibliographic instruction since the 1970s, delivered her observations of instruction for lifelong learning.

Speeches by major speakers are printed in the order in which they were presented. Editing for style was minimal to maintain the flavor and originality of each session. Readers are reminded that spoken presentations will always vary in readability.

Specific instructional methods and the evaluation of sources were addressed in the instructional and poster sessions given in addition to the major speeches. In a departure from tradition, speeches from the brief twenty-minute instructive sessions have been included in their entirety. The abstracts from poster sessions and accompanying handouts have been included.

The LOEX Clearinghouse most gratefully acknowledges the contributions of the following companies: Baker & Taylor, Blackwell North America, Mountainside Publishing, Pierian Press, and University Microfilms International. Thanks also go to individuals who assisted in conference preparations: Carolyn Kirkendall, Martha Perry, Vicky Young, Keith Stanger, and Morell Boone. Special thanks go to each conference participant--your enthusiasm really made the conference a success!

Glenn E. Mensching, Jr.
Instructor, Learning Resources & Technologies

Teresa B. Mensching
Director, LOEX Clearinghouse

Information Literacy:

Revolution in Education

Dr. Patricia Senn Breivik

It did not occur to me until after I received the printed brochure for this conference that my inability to be a supporter, any longer, of library instruction may make me an inappropriate speaker for the 17th Annual LOEX Conference on Library Instruction. When I spoke at the fourth LOEX Library Instruction Conference in 1974 I was a very strong supporter of library instruction and continued to be so for many years. I have even written two books on the subject, which were major undertakings of love. I now believe, however, that library instruction encompasses too small a concept for the needs of education in an information society.

Library instruction by its name implies that it is instruction for use of libraries only. It implies that its value only extends as far as the walls of libraries. (The only thing worse is bibliographic instruction, which if you ask the uninitiated, has something to do with writing bibliographies.) Now you know, and I know, that good library instruction has always transcended what its name implies, but we need to ask ourselves whether part of the almost total invisibility of libraries in the educational reform reports, that started with *A Nation at Risk*[1] in 1983, has to do with how we position ourselves and by the labels we attach to our work.

And yet I am talking about more than simply a label. I am talking about how we go about our instructional activities, what our goals are, how we do our planning, and how we evaluate what we do. Perhaps I can best explain what I mean by telling you of a visit I made to Littleton High School, outside of Denver, last fall.

The school had produced an outstanding strategic plan that, with very great insight, looked at

Breivik is Director of Auraria Library.

the educational demands at the secondary level in an information society and addressed the changes that needed to occur. Implied throughout that document was a new and expanded role for the school library media center, but nowhere did the words library, librarian, or information literacy appear. When I met with the principal and we began exchanging ideas, he immediately saw the missing element that I was representing and asked me to come meet with a group of teachers and curriculum coordinators to talk about library instruction. He and the school librarians provided me with some good background information, and I also knew that there were real library supporters among the teachers. Key among these was the social studies curriculum coordinator, who alerted me right before our formal time together that he was going to be asking me how to move beyond the treasure hunt of the freshman year into a structured library instruction sequence for four years. That was, in fact, the first question asked, and my response was that he was asking the wrong question.

I then proceeded to talk about the need for active learning, learning that prepared students for lifelong learning by allowing them to become familiar with and effective users of the information resources that would be available to them throughout their lives: books, journal articles, television, online databases, government agencies, and others. We talked about expanding the walls of the classroom to encompass the learning resource center and further to encompass the community. A number of the faculty stayed around after the others had left, and one of them commented that they had invited me for the wrong meeting. I should not have been asked to speak about library instruction, he said, but to meet with their school restructuring committee. They well understood, and agreed, that we were not talking about an added-on instructional component on how to do library research, but rather what we had been talking about went to the very core of how their school is organized and how their students learn.

It is that concept--the concept of resource-based learning--that is so needed today to address the problems and the opportunities inherent in providing education in an information society. It is that learning environment, created by having individuals use a wide range of real world resources instead of placing so much dependency on lectures and textbooks, about which I wish to talk to you today. And I must say that I was very pleased to see that the theme of this particular LOEX conference addresses those issues of breaking out of the walls of the library into the influencing of the entire educational process. I look forward, as eagerly as you do, to the sessions that

are before us today and tomorrow.

Let's talk about the environment in which we are discussing information literacy. This conference is taking place at an ideal time. We are in the midst of a series of unique occurrences that over the next two to three years should provide an unparalleled opportunity to advance the understanding of the role of librarians, library resources and services, and information literacy in quality education. Let me start by highlighting a number of those events that have happened recently and that will be forthcoming in the near future.

First, I hope that many of you have seen the book that Bob Wedgeworth and I edited entitled *Libraries and the Search for Academic Excellence*.[2] The book grew out of a national symposium of that title, which brought together leaders from higher education and librarianship from across the country to take the first serious look at the potential role of libraries in meeting the challenges presented by the educational reform issues of the eighties. Only one report seriously looked at this issue; it was Ernest Boyer's *College: The Undergraduate Experience*,[3] which was published after the symposium was planned. We were fortunate to have Boyer, who is president of the Carnegie Foundation for the Advancement of Teaching, speak at the symposium, and the book contains not only his speech but a number of papers that are co-authored by educators and librarians.

One of the outgrowths of the symposium was the formation of the American Library Association Presidential Committee on Information Literacy. (A copy of its report was given to you in your conference packets.) Again you will note the presence of outstanding educational leaders on the committee, and I am happy to say that they are still actively involved in the dissemination of the report to ensure that the concerns raised in the report are brought to the attention of other educational leaders across the country. None of us wants the report to become a dust collector. In addition, the four national educational organizations, which were represented on the committee, are all committed to being founding members of a national coalition on information literacy, which is in the process of being formed this summer.

The report says that to be information literate, a person must be able to recognize when information is needed and have the ability to locate, evaluate, and use effectively the needed information. It explores the importance of this aspect of the critical or higher thinking literacies as being essential to the quality of individuals' lives, to business, and to our democratic way of life. Not only do the educational leaders, who were on the committee, subscribe to the concepts in the report, but one of the most exciting parts of being chair of the committee has been talking with a wide range of educators and seeing the "light bulb go off" as they realized the importance of information literacy to their concerns. One president, whom I knew slightly through my work with the American Council on Education, had dictated a fairly perfunctory thank you when I sent him a copy of the report and commented that he was going to read it as soon as he had dictated my letter. The letter, however, concluded with a P.S., which said, "I just finished the report of the Presidential Committee on Information Literacy. It is excellent--I am sharing it with my deans, librarians, et al. Thanks much." He also sent me a copy of a speech he had made earlier. I dealt with an educational issue of great concern to him that he now understood to be related to information literacy.

Information literacy does strike very responsive chords with thoughtful educators--with people who have been struggling with the issues raised in the reform reports in terms of more active learning, preparing people for lifelong learning, and active citizenship. I believe that as librarians place the report in the hands of educators, as information on the report appears in educational journals, as information literacy is further explored at the White House Conference on Library and Information Services, and as the work of the national coalition on information literacy gets underway (with founding members such as the national Council on Independent Colleges) that the potential exists for an unprecedented favorable climate for the incorporation of information literacy efforts into the curriculums of our colleges and universities.

One such article has already appeared in the winter issue of the *Educational Record*,[4] and University of Colorado President E. Gordon Gee and I have collaborated on a book entitled *Information Literacy: Revolution in the Library*[5] (a title that lent itself with slight modification to the title for this speech). The book is in the process of being released by MacMillan under the auspices of the American Council on Education. The focus of the book is a challenge to presidents and other academic officers to take a new look at their libraries as tools of empowerment to accomplish campus priorities. As you can tell by the title, there is much emphasis on information literacy. Efforts are also underway at both the higher education and K-12 levels. You will have noted my emphasis on the involvement of nonlibrary educators in these comments.

Since it is not realistic to expect many academic officers to read articles from library journals and since such articles, even if read, seem self-serving, it is the use of the K-12 and higher education press and the authoring of articles and books by nonlibrarian educators on this topic that will better help create a new and more favorable climate for library services. The question is, what do we need to do to be prepared to take full advantage of a more hospitable climate?

Let me emphasize that the climate will be supportive of library instruction efforts, but it will also allow us to make a more profound impact on education **if** we are willing to move beyond current programs to becoming involved with restructuring efforts and use our influence and expertise to support resource-based learning with a goal of creating lifelong learners who are so because they are information literate.

The Needs

To take full advantage of the window of opportunity that will be available to us in the coming years, I believe that there are three pressing needs that we must address. First, we need to reassess the priorities within our libraries. How important is control to us? There are strong elements of the current information literacy thrust in the old library-college movement. The emphasis in the latter, however, was on the library taking control of the educational process. This approach has no sex appeal for anybody who was not a librarian and, therefore, was doomed to failure. But if we are talking about the restructuring of the learning process, we are talking about turning over to classroom faculty much of our control of what and how information management skills are mastered. It will probably mean giving away those library instruction courses for credit, which were fought for so hard and long. It may well mean increased working behind the scenes in curriculum planning with faculty as opposed to being on the front line with students. It may mean less credit for librarians as instructors, which may present some problems for promotion and tenure decisions. Is it our priority to improve the quality of instruction even at the expense of giving up direct control of library research programs?

Second, is evaluation and applied research a priority to us? Are we willing to commit staff and money to research and to move away from pre- and post-library tests to deal with evaluative issues such as student retention and measurements of academic performance in subject areas? If information literacy is to have meaning, it must have meaning within the curriculum.

Third, are we willing to set a higher priority on services than on collections? I do not mean that building collections is not important, but the percentage of the budget going into acquisitions is often the most sacred of all expenditures. If our large collections and concerns for preservation did not win us any attention in the recent round of reform reports, it is unlikely that such an emphasis in the future will change how libraries are perceived. As long as the primary criteria for ranking libraries continues to rest on size of collections and journal holdings, we shall be perpetuating the warehouse image of libraries and librarians as clerical employees. The very present realities of the information explosion and our too limited budgets should force us to develop new criteria of quality.

These priority issues of who has control, what we measure, and how we evaluate services in relation to collections are crucial determinants of how effectively we, as professional librarians, can support quality education in the Information Age. They are all difficult issues to address, and it is not enough that we should agree here today. There needs to be consensus building in our individual libraries and in our profession as a whole, quickly enough to take advantage of the current window of opportunity to engage faculty and academic administrators in effective dialogue.

Another need I would touch on just in passing. I believe that people concerned with the educational function of libraries must get into more influential positions in designing library systems. Far too many online catalogs are simply remakes of the card catalog. We need to be designing systems that are truly user-friendly, and that allow for access to collection holdings information and other databases from home or office so that they may be accessed twenty-four hours a day, seven days a week. We must not make people dependent on the knowledge of the Library of Congress subject headings. To use these systems we must, in fact, begin to insist on user-friendly **information** systems as opposed to **library** systems--just as we must move beyond programs of **library** instruction to **information** literacy.

The final need is in some ways the most important. We need a sharable vision. I have already touched upon the importance of opening up dialogues with campus personnel in terms of campus educational priorities, but we also need a vision to drive those dialogues to desired outcomes. We need a vision for what quality education can mean in an information society, and to be able to articulate that in a meaningful way with faculty and educational leaders both on our campuses and at the state level.

Let me just paraphrase for you from the Information Literacy Report[6] one vision of what an Information Age college might be like.

The college would be more interactive, because students, pursuing questions of personal interest, would be interacting with other students, with faculty, with a vast array of information resources, and the community at large to a far greater degree than they presently do today. One would expect to find every student engaged in at least one open-ended, long-term quest for an answer to a serious social, scientific, aesthetic, or political problem. Students' quests would involve not only searching print, electronic, and video data, but also interviewing people on and off campus. As a result, learning would be more self-initiated. There would be more reading of original sources and more extended writing. Both students and faculty would be familiar with the intellectual and emotional demands of asking productive questions, gathering data of all kinds, reducing and synthesizing information, analyzing, interpreting, and evaluating information in all its forms.

In such an environment, faculty would be coaching and guiding students more and lecturing less. They would have long since discovered that the classroom computer, with its access to the libraries and databases of the world, is a better source of facts than they could ever hope to be. They would have come to see that their major importance lies in their capacity to arouse curiosity and guide it to a satisfactory conclusion, to ask the right questions at the right time, to stir debate and serious discussion, and to be models themselves of thoughtful inquiry.

Faculty would work consistently with librarians, media specialists, and instructional designers to ensure that student projects and explorations are challenging, interesting, and productive learning experiences in which they can all take pride....It (would not) be unusual to see a librarian guiding a task force through its initial questions and its multi-disciplinary, multi-media search--all the way through to its cable or satellite presentation. In such a role, librarians would be valued for their information expertise and their technological know-how. They would lead frequent in-service faculty workshops and ensure that the college was getting the most out of its investment in information technology.

Because evaluation in such a college would also be far more interactive than it is today, it would also be a much better learning experience. Interactive tutoring software that guides students through their own and other knowledge bases would provide more useful diagnostic information than is available today. Evaluation would be based upon a broad range of literacy indicators, including some that assess the quality and appropriateness of information sources or the quality and efficiency of the information searches themselves. Assessments would attend to ways in which students are using their minds and achieving success as information consumers, analyzers, interpreters, evaluators, and communicators of ideas.

Finally, one would expect such a college to look and sound different from today's colleges. One would see more information technology than is evident today, and it would be important to people not only in itself but also in regard to its capacity to help them solve problems and create knowledge....One would hear more discussions and debate about substantive, relevant issues. In the halls, in the cafeteria, and certainly in the classroom, one would hear fundamental questions that make information literacy so important: "How do you know that?" and "What evidence do you have for that?" "Who says?" and "How can we find out?"

Maybe that is not quite the vision that would fit your college or university. Maybe your vision needs to be focused more around assessing learning outcomes. Maybe your vision needs to be couched in terms of writing and information literacy across the curriculum. The exact vision and the exact wording does not matter. What is important is that the vision is one that matches your particular institution and that provides an avenue for faculty and administrators to see library personnel and resources as an integral part of quality education.

The Challenge Before You

In a way I envy you. Many years ago I was working as a reference librarian at Brooklyn College when an open admissions policy was adopted in the spring to become effective the following fall. There was no cooperation among the city university campuses. Each campus designed its own way of meeting the unique needs of students, who a year earlier would not have been allowed onto their campus. I will always remember the library assignment given to these students to introduce them to the library. The first question was, "What are the differences between the Library of Congress and the Dewey Classification systems?" The preposterous nature of such an introduction for academic at-risk students coupled with their obvious desperate desires to succeed angered me and deeply moved me.

Years later, as the basis for my doctoral dissertation, I undertook a controlled experiment to see if what I then called information management skills could help at-risk college freshmen succeed academically. Some of you may have read the book that I wrote from that experience,[7] but the book failed to express the extreme personal satisfaction that came from knowing the difference --the lifelong difference--that I was able to facilitate in the lives of some of the students. It happened at different times; but when those particular moments came, when suddenly students felt in control of the information environment of their college experiences, their faces were like Christmas tree lights suddenly blazing forth. The wonderful empowerment! The knowing they were in control! The knowing that they could succeed! Nothing I do as an administrator, equals the joy, the exhilaration, and satisfaction of those experiences; and, as a Christian and a mother, I believe that nothing else I have done professionally has been more important in ultimate terms.

My job in more recent years has been to contribute toward opening windows of opportunity in libraries, which I have directed, and that broader window that now stands open before you. Yours is the challenge, the opportunity--indeed, the privilege--of walking through that window and bringing students along with you. It is up to you to create a vision for your campus and promote it so effectively that it becomes a reality in the lives of today's students.

In the more than a dozen years that I have been involved with library instruction, I have seen it attract the best and the brightest of librarians entering our profession. Initially they faced battles to convince their own colleagues and their directors that library instruction had a legitimate place among basic library services. While I am not sure that all of you here have library directors who are firmly committed to an expanded educational role for librarians, certainly our profession stands solidly behind this commitment as evidenced in the Access to Information priority of the American Library Association, which includes among its goals that instruction in information use should be available to all.

But the challenge before you is perhaps even more daunting than that of a decade ago. You are not being asked to convince your colleagues and your library directors but to convince your campus faculty and your academic vice presidents. You are being asked to convince them that information literacy is not only important to quality education but, indeed, that it is the very basis by which the learning process can become more active and by which students can be prepared for lifelong learning and active citizenship.

To do this you must venture out into the larger sea of higher education of which librarianship is only a small part. But just as a small amount of a chemical added to a much larger solution can act as a catalyst for major transformation, so too can you affect a major change in learning across our campuses today. This is the challenge before you: to help in the reform of learning and to make a difference in the lives of current and future citizens. This I believe you can do. This I hope you will resolve to do before you leave Ann Arbor.

NOTES

1. U.S. Department of Education. National Commission on Excellence in Education. *A Nation at Risk: The Imperative for Educational Reform.* (Washington, DC: The Commission, 1983).

2. *Libraries and the Search for Academic Excellence*, ed. by Patricia Senn Breivik and Robert Wedgeworth. (Metuchen, NJ: Scarecrow Press, 1988).

3. Ernest L. Boyer, *College: The Undergraduate Experience in America.* (New York: Harper & Row, 1986).

4. Patricia Senn Breivik and Ward Shaw, "Libraries Prepare for an Information Age," *Educational Record* (Winter 1989): 13-19.

5. Patricia Senn Breivik and E. Gordon Gee, *Information Literacy: Revolution in the Library.* (New York: MacMillan, 1989).

6. American Library Association, Presidential Committee on Information Literacy, *Final Report.* (Chicago: The Committee, January 1989).

7. Patricia Senn Breivik, *Open Admissions and the Academic Library.* (Chicago: American Library Association, 1977).

REFERENCES

Breivik, Patricia Senn. "Making the Most of Libraries in the Search for Academic Excellence." *Change* 19 (July/August 1987): 44-52.

Breivik, Patricia Senn, and Robert Wedgeworth. *Libraries and the Search for Academic Excellence.* Metuchen, NJ: Scarecrow Press, 1988. Papers from a National Symposium sponsored by Columbia University and the University of Colorado, New York, 15-17 March 1987.

Hardesty, Larry, Nicholas P. Lovrich, Jr., and James Mannon. "Library Use Instruction: Assessment of the Long-Term Effects." *College & Research Libraries* 43 (January 1982): 38-46.

Hyatt, James A., and Aurora A. Santiago. *University Libraries in Transition.* Washington, DC: National Association of College and University Business Officers, 1987.

Lewis, David W. "Inventing the Electronic University." *College & Research Libraries* 49 (July 1988): 291-304.

"The Literacy Gap." *Time* 132 (19 December 1988): 56-57.

Moran, Barbara B. *Academic Libraries: The Changing Knowledge Center of Colleges and Universities.* ASHE-ERIC Higher Education Research Report, no. 8. Washington, DC: Association for the Study of Higher Education, 1984.

Cornell University's Information Literacy Program

Jan Kennedy Olsen and Bill Coons

Introduction

Today we are making the transition from an industrial society to a post-industrial society, which is also called an information society. The characteristics of this society are not machines, manufacturing, and manpower as of the industrial society, but ideas, information, and knowledge to be used for innovative solutions to society's problems.

The cultural, social, and economic disturbances of this transition are so deep and so dramatic that we are considered a society in revolution. Why is this so? What is driving this?

Trigger Technologies

The explanation lies in looking at the history of revolutions that have resulted in the shift from one society to another. At the heart one can find a trigger technology. For example, in the case of the industrial revolution, the trigger technology was the steam engine; it supplemented man's muscle power, spawned new machines, which produced new goods; it opened the door to mass production. It touched every aspect of human life--it put the tractor on the farm, the typewriter in the office; it produced the daily newspaper. It pulled mass literacy into society. It created new social, economic, cultural, and political structures. It created an industrial society in which the key economic resources were manpower, manufacturing, and machines.

Today, the trigger technology of the information revolution is the computer and telecommunications. The driving force of this technology is its power to store massive amounts of information

Olsen is Director and Coons is Information Literacy Specialist at Albert R. Mann Library at Cornell University.

in a small space, to organize it, retrieve it, regroup it, and distribute it, all with lightning quick speed. It supplements not man's muscle power as in the industrial revolution, but man's brain power; it can generate types of information that before have been unthinkable. It is creating a society in which information is becoming a commodity. But information is an unusually powerful commodity. It provides the heart of the development of knowledge, the basis for innovations, the resources for an informed citizenry, and thereby, becomes the key commodity for the progress of society. Today the success of nations will depend upon the availability of leaders, professionals, and citizens who have been educated to understand the power of information, have developed the capabilities of finding it, using it, and generating it for decision making and the production of innovative solutions to society's problems.

It should be said that education has failed if it does not produce citizens and leaders who are capable of exploiting information.

The need for the people to exploit information is not a new concept in a democratic society; information has always been the essence of a democracy. That information, however, has been based in the print tradition. Today, information is produced by the computer, stored in electronic form, manipulated in complex ways, and distributed via telecommunications. This technology has infused information with a new power, a new dominance, and a new level of significance in our society. Information has now become a strategic commodity in the global economy. The Japanese and European governments, and a host of other nations have already perceived the need for a competitive edge in information technology. Within the United States the power of the people to exploit information is certainly a matter of supporting a democratic way of life, but today it is also at the heart of this nation's ability to remain as a leading world power.

Expanding Literacy Skills

Increasingly as we move towards the twenty-first century, this technology will be the only means of generating and storing information. To be in a position to exploit information, that is to create, locate, use, and distribute information, we will have to shift our perceptions and abilities related to information formats. We will have to acquire a new bundle of information skills, which will be fundamental to functioning in society. I submit that, in fact, we will have to expand the traditional skills of literacy. This new literacy is not simply about programming computers, or working a computer; it is not about computer lit-

eracy. That is too narrow. This new level of literacy has to do with understanding the role and power of information in society, its use and misuse; of being able to handle the varieties of information formats; of understanding the systems used in organizing information; of being able to generate information and manipulate it using electronic processes.

The foundation of this new literacy is the social, economic, and cultural change being driven by the increasing use of information technology. There is already precedent in history for the influence of technology on literacy. History shows that literacy is dynamic, not static; it changes in response to the demands of its times.

Literacy can be defined as having the skills one needs to make the connection to the information necessary to survive in society. Literacy as we know it today is manifest in the ability to read and write. As Benjamin Compaine of the Center for Information Policy Research at Harvard University points out, this has not always been the case, however. Before the written record came into widespread use in eleventh-century England, the oral tradition dominated. To be literate meant the ability to compose and recite orally. The spoken word was the legally valid record.

The emergence of the quill pen, and the producing of written texts on paper were the beginning of the technologies that have brought us to our current concept of literacy; in addition, the steam driven rotary press, the spread of railroads, and innovation in the manufacturing of paper have also played a significant role in developing the skills of literacy and allowing mass society to connect to the information needed to function in society. The current notion of literacy has evolved from the technology of the quill pen, paper, movable type, and the mechanically powered rotary press.[1] The bundle of skills we call literacy has evolved with technology. Today, the dominant technology is the computer and telecommunications. It is forcing a fundamental innovation in the conceptualizing and use of information.

Educating for an Information Literate Citizenry

We are proposing that true literacy, in an era when information is a strategic global commodity, has to include information literacy. We define information literacy as understanding the role and power of information, having the ability to locate it, retrieve it, and use it in decision making, and having the ability to generate and manipulate it using electronic processes. In short, information literacy is a necessary expansion of the traditional notion of literacy, a response to the revolution in which we are living.

Among the most concerned about the implications of information technology in society should be educators, particularly in terms of curriculum design.

In the literature of education today one can find extensive acknowledgment of the reality of the information era. One can also find extensive examination of what constitutes an excellent undergraduate education for the 1980s, with particular concern expressed for the state of student literacy. Interestingly, however, it is not possible to find any discussion at all of the implication of the information age for traditional literacy and the responsibility of undergraduate education to respond to this. For example, the report *A Nation at Risk*[2] certainly recognizes that effective participation in our "Learning Society" requires each person to be able to manage complex information in electronic and digital form, and therefore places great importance on computer literacy. This is not enough; it is too narrow. The forward-looking discussion paper by Benjamin Compaine does actually address a concept of "New Literacy."[3] He first asserts that computer literacy is not enough and then strongly presents the possibility that a new literacy might indeed evolve as the result of the information age. This is not enough either. The development of a level of literacy essential to functioning in today's society cannot be left simply to evolution. Information literacy is as fundamental as reading and writing. It has to be cognitively developed.

Mann Library is committed to teaching a cohesive information literacy curriculum as part of the undergraduate education at Cornell. The overall goal of the program is to educate and motivate students to become sophisticated in their awareness and abilities to use information and information technology.

Institutional Context

The Albert R. Mann Library is the second largest of sixteen libraries within the Cornell University Library system. Mann is also the land grant university library for the State of New York and has extensive collections in agriculture and life sciences, human ecology, and various social science disciplines such as communication and education. Mann excels in the innovative application of information technologies and possesses an exceedingly strong public service ethic.

In the Public Services Division there is an unusual mix of individuals--a programmer, statistician, database interface design specialist, computer files librarian, and two information literacy specialists. Elsewhere in the library we have another programmer and a cataloger who are becoming involved with database construction issues. By creating such a mix of competencies amongst the sixty FTE staff, Mann Library is trying to influence how information is structured, organized, and accessed.

The Mann Library information literacy program is embryonic within the College of Agriculture and Life Sciences and is entering its third year. It has succeeded because of strong administrative support, available monies to subsidize tools and access, quality collections and services (established credibility), collegial links with faculty, a dovetailing with educational reform agenda, and the presence of talented, versatile colleagues. With these also exists a certain evangelical drive, desire, and passion: if one does not believe in information literacy, it will not happen.

Rationale

Librarians have a particular responsibility to produce students who understand the importance of information and have the competence to locate, evaluate, and manage it. And "people who do not educate themselves--and keep educating themselves --to participate in the new knowledge environment will be the peasants of the information society."[4] Cornell University has a strong commitment to ensure that our students have the knowledge, motivation, and scope of abilities necessary to become aware and sophisticated producers and users of information.

Definitions of Information Literacy

One of the current definitions of information literacy is that it is "the set of information concepts, knowledge and skills required to function effectively in society"; it incorporates the "ability to structure, acquire, analyze and synthesize information." Teaching information literacy involves "communicating the power and scope of information to students and instructing them in how it is organized, retrieved and managed." (That definition, and a slightly modified version of Mann's goals and objectives, were adapted by the ALA Presidential Committee on Information Literacy and are available from ACRL.)[5]

Other definitions exist. In 1983, Forrest Woody Horton, Jr., wrote that information literacy "means raising the level of awareness of individuals and enterprises to the knowledge explosion, and how machine-aided handling systems can help identify, access and obtain data, documents and literature needed for problem solving and decision making."[6] And in 1984, Benjamin Compaine reported that the new literacy was "the bundle of information skills that may be required to function in society."[7]

Marin Tessmer of Denver's Auraria Library, defined information literacy in 1985 as "the ability to effectively access and evaluate information for a given need."[8] In 1986, William Demo, the director of Tompkins County Community College, said that information literacy is "a new intellectual skill that will enable us to be masters of new communications and information technologies."[9] Also in 1986, Robert S. Taylor said that "There is an unfortunate tendency to equate computers and information, and hence to mistake computer literacy for information literacy. Computer literacy, however, is not enough and never will be enough for intelligent survival. True information literacy is made up of the effective combination of a number of knowledges and skills...the kinds of knowledge and capabilities that any educated person will need to operate effectively in an information-rich technological society."[10]

THE DEVELOPMENT OF MANN'S INFORMATION LITERACY PROGRAM

Information Literacy Specialists: Mann's information literacy program formally began in June of 1986 when a job was posted for a Coordinator of Information Literacy. This excerpt describes part of the position: "The Coordinator of Information Literacy serves as the administrator of the Mann Library Information Literacy Program. Develops a plan to teach users about the power and variety of information and how it is organized, retrieved and managed. Includes both print and electronically stored information. Duties include planning, coordinating, designing materials, promoting, scheduling and evaluating the program. Includes active participation in the teaching programs for students, faculty and staff." In August of 1987 Mann hired an additional information literacy specialist to assist our existing program with business and finance students and to lead the planning and development of the program for biological sciences undergraduates.

Planning: Our planning process includes identifying goals and objectives, organizing them into a cohesive curriculum, developing instructional strategies and techniques, analyzing the curriculum and the majors, implementing instruction, and revising, evaluating, and expanding our program.

Course Selection: The process of selecting courses and faculty was complex and evolved over time. Fortunately, our director had already established a base of working relationships with the faculty and the dean, and our excellent collections and service helped to emphasize that we weren't using hollow words and empty promises. The fact that we realized where we wanted to go, were

going to start small and expand outward, and weren't going to over-extend ourselves, were very important to our credibility with the faculty.

We also have at Cornell an unusual opportunity. The CALS Office of Instruction for the last three years has sponsored a weeklong retreat dedicated to improving the quality of undergraduate education; twenty faculty are invited to the secluded retreat fifty miles from the university, and since its inception, Mann has been able to place two librarians. As a result, we have been able to form many connections and bonds with our faculty, which are stronger than those formed by infrequent reference desk transactions. The faculty recognize that we go through the same processes as they do as they plan for classes, we have the same aspirations and goals, and we have a body of knowledge and training behind us. We are changing the attitudes of faculty.

We looked at the twenty-two academic departments, the number of students enrolled in various majors, the faculty who taught, and who the department chair was at that time. We narrowed the twenty-two down to a short list of four or five and subjected them to a critical examination.

We selected the Department of Agricultural Economics. That department has 700 undergraduate business and finance majors within a specific discipline, so it was discrete and we could identify, work with, and track them over time. We also looked at some other factors: the fact that the dean of the College of Agriculture and Life Sciences is a former faculty member of that department wasn't a key factor, but it was a consideration.

Within that department, we looked for the innovators and early adopters and those faculty who were either trying to reach tenure or had reached tenure and had considerable momentum. As part of the process of selecting classes, we would ask the students about their professors and classes. Did the student like this class? Is the professor well respected or not? The reason for asking the students these questions was that we didn't want to choose a class, even if it had the right body of students and an assignment that would be appropriate for information literacy skills training, if the class was taught by a professor who was not favorably viewed by the students. We wanted to be connected with winners. We also looked at content: we couldn't choose any classes in which there was nothing to tie into as an information resource, either library based or in a remote database. In those classes that had no other previous assignment, or used information in any way, if the potential was there, the professor was right, and the class size was right, and it was in the sequence we were looking for, we went after them as well. Overall, we looked at impact, exposure, and the number of students we could reach.

We began the selection process inhouse and then used the formal channels that exist within the college. We went to the Agricultural Economics Undergraduate Program Committee, the committee that approves new classes and course changes for that major, and we asked them for suggestions and recommendations. We had a separate meeting with the dean and the chair of the department and the director of Instruction for our college. We made them aware of what we were doing and alerted them to our goals and our efforts. We also went to individual faculty and key faculty within the department--people who others in the department went to for advice. We wanted them on our side as well--so we informed them of what we were doing, we asked them for their support, and we asked for their suggestions. It was the partnership idea--it wasn't us telling them what we thought was right, it was "Here's a good idea, we think it will benefit the students, here's why it will benefit them, we think these classes might be appropriate, can you suggest other ones for us?"

Finally, in presenting ourselves to the selected faculty, we prepared tight documentation proposing our course of instruction with possible assignments and tools to be taught. This preliminary planning helped to show that we were serious in our efforts and capable of meeting the demands the faculty might place upon us. It also helped to demonstrate our case and win the faculty over.

Core Program Elements: We believe that information literate students are created--they just don't happen. However, one fifty-minute class over four years is not going to create information literate individuals. So we have developed a series of goals and objectives, which are applied in a sequence of specific classes from the sophomore to senior year. (For the first-year students we do not do anything. We made a decision to leave the freshmen alone. They're adjusting to the university environment, it's their first time away from home, they're learning study skills, they have many required courses, and much of what they do doesn't require the use of information resources. Quite simply, freshmen weren't a good fit for our program.)

There are five overarching goals and within them a number of objectives. (See Appendix I.) The five goals are 1) understand the role, power, and uses of information; 2) understand the variety of contents and formats of information; 3) understand systems for organizing information; 4) develop the capability to retrieve information; and 5) develop the ability to evaluate, organize, and manipulate information.

We use an acronym - AASK - to describe the components of one facet of our program: in-

fluencing attitudes about libraries, information, and librarians, raising awareness to the role and value of information, improving skills (transferable capabilities), and increasing knowledge (concepts, tools, and strategies). We talk about the range of resources and teach how print and electronic resources complement each other.

These elements are taught within a framework --they do not just happen haphazardly. Our instruction is a cohesive program (Appendix II). The five classes we use to reach our students are as follows:

Sophomore Year
    Fall   Introductory Statistics (AE 310)
    Spring   Financial Accounting (AE 221)

Junior Year
    Fall   Marketing Management (AE 342)
                     Managerial Accounting (AE 323)
    Spring   no classes in the program

Senior Year
    Fall   no classes in the program
    Spring   Business Policy (AE 424)

Enrollment in these classes ranges from 160 (AE 424) to 600 (AE 221). The context of our instruction (examples of some specific class assignments may be obtained from LOEX) is based upon a matrix of these classes against the goals and objectives; some objectives are accomplished twice, others only once. The goal that we're aiming for is, over time, to address all of the objectives within the classes. We are giving the students information skills that build upon previous efforts and that are transferable to other tools and future learning environments. We are trying to create future professionals who value information, and value librarians as key players in that process.

Student Outcomes/Benefits

We anticipate that students who have completed Mann Library's Information Literacy Program will appreciate the value of information; be aware that proper, timely information is a valuable tool that can substantially improve decision making; recognize the need to evaluate the accuracy of information; be able to navigate physically within and among the libraries at Cornell; possess a working knowledge of key discipline information retrieval resources; have a working ability to use electronic information technology and sources, with the potential to transfer that skill/knowledge to other circumstances; improve their class assignments by retrieving more relevant information in less time, allowing more time for analysis and presentation of information; and acquire the knowledge and skills that not only directly improves their college experiences, but also their performance in future professional careers and in society at large.

Evaluation

Mann Library has received ALA's Carroll Preston Baber Award to develop formal mechanisms to evaluate the success and usefulness of our program. We need to know if learning has taken place, and if it has, was it of any value? With the assistance of this grant we will survey employers to determine what information skills they expect recent college graduates to have and we will develop a standardized test designed to assess students' information literacy status.

Expansion

Within Cornell, there is a President's Fund for the Improvement of Undergraduate Education, a discretionary endowment of $5 million. Mann, with the strong endorsement of the dean of the College of Agriculture and Life Sciences and the director of the Division of Biological Sciences, submitted a proposal on "Information Technology and Literacy for Biological Sciences Undergraduates." In competition with faculty from throughout the university, Mann Library was awarded this grant of $120,000 for 1989-1991 to develop a scholars' workstation for students and address issues of interface design. Specifically, the tasks for this grant are to create local area networks and connect them to the campus backbone network, to mount biological information resources on Cornell mainframes, to link information resources to users by creating a gateway program (interface design), and to instruct students in information literacy skills at appropriate points in the biological sciences curriculum.

Lessons Learned

Over the past three years we have learned a variety of lessons. Some of them are that all students do not take classes in sequence; students would prefer more hands-on time; assignments that involve the use of information resources work best when they relate to a real need; if a class changes faculty hands, we begin anew; having the same librarian doing the instruction has some benefits (students can identify a specific face, learn the teaching style, and form stronger bonds) and some detriments (a program should not be too dependent on one person; some students freeze frame the face and place it in a box that equates the same face with the same lecture). Additional lessons are that changes in the content or format of any one class may drastically affect the content of others and require a change in teaching methods or tools taught; preparation and coordination time exceeds that required for bibliographic instruction classes; and each lecture must be prepared from year to year and can't be pulled from a file and used without modification.

Conclusion

T.S. Eliot has said that "Hell is a place where nothing connects with nothing." With information literacy we're trying to forge the links that will enable our graduates to make appropriate connections to gain more leverage with information. "Developing information skills--becoming information literate --is not something, however, that's completed within the limits of a school term, whether at the secondary school level, in the community college, or beyond. Just as we increase our language and expression skills, we become more masterful in our use of information over time. Along with the traditional, basic literacy skills, information literacy forms the common prerequisite for lifelong learning."[11]

NOTES

1. Benjamin M. Compaine, *Information Technology and Cultural Change: Toward a New Literacy.* (Cambridge, MA: Center for Information Policy Research, Harvard University, 1984), 6.

2. U.S. Department of Education. National Commission on Excellence in Education. *A Nation at Risk: The Imperative for Educational Reform.* (Washington, DC: The Commission, 1983).

3. Compaine, 6.

4. Cleveland Harlan, "Educating for the Information Society," *Change* 17 (July/August 1985): 21.

5. American Library Association, Presidential Committee on Information Literacy, *Final Report.* (Chicago: The Committee, 1989).

6. Forest Woody Horton, Jr., "Information Literacy vs. Computer Literacy," *Bulletin of the American Society for Information Science* 9 (April 1983): 16.

7. Compaine, 6.

8. Patricia Senn Breivik, "A Vision in the Making: Putting Libraries Back in the Information Society," *American Libraries* 16 (November 1985): 723.

9. William Demo, *The Idea of 'Information Literacy' in the Age of High Tech*. ERIC ED 282 537 (1986), 4.

10. Robert S. Taylor, *Value-Added Process in Information Systems*. (Norwood, NJ: Ablex Publishing Corp., 1986), 275.

11. Demo, 4.

INFORMATION LITERACY PROGRAM

Albert R. Mann Library
Cornell University

Encompassing Goals

Students within the colleges and divisions which Mann Library serves, after the course of their four undergraduate years at Cornell, should possess the following core information literacy competencies (each of these core competencies contains subordinate objectives). College of Agriculture and Life Sciences, College of Human Ecology, Division of Biological Sciences and Division of Nutritional Sciences students will:

A. Understand the role and power of information in a democratic society;

B. Understand the variety of the content and the format of information;

C. Understand standard systems for the organization of information;

D. Develop the capability to retrieve information from a variety of systems and in various formats;

E. Develop the capability to organize and manipulate information for various access and retrieval purposes.

9/12/87

Jan Kennedy Olsen and Bill Coons: Appendix I

INFORMATION LITERACY PROGRAM

Albert R. Mann Library
Cornell University

Subordinate Objectives

Goal A:

Understand the role and power of information in a democratic society.

Objectives:

Students can describe and understand:

1. How scholars and researchers use information and keep currently informed;

2. How practicing professionals use information and keep currently informed;

3. How the use of information can improve the quality of scholars' and professionals' work;

4. The commodity nature of information: who generates, controls, and uses information. In particular, the role that governments play in the dissemination and control of information;

5. The costs of misinformation, the possibilities of abuse and its consequences.

9/12/87

Jan Kennedy Olsen and Bill Coons: Appendix I (continued)

INFORMATION LITERACY PROGRAM

Albert R. Mann Library
Cornell University

Subordinate Objectives

Goal B:

Understand the variety of the content and the format of information.

Objectives:

Within their discipline, students can:

1. Distinguish popular from scholarly treatments of a subject;

2. Distinguish between primary and secondary sources;

3. Define various standard formats for the storage of scholarly information, e.g. print, microform, optical, floppy and compact disk, and magnetic tape;

4. Evaluate the quality of information and the usefulness of the content and format of a particular information tool based on relevant criteria;

5. Identify appropriate print or computerized information resources and references in their discipline, e.g. encyclopedias, directories, indexes, and describe their value.

9/12/87

Jan Kennedy Olsen and Bill Coons: Appendix I (continued)

INFORMATION LITERACY PROGRAM

Albert R. Mann Library
Cornell University

Subordinate Objectives

Goal C:

Understand standard systems for the organization of information.

Objectives:

Within their discipline, students can :

1. Define types of databases and their organization, e.g. records, fields, and the retrieval function/process;

2. Recognize that different types of reference sources lead to various forms and formats of information;

3. Define standard terms such as bibliographic citation, periodical index, abstract, and citation index;

4. Differentiate between the types of materials typically represented in a library's catalog and those that are not;

5. Determine the index structure and access points of print or computerized information resources.

9/12/87

Jan Kennedy Olsen and Bill Coons: Appendix I (continued)

INFORMATION LITERACY PROGRAM

Albert R. Mann Library
Cornell University

Subordinate Objectives

Goal D:

Develop the capability to retrieve information from a variety of systems and various formats.

Objectives:

Within their discipline, students can:

1. Construct a logical plan to organize their search for information;

2. Describe the differences between controlled vocabularies and keywords and use both efficiently in their search strategy;

3. Effectively use logical operators (e.g. and, or, not) to link their search terms and intersect concepts in various electronic information systems;

4. Understand and apply the concepts of truncation and field qualification in various electronic information systems;

5. Describe and use appropriate services which are available to assist them in locating information;

6. Successfully navigate within the libraries they use;

7. Accurately interpret bibliographic citations from print and computerized information resources and locate the materials they represent;

8. Operate a standard personal computer, develop mastery of certain programs/software, and maintain a working awareness of others;

9/12/87

Jan Kennedy Olsen and Bill Coons: Appendix I (continued)

INFORMATION LITERACY PROGRAM

Albert R. Mann Library
Cornell University

Subordinate Objectives

Goal E:

Develop the capability to organize and manipulate information for various access and retrieval purposes.

Objectives:

Within their discipline, students can:

1. Use a bibliographic file management package to organize downloaded citations and personal files of references;

2. Conduct their own needs assessment, based on relevant criteria, to identify suitable software packages appropriate to a given application;

3. Use electronic spreadsheets (e.g. LOTUS) to reformat and analyze numeric data which has been either downloaded or manually entered into the package;

4. Use a word processing package (e.g. WordPerfect) to format papers, reformat downloaded references and construct bibliographies;

5. Write correct bibliographic citations for books, journal articles, and conference papers.

9/12/87

Jan Kennedy Olsen and Bill Coons: Appendix I (continued)

Cornell University
Albert R. Mann Library Information Literacy Program
Department of Agricultural Economics

	Fall 1987	Spring 1988	Fall 1988	Spring 1989	Fall 1989	Spring 1990	Fall 1990	Spring 1991
Freshman Class of 1991			AE 310	AE 221	AE 323 AE 342			AE 424
Sophomore Class of 1990	AE 310	AE 221	AE 323 AE 342			AE 424		
Juniors Class of 1989	AE 323 AE 342			AE 424				
Seniors Class of 1988		AE 424						

B. Coons 7-15-87

Jan Kennedy Olsen and Bill Coons: Appendix II

Computer Literacy, Information Literacy,

and the Role of the Instruction Librarian

Harold W. Tuckett

Introduction

I'd like to begin by sharing a few stories,
based on my own experience in working with people
and computers. They're not particularly unique
--all of you who have had to deal with patrons
and some type of computer can supply your own
war stories--but I'd like to share these anyway
because I think they sum up some of the major
points I'd like to consider later.

I was sitting at the reference desk one day
in my former position at the University of Wisconsin-
Parkside when I became interested in the behavior
of a young man who was sitting at our recently
installed CD-ROM workstation. The only CD-ROM
product we had at that time was the *Academic
American Encyclopedia*, and we'd just recently put
it out for patron use. This patron had been sitting
at the CD-ROM station for about forty-five minutes,
and he was clearly becoming increasingly enthusiastic
about using it. He was printing out a variety of
things, and after a while he called a buddy over
from a table where he'd been studying to show
him the wonders of the system. He proceeded
to give his friend a quick tutorial in the use of
the CD-ROM product, and his friend quickly began
to share his enthusiasm. After he'd gotten his
friend engrossed in the machine, this young man
wandered over to where I was at the reference
desk--it wasn't very far from the CD-ROM worksta-
tion--and began to tell me about how wonderful
a product he thought this was, and went so far
as to congratulate me--as the immediately present
representative of the library--for our having had
the wisdom to install the thing. We talked about

Tuckett is Coordinator of Automated Services, Undergraduate Library, The University of Michigan, Ann Arbor, Michigan.

the product for several minutes--I was both pleased that he had such a favorable reaction to it and a bit bemused by the extent of his obviously heartfelt enthusiasm--and then he wandered back to join his friend at the workstation.

One of the things that that young fellow said really struck me at the time, although I didn't let on how it amused me since I didn't want to dampen his enthusiasm. In the middle of his describing his reactions to the machine, he exclaimed, "That thing is really wonderful. It has **so much information** on it!"

I didn't have the heart to point out to him that the CD-ROM version of the encyclopedia really didn't have any more information on it than the printed version of the encyclopedia, which was quietly sitting on the shelf of the reference collection only about ten feet away. In fact, it actually had less, since the CD-ROM version didn't have the illustrations, charts, and so on that the printed version did.

When I shared that story with my colleagues, they were also amused--we'd long ago become aware of the power that any computerized application has for some users, for either good or ill. How many times have you seen a user who has spent hours looking for a particular citation in printed sources, absolutely certain that it existed, shrug, and give up if a quick online search also didn't find it?--never mind that the search wasn't comprehensive, or even necessarily well done; "if it's not on the computer, then I guess I was wrong." But it did occur to me later that perhaps my enthusiastic young friend wasn't so far off in his reaction to the CD-ROM, and that perhaps he'd just not expressed himself well. What is really impressive about the CD-ROM encyclopedia, as we librarians know, is the full-text access and retrieval power that it gives, as exemplified by the fact that one can, for example, simply type in "Freud," and instantly retrieve references to Freud in any article in the encyclopedia, including not only the individual biographical article on him, but also references to him in articles on art and on literature. Perhaps what that young fellow was really getting at, I thought, was the revolutionary powers of access and retrieval that the computer brings to research.

A few days later, I was on the reference desk again, and here was the same patron back at the CD-ROM station again. He'd become something of an advocate for the system--he had another friend with him, a young woman this time, and he was explaining to her the benefits of the system. She was a bit more skeptical than his other friend had been, though, and was wondering aloud why she would possibly want to use a computerized encyclopedia when the printed version had served her so well since she'd been young. She was about to go over and use some of the encyclopedias in the reference collection. Our enthusiast, however, would have none of it: "No, no, no!" he insisted, rather loudly, and patted the CD-ROM station's monitor affectionately. "This one has much more information in it than all of those put together!"

The second story that I'd briefly like to share with you is not nearly so amusing, and I suspect it's a familiar one to many of you. I was sitting at the reference desk in the Undergraduate Library at the University of Michigan not long ago. A young woman hesitantly approached the desk and said that she was having difficulty finding many books on a particular topic. I asked her what she'd tried so far in her search, and she said that she'd spent almost an hour looking in the card catalog, without much success. I asked her if she'd tried looking in MIRLYN, which is the name we've given to our NOTIS-based online catalog. I explained to her that the only materials in our collection still represented in the card catalog were those acquired before 1975, while all the newer materials acquired since then were only represented in MIR-LYN. "You mean I have to look in those computers?" she asked, very nervously, and a look of panic was in her eyes. I adopted my most reassuring manner, went over with her to the online catalog, and spent at least fifteen minutes with her--arguably longer than I should have, since it was a very busy night and people were lined up several deep at the reference desk--showing her how it worked and reassuring her that she could use it. When I left her to go back to the desk, the patrons there kept me quite busy for the next forty-five minutes or so, but when it finally quieted down, I glanced over to the catalog area. The young woman I'd been helping earlier with MIRLYN was still there, but she was no longer sitting at an OPAC terminal, even though there were several available. She looked lonely and despairing, and obviously still hadn't found what she wanted. She actually looked close to tears. She'd gone back to trying to use the card catalog.

What is the point of opening a paper that will, I hope, deal with some important themes for both our users and for our profession with two such seemingly dissimilar personal stories? I think that these two stories are really much more similar than they might appear to be at first glance, and I think that they illustrate some of the themes and concerns that I'd like to share with you today much more forcefully and eloquently than any dry recitation of statistics could. Because in spite of all their personal computers that have been purchased in the last decade or so, in spite of the array of online systems that commercial vendors have introduced, in spite of all the online catalogs that have become available in libraries, and in spite of all the end-user searchers we've trained or software packages we've purchased or microcomputer centers we've opened, there are still far too many of our patrons who have no concept whatsoever of the relationship between the printed and online versions of something as basic as an encyclopedia. Or, there are those who are so fearful of using a computer that they persist in using older, less threatening means of gathering information even when they know that the results of doing so will be less than adequate information retrieval. As we go on now to consider things like "computer literacy" or "information literacy" --things that can get fairly theoretical or technical--let's not forget that as public services librarians what we're really talking about is doing what we can to ensure that none of our patrons will have to go without needed information because she can't or won't use a computer.

The purpose of this paper is to consider all those aspects of what we can call "information literacy" that somehow relate to the use of a computer. I'd like to begin by considering the relationship of "computer literacy" to "information literacy," to examine various definitions that have been proposed for each, and to suggest a model that might help clarify matters. Then I'd like to focus on instructional roles that seem to me appropriate for librarians to play pursuant to these concerns, and to look at examples of such roles in two different libraries with which I've been affiliated. Finally, I'd like to consider the implications that librarians' involvement with computer literacy instruction will have both for our bibliographic instruction programs and for our professional roles.

Computer Literacy vs. Information Literacy

It has become something of a cliche to note that we live in the Computer Age and/or the Information Age. Since *Time* magazine named the microcomputer its "Machine of the Year" in 1983, there has been much attention paid to the role of the computer in our lives. Similarly, much has been made of the "information explosion" and both the geometric increase in the amount of information available and the difficulty inherent in both managing and using that information. The use of the powers of the computer to assist in managing and using information has been a natural and vital use of that tool, as has been the widespread harnessing of computer technology to make available still more sources of information.

Yet, studies continually remind us that there are still millions of people who don't know how to use a computer; and even among those who use computers daily in their work, there is often no more than a scant understanding of how the machine works or of what it could potentially be used for. As computer use becomes increasingly critical for those who need to have access to information, it seems useful to consider what exactly we mean by "computer literacy," and exactly how this relates to a person's information handling ability.

Defining Computer Literacy

There has been a great deal of discussion, in the literature of many disciplines, of what "computer literacy" involves; some have even looked at it from a librarian's perspective. Generally speaking, current definitions of computer literacy tend to emphasize the ability of people to use the computer as a tool to accomplish something, as opposed to earlier definitions that stressed understanding how it works or how to program it. Forest Horton states that

> [the popular press has] helped educate us to the incredible spectrum of machine problem-solving capabilities. For our purposes, we might call this consciousness-raising "computer literacy." Computer literacy has to do with increasing our understanding of what the machine can and cannot do.[1]

And the University of Cincinnati's Computer Literacy Steering Committee (which included several U of C librarians) defines computer literacy as

> a working knowledge of computers. This knowledge should be at a level compatible with other knowledge and skills a student is acquiring in school or that faculty or staff members need to function effectively in their positions. It is a knowledge based upon understanding how computers can be used as a tool to help one learn, teach, solve problems and in general become more productive. The goal is to teach faculty, staff, and students enough to make them users of some computer system.[2]

These two definitions get at two important points about computer literacy--that it includes a general understanding of what computers can do for us and that we can use them to accomplish something. I would add a third requirement for a person to be considered computer literate, and that would be that that person demonstrate a certain amount of **self-reliance** in his or her use of computers; I don't think that this can be over-emphasized. Just as when we read in the literature on critical thinking and active learning that a certain amount of confidence and self-reliance is a trademark of the independent learner, so, too, it seems to me that it is an essential characteristic of someone who is computer literate. I've worked with far too many people--and many of you can probably add your own examples--who have been given only a minimal and inadequate amount of computer training to think otherwise. There are far too many people using computers today who know just enough to, for example, turn on the machine in the morning, and follow the series of cookbook-like steps written down next to the machine far enough to boot up the word processing program successfully and begin work on a document. But should anything go wrong, should they even in some cases make a single mistake in the order of those initial steps, they'll be completely lost, and need to call on someone else for assistance. I'm not exaggerating at all when I describe these poor helpless souls, and I'm certainly not necessarily blaming them for the poor training that they've received. But it seems to me that someone who has so little independence at the terminal and is so completely dependent on others should anything go wrong cannot reasonably be called computer literate, even though they may use the machine every day, have some idea of what the machine can do for them, and can use it to accomplish something.

A final way of considering what we might define as computer literacy might be to consider some instructional goals related to it. When I was at the University of Wisconsin-Parkside, the library there had developed a fairly extensive instructional program for its users in basic microcomputer literacy; I'll describe this program in greater detail a bit later. What seems pertinent to discuss now is that, pursuant to that instructional program, we developed specific instructional objectives for the teaching of microcomputer literacy, which included behavioral objectives for measuring the student's knowledge of essential microcomputer-related concepts and of the abilities and limitations of microcomputers, the student's ability at performing basic microcomputer-related skills, and the confidence and self-reliance of the student in using a microcomputer; these included the following:

INSTRUCTIONAL OBJECTIVES

1. The student will be able to make effective use of microcomputer software. The student will

- demonstrate the use of a keyboard, disk

drive, and printer;
- define basic concepts (e.g., hardware, software, memory, storage);
- demonstrate formatting and backing-up data disks;
- state the abilities and limitations of using a microcomputer to increase productivity or solve a problem; and
- demonstrate confidence and self-reliance when using microcomputers.

2. The student will understand the services, policies, and procedures necessary for use of the Library/Learning Center's microcomputer area. The student will

- identify the types of microcomputers and printers available for use in the area;
- demonstrate log-in and reservation procedures for use of the equipment;
- identify microcomputer assistants as a source of help with equipment and programs;
- identify software relevant to his/her needs and locate it in the Library/Learning Center;
- identify reference librarians as a source of help in identifying appropriate software; and
- state copyright laws and licensing restrictions concerning the use of software.

Defining Information Literacy

As can be seen by, among other things, the theme of this conference, there has been much concern in recent years with what has come to be called "information literacy," which is coming to be looked at as a superset of computer literacy. It has been variously defined; at an open forum sponsored by the Library Instruction Round Table at the 1986 Mid-Winter conference, it was described as

the ability to effectively locate, evaluate, and communicate information for a given need...[it] is an integrated set of skills, knowledge, and attitudes...[that is] maintained through changes in technology and resources...[and is] distinct from, but related to...computer literacy.[3]

Another possible definition was given in a recent article by Breivik:

To accomplish this (active learning), students need to become "information literate," whereby they

- understand processes for acquiring information, including systems for information identification and delivery;
- can evaluate the effectiveness of various information channels, including libraries, for different kinds of needs;
- master basic skills in acquiring and storing their own information (e.g., database skills, spreadsheet and word processing skills, and book, journal, and report literature);
- are articulate, responsible citizens in considering public policy issues relating to information (e.g., copyright, privacy, privatization of government information, and issues yet to emerge).[4]

And Horton, emphasizing technology and the vast information systems facing librarians and their clientele, says

Information literacy, then, as opposed to computer literacy, means raising the level of awareness of individuals and enterprises to the knowledge explosion, and how machine-aided handling systems can help identify, access, and obtain data, documents and literature needed for problem-solving and decision-makings.[5]

The Relationship of Computer Literacy to Information Literacy

We can see, then, that computer literacy and information literacy are separate but related concepts. I'm not sure that it's particularly important that we define the exact relationship between them--whether, for example, computer literacy is actually a subset of information literacy, or whether they stand as separate, distinct, but related sets of skills and knowledge. What is important, it seems to me, as we consider the librarian's role in promoting information literacy, is the extent to which computer skills and knowledge permeate every level of information literacy, and how that affects what we as librarians are responsible for teaching our users.

One way to think about this might be the following. Horton, in his article, makes a really interesting observation about information literacy. He compares Maslow's Hierarchy of Needs with what Horton describes as a Hierarchy of Information Needs. Let me quote from Horton for a moment:

Just what is the Information Age? One place to begin is with Abraham H. Maslow's idea of a hierarchy of basic needs.

According to Maslow, man has values and tries to reach for and achieve his full potential. In his 1968 book *Toward a Psychology of Being*...Maslow described a pyramid or hierarchy of five levels of values and needs, with survival or physiological needs and values at the lower level. He put spiritual or "self-actualization" needs and values at the top.

Maslow said that all the needs and values on the hierarchy are important...As lower level needs are satisfied, then higher level needs can be addressed progressively.

It is possible to juxtapose human physiological and psychological needs, on the one hand, with human information needs on the other...[6]

Horton then proceeds to describe a hierarchy of information needs similar to Maslow's; whereas Maslow describes needs for, progressively, biological-physiological, security, social, ego, and self-actualization needs, Horton posits a hierarchy encompassing needs for coping, helping, enlightening, enriching, and edifying information.

It seems to me that we might usefully borrow such a model to help us think about information literacy, particularly in its relationship to computer literacy. If we think about information literacy not so much in terms of needs, but in terms of skills and knowledge, then we may be able to construct a useful hierarchy that would describe the skills needed by an information literate person. Such a hierarchy would be useful, by focusing on skills rather than needs, in operationalizing the concept of information literacy as something that could be addressed as operational goals for a BI program; it would also be useful, I think, in making clear how computer literacy relates to information literacy.

This transparency (see Figure 1) illustrates the beginning of my thoughts about such a hierarchy. I'm not sure it's fully worked out yet, but notice that it does elaborate, if somewhat simply, a progression of information handling skills that could tell us something about the information literate person.

At the lowest level, which I've called the level of *Simple Information Skills*, we can see that a user is able to make use of one simple information-related tool; they can use a computer to accomplish some purpose, for example, or they can use a single library access tool like a card catalog or an index.

At the second level, which I've called the level of *Compound Information Skills*, the person is able to combine the use of simple information tools into some sort of a search strategy or is able to use one collection of simple information tools effectively together. Examples could include designing a search strategy for a research paper, using a particular library's collection, or becoming familiar with the databases available on one particular online service.

At the highest level, which I've called *Complex or Integrated Information Skills*, the person is able to make use of a wide variety of information networks, can evaluate and re-think the use of information gathered from a variety of sources, and generally understands the "big picture" of information use.

This model may not be fully worked out yet, but it seems to me that even as it stands it tells us some useful things. It illustrates for us how obtaining information literacy consists of a series of progressively complex steps--this can be useful in thinking about the design of BI programs, for example. More to the point for present purposes, it illustrates clearly how computer literacy is intimately related to information literacy: it is both a basic level skill, necessary for any sort of advancement up the hierarchy, and it is a set of skills and knowledge that is further needed at each step along the hierarchy. Put in this way, we can see that computer literacy is a vital component of any program of information literacy instruction; while you can be computer literate without being fully information literate, you cannot possibly be information literate today without also being computer literate.

Librarians and Computer Instruction

One of the most important questions, which arises from the preceding discussion, has to do with what the appropriate instructional role or roles might be for librarians in relation to computer and/or information literacy. It follows from the preceding discussions that there are at least two ways librarians might be involved in instructional activities related to the computer--as instructors directly in computer literacy itself or as instructors in those aspects of computer use that are most directly related to areas of the librarian's traditional mission and expertise.

Another way to think about this might be the following. Katherine Chaing, who's also from Cornell, described in a 1986 paper presented at the ACRL National Conference in Baltimore, what I think is a very useful hierarchy of levels of support that librarians at Cornell will supply for various software packages purchased by the library. While she was specifically talking about levels of support for specific software packages, I think

her levels of support can be appropriated to consider more broadly what levels of involvement we librarians might have with regard to different types of computer literacy instruction. Chaing's levels are as follows:

Our most basic level is reference; we have minimal knowledge of a program, are aware of what is available, where packages are indexed, and the individuals on campus willing to consult.

Our second service level is formal group instruction, either in the concepts and/or the use of categories of programs, or of individual packages; this requires we maintain a working knowledge of the programs involved.

Our highest service level is consulting. In certain areas we give individual instruction and advice on the concepts or use of categories of programs and individual packages. An indepth knowledge of a program is required at this level.

We are committed to the consulting level for bibliographic file management programs, expert systems for the microcomputer and online search aids/gateway programs...[7]

Perhaps the strongest or most radical call for academic librarians to become actively involved in offering various and comprehensive microcomputer services, including extensive instructional services, is in the 1984 article by Guskin, Stoffle, and Baruth entitled "Library Future Shock: The Microcomputer Revolution and the New Role of the Library." Among the arguments raised in this article for a central role for librarians in campus microcomputer activities are the following:

- The microcomputer is a powerful "information management and retrieval tool," which provides access to online and other information, some of which has become either cost-prohibitive or unavailable in paper format and to which libraries have an obligation to provide access.
- The library is the only place on campus organized to handle the information needs of large numbers of users and therefore, to facilitate campuswide access to microcomputer technology, libraries should develop and maintain extensive microcomputer labs to enable users to use microcomputers as they would other instructional materials.
- Because they have strong interpersonal skills, a concern for the information problems of

unsophisticated users, and a knowledge of information needs globally, beyond specific disciplines or specific campus units, librarians, and not computer center staff, should become the central campus resource for the new information and communication technology, providing both teaching and consultational services and the link between the information user and the new information technology.[8]

Exactly what roles librarians will adopt will vary, based on a variety of factors and local considerations, but it does seem to me that any library that is concerned with instruction in information literacy will have to assume the responsibility for at least part of the computer literacy instruction of its clientele.

In thinking about this, it might be useful to examine the experiences of two specific libraries in offering a variety of computer-related instruction to their users. We've already heard to some extent about the programs at Cornell. Two other libraries that might offer useful examples are the libraries at the University of Wisconsin-Parkside and at the University of Michigan. The former is an example of a library at which librarians assumed a very comprehensive role for providing instruction for the campus in both basic computer literacy and in the broader concerns of information literacy. At Michigan, on the other hand, other units on campus are providing instruction in basic computer literacy skills, and the library has been free to develop more narrowly focused computer instructional programs.

Specific Programs: The University of Wisconsin-Parkside Experience

In the fall of 1982, a microcomputer lab was made available to the users of the Library/Learning Center at the University of Wisconsin-Parkside. The library was chosen as the site of the lab because of the library's service orientation, its long hours, the ability to acquire and circulate a software collection, and, not insignificantly, because librarians had actively sought to administer such a lab, while the campus computing center at that time had little or no interest in microcomputers. Two of the major goals of the lab were to support the curriculum and to provide a facility for general computer literacy for all L/LC users. It's probably also worth pointing out that, while the lab would grow considerably over the course of the next several years, it remained, at least until I left UW-Parkside in the summer of 1987, the only general purpose microcomputer lab for this campus of approximately 5,000 students.

Shortly after the lab opened, librarians quick-

ly came to realize that there was a strong need to offer general microcomputer instruction to L/LC users. Most of the initial users of the microcomputer lab, in fact, were computer science students and "hackers"; with hindsight, this probably shouldn't have been surprising to us, but it was at the time. While we didn't have anything against these users, they clearly weren't who we considered to be the primary clientele for the lab; we had a clear charge, which we took seriously, to promote general computer literacy for everyone on campus, and to help faculty and staff apply microcomputers to their teaching and research. But many faculty and students either did not know microcomputers could be applied productively to their research and teaching needs or assumed that one needed to know how to program to use the microcomputers. Additionally, those few initial nonhacker users who tried to make use of the lab weren't able to get much help with their questions or concerns; while we had hired a computer science student to work in the lab and provide general trouble-shooting and hardware maintenance and support, he clearly wasn't able to work with faculty in the manner or at the professional level that they were used to in working with librarians for other matters relating to the library's collection or services. Clearly, if the lab was going to be able to live up to its announced mission and become a fully integrated part of the library's collection and services, we the librarians were going to have to do something.

To respond to these needs, two librarians from the public services staff developed and began regularly offering a two-hour, hands-on, general orientation workshop to introduce students, faculty, and staff to the use of microcomputers. This workshop focused on introducing participants to basic concepts of computer literacy, such as definitions of hardware, software, memory, and storage, and on providing a hands-on introduction to the variety of nonprogramming applications that microcomputers can provide. The response to these initial workshops was both overwhelming and positive. After the need for follow-up workshops on several specific applications--word processing, file management, and electronic spreadsheets--became apparent, workshops on each of these applications were developed and team taught the following semester.

After approximately one year, the seven reference/instruction librarians in the public services division reached the collective decision that they should all participate in this program of microcomputer instruction. All librarians had been gradually increasing their own computer literacy by attending inhouse hands-on workshops similar to the orientation workshops and by using micros themselves for personal productivity. The team teaching method allowed those who had not yet taught workshops to work initially with one of the more experienced workshop leaders; while assuming this role was initially stressful for some, they also found it to be stimulating and rewarding. The participation of seven librarians as instructors allowed the microcomputer instruction program to expand in two ways: first, an additional workshop on the use of bibliography management software was developed and offered regularly; second, as the lab itself grew by adding first IBM and then Macintosh microcomputers to its initial collection of Apple II machines, we were also able to develop introductory and application-specific workshops for each brand of microcomputer available in the lab.

As time went on and as librarians increased both their level of computer literacy and awareness of the rapid changes occurring in the area of information technology, we became aware that the objectives of the microcomputer instruction program should be expanded beyond simple instruction in general computer literacy and the use of generic applications packages. The potential applications of microcomputers to library research and information retrieval tasks became more apparent with new information becoming available--in some cases, exclusively--in machine-readable format, whether on floppy or optical disks or via telecommunications. An online catalog with remote dial-up access capability was also soon to be implemented and we were beginning to consider what decentralized access to information about the library's collection would mean. Librarians became convinced that instruction in what we came to call information literacy--the skills and knowledge necessary to find and use information, regardless of its physical location or format--was an important goal of the bibliographic instruction program and that microcomputer literacy was an important subgoal.

We therefore developed a series of seminars directed at faculty on the use of microcomputers specifically as a tool to enhance library-related research and teaching tasks. Included in the series were presentations on end-user online searching, on management of bibliographies and research notes using a variety of both traditional and free-form file managers, bibliography managers, and outlining and indexing software, and on presentation graphics (the library at UW-Parkside included a Media Services division). Unlike the workshop series, which emphasized a hands-on approach, the seminars were more conceptual in nature. We demonstrated relevant software, but little hands-on experience was offered. By emphasizing the concepts behind using the micro for a variety of research and teaching tasks, and by targeting the sessions at faculty members, we hoped that faculty members would then be able to take this new knowledge and develop their own applica-

tions of it to best suit their research needs and the individual computer needs of their classes.[9]

As a final note, it should be mentioned that in addition to the formal programs of instruction, which we developed, librarians also functioned extensively as consultants for certain software packages we were particularly familiar with and we also provided a separate facility within the micro center so that computing center staff could provide consulting services for faculty and staff.

Specific Programs: The University of Michigan Experience

The situation relating to computer and information literacy instruction at the University of Michigan is, as you might imagine, quite different. For several years, the campus computing center has been providing a number of courses in basic computer literacy and in the use of applications packages supported by them for the campus community of over 34,000 undergraduate, graduate, and doctoral students and over 2,700 faculty; with these basic needs being met in this way, this has left the library free to develop instruction in those aspects of computing most closely related to its own goals and expertise. Further, as bibliographic instruction activities are decentralized at over twenty campus libraries, a variety of different approaches are being utilized. These have ranged from a recent seminar series developed and taught by librarians from the Graduate Library entitled "Computer Use and the Humanities Scholar" to a long-standing program of workshops on searching the MEDLINE database, which is taught by librarians in the Medical Library. I can probably best comment on one particular ongoing series of workshops, which was developed under the auspices of the University Library system as a whole, is marketed to the entire campus community, and is taught by librarians from a variety of libraries on campus. I can also mention areas of consulting expertise that have been developed by some librarians on campus. Further, I can also briefly mention those activities that have been undertaken within the Undergraduate Library's microcomputer center, which I supervise, and some ways in which developments in information technology have had an impact on our traditional bibliographic instruction program. Finally, I can mention some fairly exciting possibilities that are either beginning or being planned for the future.

University Library Courses

The workshop series, mentioned above, is called University Library Courses. It is marketed as one component of a much larger series of computing courses on campus, and is open to all faculty, staff, and students. These university library courses began a few years ago and initially covered instruction in searching commercial online databases for the campus community. I continue to teach online searching sessions several times a semester as a part of this series, including sessions on BRS, DIALOG, and occasionally on other systems such as Wilsonline. The curriculum of the university library courses has gradually been expanded to include a variety of other workshops, including one that I teach on personal bibliography management using ProCite software. Sessions taught by other librarians include personal file management using both IBM and Macintosh computers, accessing national information utilities like RLIN, accessing MIRLYN, our NOTIS-based online catalog, accessing specialized or inhouse databases maintained by the library on the campus network, and most recently teaching end-user searchers to search the databases of commercial vendors, which the University Libraries have leased or purchased and mounted on the campus network. This is one of the exciting developments that I mentioned earlier, and represents the major direction in providing end-user searching currently being pursued by the University of Michigan libraries. We presently have MEDLINE mounted on the network and are conducting workshops on its use. Future plans call for the mounting of additional databases from other vendors (such as a number of those from the H.W. Wilson Company), and instructional sessions for those will be developed as needed.

Consulting

I serve as a campuswide consultant for the ProCite bibliographic management software package, a role I assumed as part of an agreement with the producer of that software whereby the Undergraduate Library's microcomputer center can receive multiple copies of that software at a reduced charge. I also act as a consultant for the persons trained as end-user searchers in the university library courses; I provide consulting in person, over the telephone, and over the campuswide electronic mail system. Other librarians on campus perform similar roles; for example, librarians in the Medical Library have long acted as consultants for searching the MEDLINE database.

The Undergraduate Library Microcomputer Center

In the Undergraduate Library's microcomputer center, we have offered workshops in various applications packages and on some generic computer topics such as use of the campus network, network conferencing system, and network message system on an on-demand basis. These have been taught both by myself and by the paraprofessional who reports to me and who is responsible for much of the day-to-day operations of the center. We do not have as elaborate a program of general computer literacy workshops as was developed at UW-Parkside, however.

In addition to providing direct instruction, we also allow faculty to reserve and use the classroom area of the micro center to teach their students microcomputing concepts pertinent to their individual course needs, and we operate a reserve service for faculty who wish to place software on reserve for their students' use.

Computers in the Traditional BI Program

Advances in information technology have, of course, also had an impact on the Undergraduate Library's bibliographic instruction program as they have for other libraries on campus. For example, the introduction and highly enthusiastic acceptance by our users of several CD-ROM products in the Undergraduate Library have led to the incorporation of instruction about these products in BI sessions. In the freshman-level psychology classes, which are the largest single component of our BI program, we now not only teach students to use the printed *Psychological Abstracts*, but also how to search *PsycLit* on CD-ROM.

The introduction of MIRLYN, our online catalog, has also obviously had an impact on our BI program. This is particularly true since MIRLYN is mounted on the campus computer network and is therefore accessible not only from within the library, but from anywhere on campus--in dozens of campus computing clusters, dorm microcomputer centers, faculty offices--and indeed from anywhere off campus where persons can dial in with a micro and modem. Instruction in MIRLYN has therefore often had to include a discussion of remote access options. This will be increasingly true as other databases are added to the network, as has been done with MEDLINE, as mentioned earlier.

This increasingly decentralized access to information raises new challenges and exciting new possibilities for our BI program. I'd like to mention just one such possibility, although it's only at the idea stage and hasn't been implemented. Almost all of the dorms on our campus have their own small libraries, small collections of reference books, popular reading, magazines, and so on, which are generally run by a library school student. Many dorms also have microcomputing centers on site. In the past, the Undergraduate Library and the dorm libraries have conducted various joint presentations, workshops, or events in the dorms for the students who live there. One idea, which we've been thinking about since MIRLYN came online, would be to conduct open workshops in the dorm microcomputer centers showing students how to access MIRLYN (and, presumably, other network databases) directly from the dorms. This would allow a scenario something as follows. Students are studying around midnight in their dorm room. They realize that they need to find out what information exists on their topic in the library. They leave their dorm room and walk about twenty feet down the hall to the dorm microcomputer center. They dial into MIRLYN, conduct a search for books; switch over to *Social Sciences Index* and identify some journal articles on their topic; switch back to MIRLYN to find out which campus libraries own those journals; and then switch over to the campus electronic mail system to send a message to the Undergraduate Library's electronic reference mail box (a service, by the way, which we do currently provide) asking for advice in conducting further research. The next day they go to the library to obtain the materials they identified, and later check their E-mail to find our reply to their reference question. All the technology exists on campus today for students to be conducting research in this way; and the possibility of our conducting "decentralized" bibliographic instruction in the dorms seems a perfect match for this type of decentralized access to information.

Conclusion and Implications

What conclusions can we draw from all of this? This paper has attempted to do several things: to examine the concepts of computer literacy and information literacy, to look at the possible relationships between the two, and to suggest what that relationship might mean for the instructional role of librarians. As we consider what that instructional role might be, it's clear that whatever answer we arrive at will have at least two sets of implications--there will be implications for our users, and there will be implications for ourselves and our professional roles.

All of our users have been and will continue to be affected by the rapid and ongoing changes in information technology and in the sheer amount of information continually being produced and disseminated. The challenges they face are diverse. For some, like those considered in the stories at the beginning of this paper, the challenges are simple yet daunting; a lack of computer literacy may result in a user being unable to obtain the information that she needs from the library's online catalog, or a lack of information literacy may preclude a user, even though he's computer literate, from being able to make reasonable distinctions between different potential sources of information. Even our most sophisticated users, however, still face difficult challenges as they face a bewildering array of sophisticated information systems and need to acquire new sets of skills to help them access, retrieve, and utilize information from a variety of sources and in a variety of formats. The extent of the instructional roles that librarians choose to play in relation to the new technology will have a direct effect on the success or failure of these users in dealing with the demands of the Information Age.

And for ourselves, increasingly decentralized access to information and increased awareness on the part of our users of a variety of different information systems and sources will have a direct effect on the roles that we will have to play, at least if we wish to remain valid as a profession. It seems to me that our roles as public services librarians will be increasingly concerned with consulting with and teaching users about the whole variety of new information technology, and will be much less concerned with the direct provision of information per se. And if such consulting and instruction is to be sufficient to meet the needs of our users, it will have to include within it a whole range of concepts that we could never have foreseen as little as a decade ago.

One thing does seems certain. If we are going to be able to help our users meet all of the demands of the Information Age, then the goals of our bibliographic instruction programs will have to be broad enough to meet that challenge. And saying that our goal is simply to "teach them about using the library" just isn't going to be good enough anymore.

NOTES

1. Forest Woody Horton, Jr., "Information Literacy vs. Computer Literacy," *ASIS Bulletin* 9 (April 1983): 14.

2. James W. Hart, "The Library's Role in Fostering Computer Literacy," in *Issues in Academic Librarianship: Views and Case Studies for the 1980s and 1990s.* (Westport, CT: Greenwood Press, 1985), 183-184.

3. Pamela Englebrecht and Linda Richardson, "Open Forum on Information Literacy," *LIRT News* 8 (March 1986): 1.

4. Patricia Senn Breivik, "Making the Most of Libraries in the Search for Academic Excellence," *Change* 19 (July/August 1987): 46-47.

5. Horton, 16.

6.   Horton, 14-15.

7.   Katherine S. Chaing, "Computer Accessible Material in the Academic Library: Avoiding the Kludge," in *Energies for Transition: Proceedings of the Fourth National Conference of the Association of College and Research Libraries, April 9-12, 1986, Baltimore, Maryland.* (Chicago: American Library Association, 1986), 69.

8.   Alan E. Guskin, Carla J. Stoffle, and Barbara Baruth, "Library Future Shock: The Microcomputer Revolution and the New Role of the Library," *College and Research Libraries* 45 (May 1984): 180-181.

9.   Linda J. Piele, Judith Pryor, and Harold W. Tuckett, "Teaching Microcomputer Literacy: New Roles for Academic Librarians," *College and Research Libraries* 47 (July 1986): 375-376.

MICROCOMPUTER LITERACY AND INFORMATION LITERACY: A SELECTED BIBLIOGRAPHY

Public Access Microcomputers in Academic Libraries, ed. by Howard Curtis, 107-122. Chicago: American Library Association, 1987.

Curtis, Howard, and Joan Lippincott. "Overview of Instructional Programs." In *Public Access Microcomputers in Academic Libraries*, ed. by Howard Curtis, 107-122. Chicago: American Library Association, 1987.

Guskin, Alan E., Carla J. Stoffle, and Barbara Baruth. "Library Future Shock: The Microcomputer Revolution and the New Role of the Library." *College and Research Libraries* 45 (May 1984): 180-182.

Horton, Forest Woody, Jr. "Information Literacy vs. Computer Literacy." *ASIS Bulletin* 9 (April 1983): 14-16.

Hart, James W. "The Library's Role in Fostering Computer Literacy." In *Issues in Academic Librarianship: Views and Case Studies for the 1980s and 1990s*, 179-190. Westport, CT: Greenwood Press, 1985.

Molholt, Pat. "On Converging Paths: The Computing Center and the Library." *The Journal of Academic Librarianship* 11 (1985): 284-288.

Piele, Linda J., Judith Pryor, and Harold W. Tuckett. "Teaching Microcomputer Literacy: New Roles for Academic Librarians." *College and Research Libraries* 47 (July 1986): 374-378.

Skill, Harold B. "Bibliographic Instruction: Planning for the Electronic Information Environment." *College and Research Libraries* 48 (September 1987): 433-453.

Figure 1
Hierarchy of Information Skills

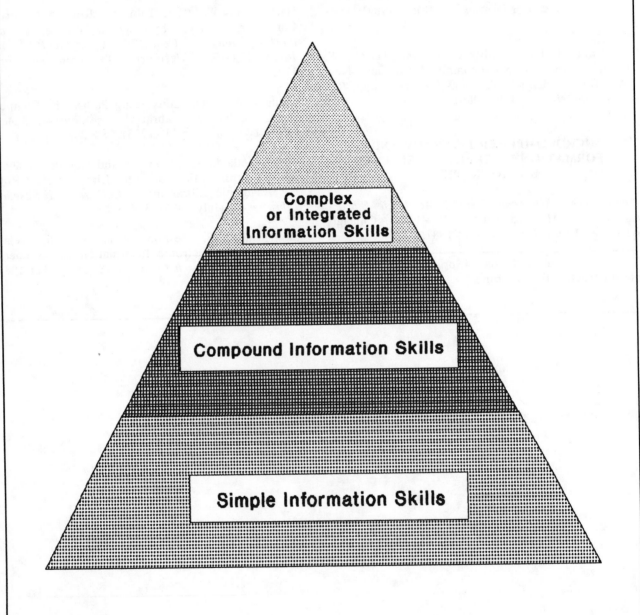

Harold W. Tuckett, Addendum

Integrating Active Learning

Techniques into the One-Hour

Bibliographic Instruction Lecture

Trish Ridgeway

Introduction

"Active learning"--it's one of today's educational buzzwords. It sounds good. It sounds like something we should use in our teaching, but what is
it? And is it possible to use active learning techniques in a one-shot bibliographic instruction lecture?
I hope today's session, which will present both
information on and demonstrations of active learning,
along with the handouts you have from me, will
define active learning and show how it can be integrated into library instruction.

After hearing about active learning, many
people are happy to discover that they have been
using some of these techniques all along; if that's
the case with you, I hope you will try some of
the other methods I suggest. If you haven't used
any of these ideas in your teaching, I hope you
will be inspired to try some. In fact, I will spend
a few minutes near the end of the session talking
about how you can change your teaching style.

Exercise One: Brainstorming on Objectives

In our first exercise, we'll use the techniques
of individual and group brainstorming to decide
upon our objectives for today's session. In brainstorming, the rules are to think of and jot down
ideas as quickly as you can, to aim for a large
quantity of ideas, and not to criticize ideas (your
own or others).

Turn to Worksheet One and do some individual
brainstorming to answer the question, "What cognitive
and affective objectives should this session try
to achieve?" For example, one cognitive objective

Ridgeway is Bibliographic Instruction Coordinator at Van Pelt Library, University of Pennsylvania.

might be, "Participants can define the various active learning techniques." You have three minutes; write down as many ideas as you can. We'll then share our ideas in a group brainstorming session.

Let's now turn to group brainstorming. Call out your ideas to me, and I'll record them on a transparency. The objectives produced by the group included the following:

Cognitive Objectives

Workshop attendees can define active learning techniques.

Participants will apply active learning principles to their own teaching.

Attendees will identify active learning techniques that are appropriate for their teaching.

Participants can identify the problems and challenges that go along with the use of active learning methods.

Affective Objectives

Participants will find active learning methods useful and desirable for their own teaching.

Workshop attendees will feel comfortable and confident when using these new techniques.

Participants will go home and convert others to the use of active learning techniques.

Participants will not worry that they have to cover everything in a lecture and thus will have time to use active learning methods.

Participants will not be bothered that they are trying something new but will have the conviction to follow their own continuum.

Attendees will overcome their fear of lack of structure in their teaching.

Participants will be creative and discover their own design for the use of active learning.

This exercise should serve as a shock technique. Using active learning techniques in the classroom requires the instructor to relinquish control. Letting the students design their own objectives is the ultimate loss of power. Do you think you could do it? It's not as bad as you think. I use this technique with undergraduates--most of them can tell you what one needs to know to use a library--but not **how** to use this library for this subject. I do prepare a list of objectives prior to the class, and students manage to name most of the cognitive ones for which I am aiming. Of course, I don't expect them to think up affective objectives, but I do want them to know that I expect them to participate and to take responsibility for their own learning.

To give you an example, in a class that is the first for education majors I project on the overhead a question such as, "To do a good term paper on an education topic, what do you have to know about this library and about library resources in education?" You can then discover how sophisticated their library knowledge is, how willing they are to participate, and hopefully motivate them by illustrating how much they don't know.

Brainstorming techniques are a good way to start a class. Individual brainstorming lets everyone take part, and brainstorming is a non-threatening method to encourage people to participate.

Exercise Two: Seat Work and Buzz Sessions on Teaching Methods

Our next technique, individual seat work, is one you probably remember from elementary school. Asking students to write an answer to a question or to complete a short exercise is a quick way to get everyone to think about the subject under discussion.

Turn to Worksheet Two, Teaching Methods & Objectives. First, try to assign a percentage for the amount of time you spend in a bibliographic instruction session to each of the items listed. We are only counting instructional activities so the time spent in passing out handouts or the professor taking roll should not count as part of the one hundred percent. Consider these categories as mutually exclusive; in other words, hopefully students are thinking while you are talking, but you should count only those times that they are thinking and nothing else is going on. On the bottom of the sheet, rank how important the objectives listed are to your teaching with number one representing the most important. You have four minutes.

Your worksheet provides a rough description of your philosophy of teaching and how you put that philosophy into action. We will use the buzz group technique to consider these ideas. First I'll explain buzz groups.

Buzz groups are made up of two to six people who work together for a very short time to consider a question, review information, or work on a simple problem. I limit my buzz group size to two or three people so no time is wasted while groups form. A buzz session can be as short as four or five minutes.

In a moment, I'd like you to form into buzz groups of two. If there is an uneven number at your table, one group can have three people. Introduce yourselves if you don't know your "buzz-buddy." In your buzz group, you will discuss your philosophy of teaching and how you put it into action. Did the worksheet provide any surprises? Does your allotment of instructional time lead to the student outcomes you consider most important? Take four minutes with one person giving his or her reaction to these questions for two minutes and then the other person taking the second two minutes.

Lecture on Active Learning Methods

I've allotted myself five minutes to demonstrate the lecture method. My main points are summarized on the workshop outline, and I hope you will consult some of the items on the bibliography if you want more information. Right now I want to present a few images that may help you remember the main ideas.

This is my concept of the ideal student: you unzip the top of the head, pour in information, and then learning and knowledge results. Students would like this too; they might be able to keep their Walkman going full blast and could still get the information. But not too many students come in the flip-top model. This concept of learning is incorrect because there is no involvement of the student, and **learning is the responsibility of the learner**. Our aim should not be to teach, but to facilitate students' learning. And we can do that by giving them as many opportunities as possible to interact with and reorganize the information, to translate it into their own terminology, and to relate it to the store of information they already possess.

Active learning gives students the opportunity to interact with information--helping them to remember more. Research has also shown that active learning activities are more effective at achieving higher cognitive objectives than are passive learning situations. If you indicated on the last worksheet that you spend most of your time talking but that you want students to achieve higher level cognitive outcomes, your methods and expectations are in conflict. Pure lecturing does not provide students with opportunities to engage actively with the information and it won't lead to higher level goals. Try tape-recording a typical BI session and then play it back and keep track of who is talking and who is thinking.

In considering affective objectives, students enjoy active learning techniques and therefore have a more positive attitude toward librarians and libraries. Additionally, techniques such as brainstorming, buzz groups, and small groups can help reinforce positive attitudes through peer pressure.

For instance, one of the small group activities that I describe in your handouts asks freshmen in an English composition class to assign a grade to a bibliography that is pretty bad and give their reasons for that grade. The groups do not give the bibliography as low a grade as I would, but they do come up with a list of things wrong with it: it's not long enough; the items are not recent enough nor scholarly enough; and not all items are relevant to the topic. I could have given them a list of criteria for a good bibliography, but I doubt they'd remember it or feel that it had much value.

One more point, students do have different learning styles. If we use only one method of teaching, it is as if we are trying to pound students of many different shapes into the same shaped hole. Using a variety of techniques will help meet the needs of students who have different learning styles.

Exercise Three: Small Groups--Teaching And/Or

Worksheet Three calls for the use of small groups. Since small group work takes so much time, I use it only for the most important objectives and usually only once, if at all, in each class session. My objective in this worksheet is to demonstrate the use of small groups, but also to give you practice in making the decisions needed to design an active learning exercise. Each group will circle the objective or objectives it wants to achieve, the amount of time it wants to use, and the activity the group will use. Then each group will design an exercise that presents the concept of "and" and "or" as logical combinations in a computer search. For example, you might design an exercise that is part of a session designed to teach students how to search ERIC on Silverplatter. What materials will you use, what topics? What instructions will you give the students for this exercise? You might want to look over the last page of your handouts for some examples and tips on active learning exercises. Divide into groups of four to six people and take fifteen minutes.

After group work, various groups reported on the exercise they designed and which activity they chose.

Conclusion

I have given speeches and day-long workshops on improving teaching and often hear from people months or years later. I'm always happy to find that people are trying new techniques, but I also hear comments such as "I enjoyed that workshop you gave; I really want to try some of your ideas but just haven't gotten around to it." That deflated my ego, but also made me think about how difficult it is to try a new style of teaching. Joyce and Weil, who are cited on my bibliography, have done a lot of research in this area, and I want to pass on some of their ideas to you.

First, before you try to change, know that it is hard and it will be uncomfortable. Recognize that changing your style of teaching is as difficult and feels as awkward as learning a new sports skill such as a correct golf swing. You have to keep at it until it feels natural.

Begin by overlearning the theory behind the new method; read as much as you can about why and how you are adopting a new technique. Find out who on the teaching staff at your institution, or at a neighboring institution, is proficient in a particular teaching method or technique and ask if you can meet with and observe this person.

Practice on a friendly audience--students who work for you, a class with which you feel comfortable, and especially a teaching buddy. Start with one small activity in a class; don't begin with a twenty-minute small group exercise; take five or ten minutes for a buzz session or a brainstorming.

Also, find a teaching buddy and try all of this together. You can sit in the back of each other's class when one of you is trying out an activity and tell the other what went right and wrong. Or you can listen to each other's audio or video tapes. You can bounce ideas off on each other and design activities together. Changing your teaching is like dieting--if you don't tell anyone you are going to do it, probably nothing will happen.

In conclusion, I hope that you have not only learned about the techniques of active learning (our cognitive objectives), but that some of your attitudes (our affective objectives) have changed as well. I hope you have an increased willingness to try active learning methods, to abdicate power to the learner by becoming a facilitator of learning, and seek approaches that lead to higher cognitive objectives.

Integrating Active Learning Techniques into the One-Hour Bibliographic Instruction Lecture
Workshop Outline

Introduction

Choosing Objectives Exercise, Worksheet 1 (Brainstorming)

Teaching Methods and Objectives Questionnaire, Worksheet 2
   (Individual Task and Buzz Groups)

Active Learning Methods (Lecture)

   Learning is the responsibility of the learner, and active learning provides students with more opportunities to organize and practice information and skills.

   Active Learning techniques more effectively lead to higher order cognitive objectives and to affective objectives.

   Breaks in the lecture help maintain interest.

   Active Learning opportunities within the lecture help meet the needs of students with different learning styles.

   Students enjoy such activities which gives them a more positive attitude toward libraries and librarians.

   Students who work on library exercises in the classroom are provided with a model of problem- solving behavior that they can emulate.

And/Or Exercise, Worksheet 3 (Small Group)

Conclusion

   If you want to try these techniques in your teaching, overlearn theory, practice with a friendly audience, start with one small activity, work together with a friend.

Definition of Methods

Brainstorming. The instructor invites class members to offer as many ideas as possible as quickly as possible; criticism is not allowed. In individual brainstorming each person writes down ideas.
Individual Task. Students work individually on a question, a paper quiz or other exercise.
Buzz Groups. Groups of from 2 to 6 people meet for a very short time to review information presented, to formulate question, to brainstorm, or to work on simple problems.
Small Groups. Within a single class period, groups composed of 4 to 6 students work on a question or problem.
Discussion. The class as a whole discusses an issue or problem. Question and answer is a form of discussion. (This technique was not demonstrated.)

Trish Ridgeway, LOEX 5/89
University of Pennsylvania

Trish Ridgeway, Addendum

Worksheet 1
<u>Brainstorming on Objectives</u>

1. What cognitive objectives (objectives that describe concepts, knowledge, and problem-solving skills, the "can do") do you think this session on active learning should focus upon?

2. What Affective Objectives (objectives that refer to changes in attitudes and beliefs, the "will do") do you think this session should focus upon?

Trish Ridgeway, LOEX 5/89
University of Pennsylvania

Trish Ridgeway, Addendum

Worksheet 2
Teaching Methods & Objectives

What percent of Instructional Time in a typical B.I. session do you spend on the following activities:

<u>Percent</u>

1. You Talking   _____

2. Students Talking to You   _____

3. Students Talking to Each Other   _____

4. Students Writing   _____

5. Students Thinking   _____

6. Students Listening to & Viewing A-V   _____

7. Other _____   _____

                                                                100%

Include all time spent on instructional activities but exclude activities such as passing out handouts, taking roll, etc. Do not total above 100%. Even though students are probably thinking and writing while you talk, count the times when they are <u>only</u> thinking or writing.

Rank the importance you would assign the following objectives in your teaching (with 1 being the most important) :

_____ Given a situation the same as the classroom demonstration, students will replicate the tasks presented in the demonstration.

_____ Students have a positive attitude towards librarians and libraries.

_____ Students will take the information that was presented in class and continue to apply it in new and different ways.

_____ Students will demonstrate their awareness of the multitude of library resources available by asking librarians to suggest additional sources.

_____ Students can recall and recite information they have received in class.

_____ Using the criteria presented in the classroom, students will evaluate the information they use.

_____ Students can list sources on a subject.

Trish Ridgeway, LOEX 5/89
University of Pennsylvania

Trish Ridgeway, Addendum

Selected Bibliography on
Active Learning Methods

Bligh, Donald A., ed. **Teach Thinking by Discussion.** Berkshire: The Society for Research
into Higher Education & NFER-Nelson, 1986.

Bouton, Clark and Russell Y. Garth, eds. **Learning in Groups.** New Directions for Teaching
and Learning, No. 14. San Francisco: Jossey-Bass, June 1983.

Brown, George and Madeleine Atkins. **Effective Teaching in Higher Education.** London:
Methuen, 1988.

Cross, K. Patricia. "Teaching for Learning," **AAHE Bulletin** 39 (April 1987), 3-7.

Frederick, Peter J. "Student Involvement: Active Learning in Large Classes," **Teaching
Large Classes Well.** New Directions in Teaching and Learning, No. 32. San Francisco:
Jossey-Bass, Winter 1987, pp. 45-56.

McKeachie, Wilbert J. and Associates. **Teaching and Learning in the College
Classroom: a Review of the Research Literature.** Ann Arbor, Mich.: National
Center for Research to Improve Postsecondary Teaching and Learning, 1986.

International Encyclopedia of Education. Oxford: Pergamon, 1985.
See articles by David Jaques, "Group Teaching in Higher Education," and by M.D. Gall,
"Discussion Methods of Teaching,"

Jaques, David. **Learning in Groups.** London: Croom Helm, 1984.

Joyce, Bruce and Marsha Weil. **Models of Teaching.** 3rd ed. Englewood Cliffs, NJ:
Prentice-Hall, 1986.
See especially Chapter 27, "How to Learn a Teaching Repertoire, Training Ourselves."

Pointers for Good Active Learning Exercises

Provide clear instructions through handouts, overhead, or chalkboard including exercise objectives,
how to form groups, definite time limits, and who will report back on what.

Insist individuals or groups make notes as they work.

Pick opportunities for active learning carefully--for an affective objective, as an introduction (or
set induction), as a review (or closure), or to stress an important point.

Remember everything will take longer than you think. Use every moment of the time allotted for
teaching activities. Ask professor to stress promptness; have students pick up handouts as they
enter.

Trish Ridgeway, Addendum

Worksheet 3
<u>And/Or Exercises</u>

Form into small groups of from 4 to 6 people to work on the following exercise:

One segment of a lecture on teaching students to perform their own computer searches is on the use of "and" and "or" in logical combinations.   Circle one (or perhaps more than one) item in each column and use the circled items to design an active learning exercise. You have 15 minutes.

<u>Objectives</u>	<u>Time</u>	<u>Activity</u>
Students can design a search strategy correctly using "and's" and "or's."	2 minutes	Question & Answer
Given a search topic and the appropriate search terms, students can show how terms should be connected.	5 minutes 10 minutes	Buzz Session Individual Seatwork
	15 minutes	Group Brainstorming
Students can describe the use of "and" and "or" when used as logical operators.	20 minutes	Discussion
Students will recognize when the incorrect use of "and" and "or" leads to bad search results.	25 minutes	Small Group
Students feel confident about their abilities to use "and" and "or" correctly during a search.		Individual Brainstorming
Students can demonstrate how they would use "and" and "or" to broaden or narrow search results.		

Describe your group's active learning exercise:

Trish Ridgeway, LOEX 5/89
University of Pennsylvania

Trish Ridgeway, Addendum

When using small group techniques, plan efficient strategies for dividing into groups by numbering seats, by handing out colored squares or numbers to seated students, or by asking students as they enter to sit only in certain chairs.

Provide students with an opportunity to look at induction exercises while class is settling down.

During group work, circulate among groups to keep students on task and to answer questions.

Make certain students have adequate information to do activities.

Repeat student remarks so all can hear. Synthesize or summarize after groups report.

Active Learning Exercises, Some Examples

Each student receives a sheet with entries from <u>Library of Congress Subject Headings</u> and an explanation of the entries. After the librarian explains LCSH, students can work individually or in buzz groups on a couple questions. This also works for such tools as the <u>ERIC Thesaurus</u>.

Bring multiple copies of indexes (Wilson, DAI, SSCI, etc.) so students can turn to the various sections as you describe them. If there is time, have buzz groups examine the tool and write a paragraph on how to use it.

Handout an example of a bibliography that might be in a freshman term paper. The bibliography should have a few very good items, several old or irrelevant items, some nonscholarly sources, and overall should rate a D or F by your standards. Have students divide into groups to grade the bibliography and list at least 4 reasons for the grade they assign.

At the end of the period in a class on locating book reviews, divide the class into groups and ask each group to locate a popular and a scholarly book review in the book review sources you have brought with you. Check out each title in advance; choose examples that illustrate some of the difficulties of locating reviews.

After a presentation on locating subject headings in history or literature, have students individually or in groups make up subject headings for books that yield some representative examples. Hold up books and project copies of title pages on an overhead projector.

As an exercise for closure, give students one or two research questions and ask them to form groups and decide what reference books they would consult for each topic and in what order.

As a lecture induction, have students brainstorm to list types of primary and secondary sources of information. The lecture will then take each type and tell how to locate them through the library.

Get a list of student research topics before the class begins. Throughout the class ask students to help out their classmates by deciding on the best periodical index to use for some of the topics, what terms they would use to locate material on others, and the appropriateness of certain reference materials for others, etc.

A pretest is especially useful for subject majors who may feel they have learned all they needed in their freshman library lecture. Some examples of pretests are a matching exercise with reference book types and their definitions, a true-false test on what can be found in the card catalog and what can't, and a test that asks what is the most important periodical index, etc., for your subject field. As a review at the end of the session, students should supply correct answers.

Trish Ridgeway, LOEX 5/89
University of Pennsylvania

Trish Ridgeway, Addendum

Information Literacy Skills:

How Students Learn Them and Why

Sandra G. Yee

"Information literacy" is a relatively new term, which has recently come to attract as much attention as "computer literacy" and "cultural literacy." Patricia Breivik wrote in a 1986 publication that information literacy "is the ability to obtain and evaluate information effectively for a given need."[1] In the same publication, she emphasizes why it is imperative that we recognize the importance of **our** role in information literacy. Bibliographic instruction librarians, as well as instructors across the curriculum, are realizing and promoting the fact that this is an "information society," that we have experienced the "information explosion," and that a clear method of dealing with this is imperative. A major thrust in the information literacy movement is its applicability across the entire curriculum--as professors no longer believe that they hold all the knowledge for a particular course, but strive to provide their students with a base of knowledge, and the ability and desire to continue gathering and processing information to add to that base.

This skill, the independent expansion of knowledge, has caused an additional focus on information literacy skills (what they are) and on how they can be acquired. It seems, simply put, that what we're all saying is that in order for students to be successful, they must acquire (or learn) information skills--they must learn how to locate information--and equally important, be able to analyze it, evaluate it, and apply it. It is in this context, of successful student acquisition of information skills, that we become concerned with the cognitive processes, which contribute to a student's ability to learn and use these skills. Information literacy skills are very basic to the process of "learning

Yee is Assistant Dean, Media and Instructional Services, Eastern Michigan University.

how to learn."

We are the experts in information literacy skills, we have been teaching them for years. We have investigated how we might present our message more effectively, how we might emphasize one aspect rather than another, what tools we might use to make our presentations more meaningful. It now seems appropriate that we consider not only how we teach these skills, but equally as important, how students learn them. How can our efforts be even more successful? What enables or prohibits student learning? What can we learn about learning that will help us be better teachers? K. Patricia Cross has written extensively on this topic. In her recent article, "In Search of Zippers," she says, "Teaching and learning are not necessarily two complimentary aspects of the same phenomenon. Learning can and does go on without teaching. Unfortunately, too, teaching can and does go on without learning."[2] Let us investigate, then, what I believe are some of the important learning processes that information literacy instructors should know in order to avoid what Cross describes.

Study of the theories of learning is useful as long as it helps us apply new or better techniques to our teaching or helps students "buy into" the importance of what's being taught. Looking at some broad principles of learning theory, and focusing on applicability may help bring these theories into perspective. Wilbert McKeachie, an educational psychology professor at the University of Michigan and an authority on "learning to learn" offers a good explanation of some of the latest thinking on how learning takes place. He explains it like this:

> For many years psychologists believed that stimulus-response connections were stamped in by rewards or "reinforcements." Memory was the reactivation of these connections. Now theorists go beyond simple reinforcement analysis of learning and memory. Some think of memory as consisting of different types of storage. The fundamental units of storage are meaningful propositions, concepts, or images. Instead of a telephone switchboard metaphor of the mind, theorists now think of semantic learning as more like the building up of structures, networks or maps. When we learn we may add more details to the maps, or we may add more connections between points on the map, or we may even construct alternative maps that are more compact and useful for certain purposes....[3]

McKeachie helps us understand that learning takes place when instructors are able to make use of what students have stored, can effectively assist students in forming new "networks" or "maps," and can facilitate the processing and retrieval of these activities. When new concepts are presented to students, each student (unconsciously) reaches back into his memory to these networks and maps. How and what is stored there is dependent upon the experiences of that individual learner, and is interpreted in relation to those experiences. Thus each student may approach information literacy skills differently depending upon prior learning and experiences that have affected this learning. It may be helpful to form a visual image of a hook, which goes into the long-term memory, finds a familiar item, pulls it into short-term memory where this familiar experience is manipulated by the current information. This certainly helps us understand why we cannot expect students who have no experience (or no internalized experience) with information seeking processes to grasp the analytical set of skills and knowledge of information literacy. Taking a student from "X" point to "Y" point must involve prior learning and experience.

In 1984 D.A. Kolb formulated an experiential learning model, which helps us build on the information from McKeachie. Kolb believes that learning involves a cycle of four processes, each of which must be present for learning to occur most completely. (See Appendix B.) The cycle begins with the learner's personal involvement in a specific experience (concrete experience). The learner reflects on this experience from many viewpoints, seeking to find its meaning (reflective observation). Out of this reflection the learner draws logical conclusions (abstract conceptualizations). These conclusions guide decisions and actions that lead to new concrete experiences (active experimentation). In a 1987 issue of *College Teaching*, Marilla Svinicki and Nancy Dixon suggest that there are instructional designs that lend themselves very nicely to Kolb's model and that may be used to enhance the learning process. They suggest activities (many of which we have already used in BI) that correspond with each of the four poles of the experiential learning model.[4]

While it is possible to design a fifty-minute lecture that incorporates the entire learning cycle, another consideration is the long-term, sequential nature of courses that may be used to build the learning cycle around. Activities will probably need to be different depending upon the discipline since Kolb has suggested that "the disciplines of humanities and social science are based in concrete experience and reflective observation, the natural sciences and mathematics in reflective observation and abstract conceptualization, the science-based professions in abstract conceptualization and active experimentation, and the social professions in active experimentation and concrete experience."[5] (See Appendixes C, D, and E.)

Exercise on Development of Learning Cycle (Group Work Session)

- Define activities appropriate within a fifty-minute lecture.
- Define a sequence of classes (and/or courses) that are appropriate examples of a learning cycle. (See Appendixes F and G.)

These explanations help us understand how information internalized by the students is transferred to their knowledge base. In addition to this understanding, it is helpful to be aware of how individual students receive and process information within the learning cycle. Experts on learning and cognition have also come to realize that all students have identifiable and preferred learning styles.[6] Many possible learning style modalities have been identified including perceptual, cognitive, emotional, and social, as well as others. Perceptual, or how a learner interacts with the environment, and cognitive, the mental processing of the information, seem most critical to information literacy instruction.

Perceptual learning styles are preferences that students exhibit for how information is received. Elements of the perceptual modality are print, aural, interactive, visual, haptic (touch), kinesthetic (movement), and olfactory (smell). (See Appendix H.) While it is important that we realize that students may gather information differently and that one method or technique of teaching may not be sufficient, it is impossible to design instruction to individually address all students' styles. Current thinking by teaching and learning experts such as McKeachie indicate that the best possible solution may be a combination of methods. This has many implications for those of us who are most comfortable with the lecture, or who feel that given the one hour for BI we can only cover everything in this way. We may want to continue to develop alternative instructional methods. The lecture, some handouts, short group discussions, and active exercises may all need to be used at one time or another in order to adequately address as many student learning styles as possible.

It is interesting to look at perceptual styles in conjunction with the learning experiences that we developed for Kolb's experiential learning model. Let's look at what we developed, and see how many different perceptual learning styles we can identify. How many more could be added?

Cognitive learning modalities also have a critical impact on information literacy instruction. Cognitive style refers to the learners' typical method of organizing, remembering, and problem solving. This is the area in which instruction librarians have concentrated efforts to teach critical thinking/problem solving as information literacy skills. For our purposes in information literacy instruction, it is helpful to discuss field independent versus field dependent modality, and the reflective versus impulsive style.

"The field-independent learner approaches a wide variety of tasks in an analytical way, separating elements from background. The field dependent individual approaches situations in a GLOBAL way, seeing the whole instead of the parts."[7] The implication for instruction in information literacy skills is apparent. If we are to develop and fine tune research strategies, evaluation, and analysis, we must be aware of the learning style differences students bring to the classroom. I'd like to share with you some characteristics of the field independent learners and field dependent learners so that we might understand the implications for us even better. As I was discussing this with one of my colleagues who is a professional in our Instructional Support Center, it was pointed out to me that librarians, as a professional group, can probably be characterized as field independent. Research is analytical and we are comfortable in that mode. Its hard to say which came first--the characteristics of the profession, or the fact that field independent learners are drawn to this type of profession. It also puts us in an interesting situation. Unless we understand that others may learn differently, it is extremely hard for us to prepare instruction that meets all needs. This may also be exhibited in the one-to-one contact at the reference desk, during which we instruct students in search strategy. We may feel that we have explained every detail, logically and clearly, only to have the student walk away more confused than before the question was asked.

When analyzing instructional methods for literacy skills instruction we need to take into account the characteristics of the field independent/dependent learners in order to maximize instruction for both. Field dependent learners may feel most comfortable with group learning, relying on others in the group to help solve problems. They may have difficulty with the organization and planning of complex problems and need very specific, detailed instructions for an assignment. On the other hand, field independent learners may be frustrated by detailed instructions, preferring to use their own analytical abilities to solve the complex problems. In this situation, group work can be very beneficial as many of you know. Learners learn best when actively involved, and when instructing others in what is being learned.

If groups are structured well, a mix of dependent and independent learners can benefit from each other. Group learning benefits from the style of the dependent learners in that they tend to have greater social sensitivity and will keep the group working cohesively.

Reflective and impulsive cognitive styles also impact our ability to teach information literacy skills. Given the ideal situation, we would like students to be reflective learners. They tend to consider various alternatives carefully before responding even if it requires a longer time period. The impulsive learner reacts with speed rather than attention to accuracy. While there is benefit to both types of learning, the reflective learner will tend to ask more questions and take a longer time to respond to problems. The impulsive learner is the kind who will want to know the answer--"don't bother me with the details!" Providing enough structure for these types of learners to internalize such information literacy skills as search strategy, analysis of sources, and evaluation of information will require a combination of many teaching strategies. (See Appendix I.)

Learning style experts are studying the impact that helping students identify their own learning styles may ultimately have. It is possible that by recognizing that a particular style exists, students may be able to employ alternative learning strategies. The concept of adapting teaching style to cognitive and perceptual learning styles must not be taken lightly. While it is beneficial for the learner to be matched with the appropriate style in terms of ease and speed of learning, it may not be the best method long term. Students cannot expect the world at large to react to their specific cognitive styles. There is something to be said for training students to change their cognitive and perceptual styles in order to better adapt to changing situations. The current bibliographic instruction trend of teaching the analytical, problem-solving method certainly can be useful in providing assistance in this regard. K. Patricia Cross analyzes this phenomenon quite well in her book *Accent on Learning*. She presents several "enlightened conclusions" regarding cognitive style and teaching that have applicability to the teaching of information literacy skills. She says,

1.   teachers and students should be helped to gain some insight into teaching and learning styles;
2.   no one method should be regarded as a panacea for all students in all subjects;
3.   there are some subjects and some skills that all students need to learn, and we need to be knowledgeable in devising cognitive strategies to teach them (i.e., information literacy skills);
4.   educators need to be aware of the cognitive

styles of students in order to provide the appropriate kinds of reinforcements.[8]

Cross seems to be saying to us in the information science field that we must recognize what and how our students learn, that we must continue to be flexible in our teaching strategies, and that we must join our fellow educators in helping students learn more about "learning strategies."

Learning style literacy is an important concept that information literacy skills instructors can use to fine tune instruction. A complicating factor, however, is **cultural literacy** and the variations in learning styles exhibited through cultural differences.

At Eastern Michigan University we have been engaged in a program to address what was discovered to be a dismal retention and graduation rate of minority students. Over the past year a number of initiatives have begun that will address this problem area. The component of the program that I have been most closely involved with is the academic support area. We have asked this question, "What can we do to better assist high risk minority students in becoming academically successful and eventually reach graduation?" Obviously, information processing skills, along with other skills, are being studied to determine the kinds of assistance that can be most useful.

As we worked on academic success support programming it became apparent that we, and the faculty in general, knew too little about what influences minority students' learning. Through our research we have discovered some differences that have prompted us to make changes in our support program. We are also discussing ways in which what we know about how these students learn, how they assimilate and process information, can be passed on to the faculty, and what we might do to help the faculty members help the students. It should not be said that our ultimate goal is to totally change either the faculty members' method of instruction or the students' method of learning. We hope to bring the two closer together so that common teaching and learning goals can be realized by both.

K. Patricia Cross tells us that it is not known how students acquire their cognitive styles, but socialization and culture seem to have a deep influence. She says, "...people probably learn habitual ways of responding to their environment early in life. These habits, spontaneously applied without conscious choice, determine one's cognitive style."[9] At Eastern, it has been extremely helpful to look at environmental and social factors of learning styles, which allow us to better prepare academic support programs (programs in learning how to learn and process information).

Janice E. Hale-Benson has compiled a great

deal of useful information on culturally based learning styles, which has been helpful in our programming. I will share some of that information with you and also explain some of the techniques that we've used to enhance our programming. In her book, *Black Children: Their Roots, Cultures and Learning Styles*, Hale-Benson describes information from two researchers on Afro-American children that indicates some learning style traits. Some of those that have most applicability to the study of cognitive styles are that Black students:

1. respond to things in terms of the whole picture instead of its parts;
2. prefer inferential reasoning as opposed to deductive or inductive reasoning;
3. prefer to focus on people and their activities rather than things;
4. tend to approximate space, numbers, and time rather than maintain accuracy; and
5. tend to be very proficient in nonverbal communication.[10]

We have also learned that minority students can be quickly discouraged by one technique or idea, and will attempt to find an alternative strategy even before the first has had time to really make an impact. For example, students may be given the assignment to write a paper with topic selection being up to the individual but having a relationship to what is currently being studied. Topic selection actually exhibits a number of difficult situations. First, selection of an appropriate topic may be difficult. Inasmuch as these students may want to respond to the whole instead of the parts, the topic selected may be much too broad. The concept of narrowing is difficult. Second, once a topic is selected, if information is not readily apparent, if the sources are difficult to identify, are checked out, or are in short supply, they will quickly move on to another topic instead of carefully working on the first. Librarians know that topic selection is difficult and it is the first step in critically thinking about a research question. How can we work with these students to identify the problem and strive to help them see the process through?

Recognition of the identifiable cognitive styles (you will probably recognize field-dependent, impulsive) has helped us in the EMU Instructional Support Center develop a few relatively successful strategies. Realizing that the students are social in nature and can effectively work in groups led us to establish regular group study sessions. Although several students might be working on different assignments the support of the group has proven to be immensely important. Students also take time out to help each other (in effect acting as peer tutors) when necessary. This has led us to recommend this method to faculty who are able to integrate group interaction in classes. I'm aware that groups are often used for "information processing" activities in information literacy (BI) sessions. Expansion or continued development of this group technique can be very useful.

A spin-off of the group study sessions combined with a peer tutoring program in content areas led us to develop a new category of peer tutors specifically for our marginal minority students. "Master Tutors" provide a more structured group study session concentrating on learning and study strategies. These sessions are very successful. Academically successful, upper-level minority students were recruited, hired, and trained in the art of helping other students learn how to learn. Included in these Master Tutor sessions is advice on information seeking and processing. The Master Tutor concept is being used in several areas around campus with significant numbers of students voluntarily making use of the services.

There is a great deal more to be discovered about minority students and learning styles in general, and specifically the effect of these cognitive styles on information literacy skills. While there is no "hard research data" to suggest that the simple programs and methods we have put into place make long-term (lifelong) differences, we do know that those students who participate in our programs have had more academic success (higher grade point averages) than those who do not. This would lead us to believe, of course, that we can make an impact on the success of these students through the study of cognitive style and cultural differences. More work needs to be done and it seems to be an area ripe for research.

In addition to the example I cited earlier about topic selection, there are other perceptual and cognitive learning style characteristics that would seem to influence our delivery of information literacy skills instruction for minority students.

As a final exercise, I would like to explore what we know about characteristic perceptual and cognitive styles and challenge you to evaluate your instruction programs utilizing this information. (See Appendix J.)

You may have noticed that I attempted to use presentation methods applicable to various perceptual and cognitive styles. I recognized my weakness in meeting the needs of field dependent learners, and tried to incorporate as many of the characteristic instructional strategies as possible: we worked in groups; you were given detailed instructions including the topic to work on. I attempted to allow impulsive learners the opportunity to feel a part of the session. (We brainstormed, or generated ideas.)

I also hope that we've managed to complete

an entire learning cycle. We have all experienced information literacy skills (both prior to this conference and during); we examined and reflected upon what we know about how they are learned; we heard an explanation about student differences in responding to our instruction; and you have been challenged to apply this information to your own program.

NOTES

1. Patricia Senn Breivik, "Library-Based Learning in an Information Society," in *Managing Programs for Learning Outside the Classroom*, ed. by Patricia Senn Breivik. New Directions for Higher Education, no. 56. (San Francisco: Jossey-Bass, Winter 1986), 47.

2. K. Patricia Cross, "In Search of Zippers," *AAHE Bulletin* 40 (June 1988): 4.

3. Wilbert McKeachie, *Teaching Tips: A Guidebook for the Beginning Teacher*, 8th ed. (Lexington, MA: D.C. Heath and Co., 1986), 233.

4. Marilla Sivinicki and Nancy Dixon, "The Kolb Model Modified for Classroom Activities," *College Teaching* 35 (Fall 1987): 141-142.

5. Sivinicki and Dixon, 144.

6. Wayne B. James and Michael W. Galbraith, "Perceptual Learning Styles: Implications and Techniques for the Practioner," *Lifelong Learning* 8 (January 1985): 20.

7. K. Patricia Cross, *Accent on Learning*. (San Francisco: Jossey-Bass, 1976), 117.

8. Cross, *Accent*, 131-133.

9. Cross, *Accent*, 119.

10. Janice E. Hale-Benson, *Black Children: Their Roots, Culture, and Learning Styles*. Rev. ed. (Baltimore: John Hopkins University Press, 1986), 42.

11. R.L. Sharpe, "A Bag of Tools," in *Best Loved Poems of the American People*, selected by Hazel Felleman. (Garden City, NY: Garden City Books, 1936), 99.

REFERENCES

Booth, Wayne C. "Cultural Literacy and Liberal Learning." *Change* 20 (July/August 1988): 12-21.

Breivik, Patricia Senn. "Library-Based Learning in an Information Society." In *Managing Programs for Learning Outside the Classroom*, ed. by Patricia Senn Breivik, 47-54. New Directions for Higher Education, no. 56. San Francisco: Jossey-Bass, Winter 1986.

Breivik, Patricia Senn, and Ward Shaw. "Libraries Prepare for an Information Age." *Educational Record* 70 (Winter 1989): 13-19.

Claxton, Charles S., and Patricia H. Murrell. *Learning Styles: Implications for Improving Educational Practices*. ASHE-ERIC Higher Education Research Report No. 4. Washington, DC: Association for the Study of Higher Education, 1987.

Cross, K. Patricia. *Accent on Learning*. San Francisco: Jossey-Bass, 1976.

Cross, K. Patricia. "In Search of Zippers." *AAHE Bulletin* 40 (June 1988): 4-7.

Hale-Benson, Janice E. *Black Children: Their Roots, Culture, and Learning Styles*. Rev. ed. Baltimore: John Hopkins University Press, 1986.

Hileand, Leah F. "Information and Thinking Skills and Processes to Prepare Young Adults for the Information Age." *Library Trends* 37, no. 1 (Summer 1988): 56-62.

James, Wayne B., and Michael W. Galbraith. "Perceptual Learning Styles: Implications and Techniques for the Practitioner." *Lifelong Learning* 8 (January 1985): 20-23.

Jones, Beau Fly. "Quality and Equality through Cognitive Instruction." *Educational Leadership* 43 (April 1986): 5-11.

Kolb, David A. *Experiential Learning*. Englewood Cliffs, NJ: Prentice-Hall, 1986.

McKeachie, Wilbert. *Teaching Tips: A Guidebook for the Beginning College Teacher*. 8th ed. Lexington, MA: D.C. Heath and Co., 1986.

Sivinicki, Marilla, and Nancy Dixon. "The Kolb Model Modified for Classroom Activities." *College Teaching* 35 (Fall 1987): 141-146.

LOEX CONFERENCE
MAY 4 and 5, 1989

INFORMATION LITERACY SKILLS
HOW STUDENTS LEARN THEM AND WHY

PRESENTED BY
SANDRA G. YEE
EASTERN MICHIGAN UNIVERSITY

I.   Learning Processes
   A. Building structures or networks
      1. McKeachie memory hooks
   B. Kolb model of experiential learning
      1. Concrete experience; reflective observation; abstract
         conceptualization; and active experimentation.
      2. Activities which correspond to the cycle: experiencing;
         examining; explaining; and applying.

II. Learning Styles
   A. Perceptual learning styles (Preferences for receipt of
      information)
      1. Print; aural; interactive; visual; haptic; kinesthetic and
         olfactory.
   B. Cognitive learning styles (Preferences for processing and
      organizing information.)
      1. Field independent: analytical
      2. Field dependent: global
      3. Reflective: longer, careful consideration
      4. Impulsive: quicker, fewer details

III. Cultural Literacy
   A. Minority students' learning styles
      1. Field dependent, impulsive
   B. Eastern Michigan University response
      1. Master Tutors

Sandra Yee: Addendum

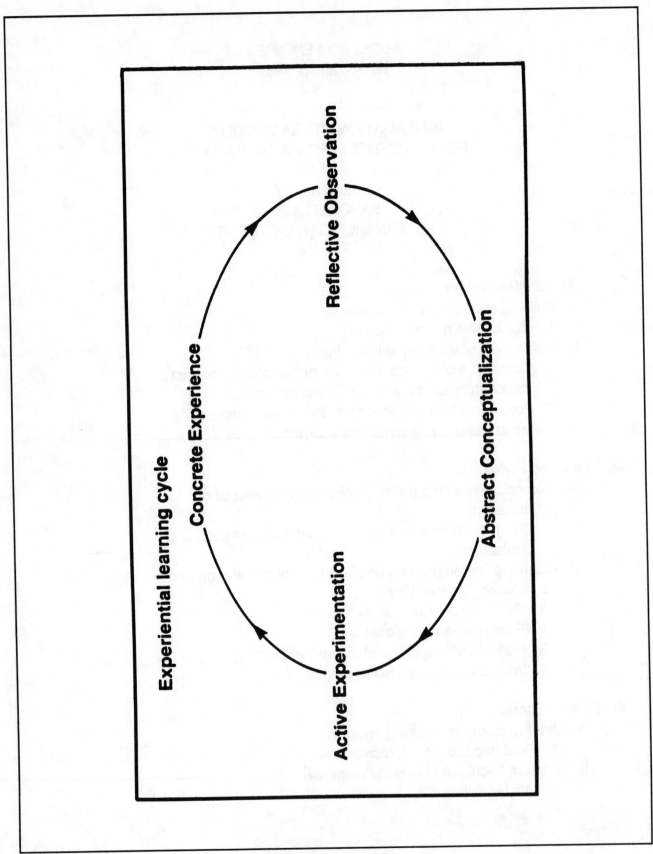

Sandra Yee: Appendix A

EXPERIENTIAL LEARNING CYCLE
INSTRUCTIONAL ACTIVITIES

CONCRETE EXPERIENCE
Laboratories
Observations
Primary text reading
Simulations/games
field work
trigger films
readings
problem sets
examples

ACTIVE EXPERIMENTATION
Simulations
Case study
Laboratory
Field work
Projects
Homework

REFLECTIVE OBSERVATION
Logs
Journals
Discussion
Brainstorming
Thought questions
Rhetorical questions

ABSTRACT CONCEPTUALIZATION
Lecture
Papers
Model Building
Projects
Analogies

Sandra Yee: Appendix B

Concrete Experience

CE
Students see films of
WW II and Vietnam

AE

Students write short
paper applying analysis
developed to reporting
on similar global events
or topics.

HISTORY

RO

Students write
personal reaction to
depictions of two
wars by media

AC

Lecture on public reaction to the
two wars plus discussion of similarities
to own reaction and attempt to identify'
reporting techniques which influence
reactions

Sandra Yee: Appendix C

EXPERIENTIAL LEARNING CYCLE

BIBLIOGRAPHIC INSTRUCTION ACTIVITIES

EXPERIENCING

Library Road Rally

Trigger film
Challenger accident

APPLYING

Group Presentation
Debate
News Report

EXAMINING

Group Brainstorming

Search Stratey Discussion

EXPLAINING

Formal 50 minute lecture

Individual discussions

Sandra Yee: Appendix D

EXPERIENTIAL LEARNING CYCLE

BIBLIOGRAPHIC INSTRUCTION ACTIVITIES

CONCRETE EXPERIENCE

ACTIVE EXPERIMENTATION   REFLECTIVE OBSERVATION

ABSTRACT CONCEPTUALIZATION

Sandra Yee: Appendix E

EXPERIENTIAL LEARNING CYCLE

BIBLIOGRAPHIC INSTRUCTION COURSES

CONCRETE EXPERIENCE

ACTIVE EXPERIMENTATION

REFLECTIVE OBSERVATION

ABSTRACT CONCEPTUALIZATION

Sandra Yee: Appendix F

PERCEPTUAL LEARNING STYLES

PRINT: Learns best through reading and writing. Easily retains information that is read.

AURAL: Learns best while listening or through verbal presentation of information. Lectures, audiotapes.

INTERACTIVE: Learns best through verbalization. Likes to talk and discuss ideas with other people.

VISUAL: Learns best through observation. Likes to see visual stimuli such as pictures, slides, etc.

HAPTIC: Learns best through the sense of touch. Has to feel objects or touch as many things as possible. Assimilates information through a hands-on approach to learning.

KINESTHETIC: Learns best while moving. Generally has to move around or have some part of the body moving while processing information.

OLFACTORY: Learns best through the sense of taste and smell.

Sandra Yee: Appendix G

COGNITIVE LEARNING STYLES

FIELD INDEPENDENCE: Analytical; separate elements from background.

FIELD DEPENDENCE: Global; see the whole instead of the parts.

REFLECTIVE: Consider alternatives carefully before responding.

IMPULSIVE: React with speed rather than attention to accuracy.

Sandra Yee: Appendix H

MINORITY STUDENTS'
CHARACTERISTIC LEARNING STYLES

PERCEPTUAL STYLES:

Aural: Generally learn best through listening. (Verbal messages are important; words must be in context to have meaning.)

INTERACTIVE: Generally learn best through verbalization. (Like to discuss and debate ideas.)

KINESTHETIC: Generally learn best while moving. (Like to move around while processing information; constant motion.)

COGNITIVE STYLES:

FIELD-DEPENDENT: GLOBAL APPROACH
    Repond in terms of the whole picture instead of parts.
    Like being with and relating to people. (Are interactive
        learners who learn well using group interaction.)
    Sensitive to the judgments of others. Tend to be guided
        by authority figures. (Look to the instructor to
        provide answers; i.e. select a topic.)
    Extrinsically motivated; respond to social
        reinforcement.

IMPUSLIVE: QUICK RESPONSE
    Quick exchange of ideas; brainstorming, group
        discussions, role plays.
    Less concern for exact accuracy.

Sandra Yee: Appendix I

EXPERIENTIAL LEARNING CYCLE

EXPERIENCING
Draw Upon prior experience
Example
Observations

APPLYING
Your Challenge

EXAMINING
Your exercises
Continued reflection
Discussion
Thought questions

EXPLAINING
My discussion
projects

Sandra Yee: Appendix J

Transforming the ACRL Model

Statement of Objectives

into a Working Tool

Rebecca Jackson

Information literacy involves knowing your way around in the information world. However, different groups of people have different needs and abilities and we, as librarians and information instructors, must be aware of what to teach to whom. A first grader cannot understand the concepts that a senior in high school can. A freshman undergraduate student working on his/her first ten-page paper does not have the same information needs as a Ph.D. student starting dissertation research. Further, if we are going to evaluate our methods for promoting information literacy, we need standards by which to test our efforts. We also need clear-cut objectives for each step along the way.

For these reasons--to help us determine the scope of instruction we need to offer, to focus on our specific aims in any instructional experience, and to evaluate our methods--we need to develop goals and objectives. Fortunately, ACRL has already helped by providing a model statement of objectives, which we can turn to for guidance. That is what we decided to use at the University of Maryland to help us develop our own statement of objectives.

Introduction to ACRL's Model Statement of Objectives

Before beginning with the University of Maryland's experience adapting the Model Statement of Objectives (Appendix 1), it is probably best to review that statement itself. The draft revision was published in College and Research Libraries News, May 1987. It starts with a fairly lengthy introduction, which describes the scope and guiding principles for the development of the model statement. That introduction is a good place to start examining

Jackson is Coordinator for Library Instruction at University of Maryland at College Park.

the statement. Based on the 1979 model statement, the newer revision expands the scope of the user groups addressed, an important addition for any academic library that finds itself serving the needs of undergraduates, graduates, faculty, administration, and outside user groups. As technology changes the range of tools and services offered by libraries, all of these groups become prospective targets for instruction in academic libraries. Further, the revised statement emphasizes conceptual processes for learning information retrieval, rather than tools. As technology changes, so do the tools and services within each particular library. Therefore, it is important to develop goals and objectives that are flexible and reflect the knowledge of information literacy rather than tools. By emphasizing conceptual processes, ACRL is emphasizing this conference's theme of information literacy.

Also described in the introduction is the theoretical framework for the development of the types of objectives used in the model statement:

1.   General objectives - describe the overall goals of the programs and what the program is intended to achieve. For example, on page three of the handout you have on University of Maryland at College Park (UMCP) Objectives (Appendix 2), the first goal is "I. How information is identified and defined by experts." The general objective further defines: "The user understands how information is defined by experts, and recognizes how that knowledge can help determine the direction of his/her search for specific information." This is a very general statement. From the general we move to the more specific.

2.   Terminal objectives - break down the overall objectives into specific, discrete, measurable results. The terminal objective for the general objective stated above is broken down into several levels. The first is "The user recognizes that disciplines use specific methods to communicate information." At the more specific level, "The user recognizes that information sources can be recorded or unrecorded sources which may appear in different physical formats." From this still fairly broad objective, we split the terminal objective into the basic and advanced users (those I will define later). The basic user "understands that sources may be found by using books, periodicals, microforms, computer reference sources, pamphlets, nonprint media such as films and tapes, and human resources." This statement is much more specific, identifying particular types of sources.

3.   Enabling (behavioral) objectives - define the specific knowledge or skills necessary to achieve the terminal objectives. These are called behavioral objectives because they define a specific

behavior that the user should be able to perform as a test of whether or not s/he has mastered that objective. For instance, an enabling objective for the above objective might be that "At the basic level, the user names four different types of information resources." The verbs used in developing enabling objectives are action verbs, specifying what the user must be able to do.

The model statement only includes the first two types of objectives. The third type, enabling objectives, should be developed by each institution, since they will, obviously, differ depending upon the tools and resources available within a particular library.

This breakdown of objectives is typically recommended by educators for use in most educational situations, and anyone who has worked with objectives before will probably be familiar with them. However, librarians have not often been expected to look at their goals in terms of educational objectives. So, in many cases, librarians are not familiar with this type of goal setting. The tendency has been to try to justify library instruction programs using general goals such as "To foster independence in library users." More and more often, though, accountability is demanded of librarians and libraries, and justification for their requests must be based on quantifiable observations; librarians must be able to pinpoint exactly what it is they want users to learn.

Finally, the introduction to the model statement has a section on how to use the statement. The authors say the statement should be used as a checklist for existing instructional programs and as a guide for developing new programs.

Basic Arrangement of the Model Statement

The model statement is divided into four major areas, which reflect the emphasis on conceptual learning:

1. "How information is identified and defined by experts." That is--the information flow within a discipline and the process of recognizing authority of information.

2. "How information sources are structured." This is what we call the bibliographic chain--myriad sources, print or nonprint, from which information can be gathered and the methods for their evaluations.

3. "How information sources are intellectually accessed by users." This point focuses on the user's recognition that there are tools available to get to the various types of information and that the methods for using these tools may vary within certain limits.

4. "How information sources are physically organized

and accessed." At this point, the aspects of individual libraries and their arrangements come into
play. How does a particular library organize its
services and resources, and does that differ from
the way other libraries do the same things? From
these broad instructional goals, more specific terminal objectives are spelled out for each of the
four goals. Librarians are encouraged to use this
statement in a kind of piecemeal fashion, selecting
those goals and objectives pertinent to a particular
program of instruction. At UMCP, we decided
to use the whole statement, but before I discuss
our experiences, let me first give you some background as to why we decided to develop objectives
at all.

Purpose of UMCP Objectives

The University of Maryland at College Park
is the largest of twelve Maryland state schools.
It currently enrolls about 36,000 students, 28,000
of whom are undergraduates. There are seven libraries in the UMCP Libraries system--an undergraduate (Hornbake), a large upper-level and graduate research library (McKeldin), and five special
subject-oriented branch libraries.

When I arrived at the UMCP Libraries in
1986, I was charged with evaluating the entire
library instruction program. Instruction had been
important to the UMCP Libraries for a number
of years, and there was already in place a fairly
complex and sophisticated program. Librarians
had developed services for the required freshman
and junior composition programs, there was a
nearly complete series of brochures for each of
the libraries and some of the special services,
there were a great many point-of-use instructional
guides and an extensive collection of inhouse, li-
brarian-produced research guides. We had slide-
tape presentations and videotapes of classes. The
librarians in McKeldin and the branch libraries
had instructional relationships with their departments for both undergraduate and graduate classes.
We even had rudimentary written objectives for
undergraduates.

However, even though we kept statistics on
how many classes we were teaching, how many
orientation sessions we provided, and how many
students were involved in each, we had no reliable
measure of how effective we were at promoting
information literacy, nor did we have a clear idea
of what we expected our students to understand
about the libraries at any given point in their college careers. Further, the libraries were experiencing, and probably will continue to experience, a process of great change, with new organization and new technology. This continuing
change meant that not only the students but also

the faculty were often uninformed about the libraries. Changes in the libraries paralleled changes
in the university as a whole. One of the most
significant of the university changes was a renewed,
stronger emphasis on the quality of education, with
a plan for restructuring the undergraduate curriculum.
Students would have smaller classes with more seminars and capstone courses focusing on integration
of the students' college coursework. What better
time for the libraries to begin to campaign for
an emphasis on information literacy and the place
of the libraries within a student's education?

Thus, to help me evaluate the library instruction
program as it was and to show the faculty that
the libraries had an interest in helping to improve
education within the university, I decided it was
time to develop a new set of objectives and goals
for library instruction. Having seen the model
statement and having attended a hearing on that
statement at ALA in San Francisco, I proposed
forming a committee to develop our own set of
objectives; I hoped we would be able to adapt
the model statement for our purposes.

Composition of Membership

I began by enlisting the support of Associate
Director for Public Services Danuta Nitecki. She
agreed that such a plan was necessary and asked
me for suggestions for a task force to write a
statement of objectives. My choice for members
on the committee was carefully planned. I wanted
to have representation from the two major libraries
and the branches. Our undergraduate library runs
a massive library instruction program, with the
freshman composition program, the junior composition program, a speech program, a zoology program,
orientation programs including those for international
and disadvantaged students, and other classes in
the lower levels of the undergraduate curriculum.
The person in charge of reference for this library
has always had a major interest in library instruction,
and so he was one of my first choices. Then there
is a library instruction liaison from both the undergraduate library and McKeldin Library; these liaisons
are my communication links with the rest of the
librarians in their respective reference departments.
Naturally, they were both important. I wanted
to include the head of reference in McKeldin Library,
but she suggested another member of the department
who works with the College of Education. Since
the government documents staff participates in
much of our instruction, the head of our government
documents unit was selected. In addition, there
were two members from the branch libraries, one
who was fairly new to our system and one who
had been around for several years and was not
as enthusiastic about instruction as the rest of

the members. With myself as chair, there were eight members on the task force--enough to divide work up into subcommittees, but not too many to be unwieldy.

Timetable

When the associate director sent the memo to begin the task force, she gave us two months to submit a first draft and another month to submit the final draft. Little did either of us know just how unrealistic that timetable would prove to be. In fact, the task force began on 15 September 1987 and submitted its final draft to the associate director on 20 October 1988. It took over a year to complete the writing process.

Review of Existing Objectives

What took so long, given the fact that we already had a model statement in front of us to work with? There were several steps to take before we even began working with the model statement. The first was to review other existing objectives. We already had a set of objectives developed for undergraduate students. How relevant were they? In addition, we had collected statements of library instruction objectives from other institutions. These were all reviewed to see how useful they could be for us at this time.

Determination of Whether or Not to Use the Model Statement

The task force members all received copies of the model statement. We spent some time deciding whether we actually wanted to use that statement as the backbone for our own objectives. We reviewed it carefully and decided that, though it seemed complex and at times ambiguous, it was useful because it seemed to cover the whole area of library instruction, it was flexible, and using an already existing model should save us time.

Level of Specificity of Objectives

Our second decision was on the level of specificity of the objectives we would create. Did we want to delineate enabling objectives, or should they be left until later? That semester, we were initiating the use of InfoTrac and other automated reference sources for end-users, such as ERIC, PsycLit, Dow Jones Information Retrieval Service, and LEXIS. We were also experimenting with some expert system applications. We anticipated many more changes, including more end-user database services, both bibliographic and non-bibliographic, a new online catalog in two to three years, and

the development of more inhouse computerized reference sources and audio-visual materials for research. Therefore, we decided that enabling objectives should be developed based on specific library instruction programs as the need for them arose.

Dividing Up the Target User Groups

The hardest decision we had to make was how to divide up our user groups. At the time, we could differentiate between levels of instruction for our freshman composition program and our junior composition program, and a level for graduate students. However, we did not know how long there would be freshman and junior composition in our curriculum, nor could we predict how the new curriculum might be structured.

To further complicate matters, we were finding that with the new information technology, including online catalogs and computerized reference sources, often faculty and graduate students were as informationally illiterate as undergraduate students. Therefore, we needed a system that would include all of our community.

We finally decided to divide users into four major groups--1) undergraduate users, 2) graduate students, 3) faculty, and 4) administration, staff, and non-UMCP-affiliated library users. Within the category of undergraduate students, we further divided into basic users (those who are at the level where their courses are basic more than subject-specific) and advanced users (those upper-level students who have begun research in their majors).

Introduction to the Whole Document

Once the divisions were decided upon, it was time to take a close look at the ACRL model statement again. We spent several weeks going over the document, almost point by point. There were several sections that all of us felt were ambiguous. We found a detailed review was necessary to get an overall picture of what each section was really about. For instance, we had great difficulty with Section 2, T3.b.4.: "The user understands the link between the information provided within a citation and the organizational structure of the source cited and recognizes the importance of the link in evaluating the usefulness of the source identified." In this case, as in several others, we struggled with the meaning of that statement, and finally simplified it to: The user understands the relationship of citations to other information sources.

Although we maintained the four divisions, within the divisions we reorganized considerably. For instance, if you look at page three of the UMCP Objectives handout and compare that with the original model statement, you can see that we omitted T1

("The user understands that individuals or groups identify themselves as belonging to specific areas and or disciplines") and T2 ("The user recognizes that individuals within these groups may combine information from information sources with original thought, experimentation, and/or analysis to produce new information"). T1 we thought was too obvious to include. T2 was not specifically about library instruction, but it is something students should be learning within their major disciplines, as germane to their majors.

Split into Subcommittees

Most of the decisions on specific changes were not made, however, until much later in the process. First, we split up into four subcommittees of two members each. Each couple was to work on the objectives for one user group; one group worked on undergraduate objectives, one graduate, and so on. This seemed the best way to actually get started with the practical problems of how to work with the model statement; the subcommittees were our first working committees.

After a few weeks, we all met together again to share our results. Although none of us had finished products, we at least had documents in front of us that bore some relationship to our particular user groups. However, this was only the beginning of a long and grueling process.

Undergraduate Objectives

After a few sessions of floundering around, trying to decide how best to handle what we had put together in our subcommittees, we finally decided, as a whole group, that we had to start with one set of objectives and work through it point by point. We chose the undergraduate objectives first because: 1. they represented the basic skills needed in library use (which would become the foundation for the other groups); 2. they would, therefore, be the longest set of objectives; and 3. since the university's primary concern at the time was for undergraduate education, we wanted to have these objectives available first.

We started with an introduction for several reasons. First, we had to have a starting point even for our basic undergraduate students. Most students have had to use either a high school or public library at some point before they begin their college studies. We chose to look at competencies developed by some of our area county school systems. From these lists we developed our own list of what we assumed students had already accomplished before they had graduated from high school. These are listed on page one of your handout on UMCP Objectives. They include use

of the card catalog (or another type of catalog); use of the *Readers' Guide to Periodical Literature* or similar periodical index; use of basic reference books such as encyclopedias, dictionaries, directories; the ability to determine from a citation basic types of publications and where to look for them; and the ability to work with a reference librarian to develop a search strategy for a subject. Although these were our written expectations, our experiences with undergraduate students led us to expect a very minimal level of competencies in any of the above areas.

Second, we had to define what we meant by basic and advanced students. At first, we had started with three groups of undergraduate students --basic, intermediate, and advanced. However, we later decided that two groups were sufficient for our purposes and our definitions. The definitions were already mentioned before and they are also listed on page one of your handout on UMCP Objectives.

From our previous floundering, we had already decided that we would develop the undergraduate objectives to be used as the basic foundation for the rest of the user groups. We would spell out very detailed objectives for this group, and for the subsequent user groups we would indicate that they were expected to have already achieved the objectives for the previous groups (the exception was for the group of administration, staff, and non-UMCP users because their needs and their backgrounds were more unpredictable). Therefore, the undergraduate objectives would be the longest, and the other groups' could be shorter, adding only the more sophisticated objectives they would need to master.

Because it was longer and more detailed, the undergraduate document took almost eight months to complete. During that time, we went through each point, revising the wording, breaking the objectives down by level, eliminating those we thought should be in another section, clarifying points, and adding items where necessary. We sent several drafts to the associate director for comment, and then made revisions based on her feedback. She also came once to speak to our group, a sort of pep talk that was much needed after weeks of agonizing over sentences, phrases, and words. She was very particular about the structure of the outline itself; if there was an A, there had to be a B. That made us focus even more on presenting a balanced, well-considered document.

As an example, page eight of your handout begins section three of the objectives. If you look at the model statement you see that many of the points are essentially the same, but in our document we rearranged them somewhat. We combined T1. a, b, and c into one statement in our document.

In section T1.d, we kept much of what was already there. However, we felt that T1.d.3 might be too sophisticated for undergraduates, so we eliminated it here and added it in the graduate objectives. Also in the graduate objectives, we added another type of access point, that of methodological and critical perspectives (as in *MLA Bibliography*).

All of this took a great deal of consideration, concentration, and discrimination. Some points we thought were repeated from section to section, some points we thought needed further explanation or complete rewording. However, on the whole, we never wavered in our belief that the model statement was a good skeleton.

Model Statement

3. How information sources are intellectually accessed by users.
General Objective: The user can identify useful information from information sources or information systems.
T1. The user understands that although any information about an information source could be used to help identify and locate it, there are certain elements of information called access points which are accepted by the research community as the most pertinent through which to identify a source.

a. The user recognizes that the "author" entry is a commonly used access point.
b. The user recognizes that the title of a recorded information source is a commonly used access point.
c. The user recognizes that the "subject" topic, or description fields is a commonly used access point.
d. The user recognizes that the use of additional access points depends on the structure and format of the source used to identify new information.
d.1. The user recognizes that each element of information found within a citation may potentially be used as an access point.
d.2. The user recognizes that information found within an abstract or summary may potentially be used as access points (usually through the method of key word searching where each word can be used as an access point).
d.3. The user recognizes that additional access may be available through codes, categories, or mapping which may not be obvious in the information source or system.

UMCP Undergraduate Objectives

III. How information sources are intellectually accessed by users.

General Objective: The user can identify useful information from information sources or information systems.
A. The user understands that although any information about an information source could be used to help identify and locate it, there are certain elements of information called access points which are accepted by the research community as the most pertinent through which to identify a source.
1. The user recognizes that commonly used access points are author, title, and subject.
B. The user recognizes that the use of access points other than author, title, or subject depends on the structure and format of the source used to identify new information.
a. The user recognizes that each element of information found within a citation may potentially be used as an access point.
b. The user recognizes that information found within an abstract or summary may potentially be used as access points (usually through the method of key word searching where each word can be used as an access point).

Another change that we made was to add a fifth category, which specifically spoke to the knowledge we expected our users to have about the UMCP Libraries and services. This section was very short and only used in the undergraduate objectives, so I will repeat it here:
V. How facilities and services are physically organized and accessed.
General Objective: The user understands how to find and use UMCP Libraries facilities and services.
A. The basic user understands how to find and use the facilities and services of the Hornbake (Undergraduate) Library.
B. The advanced user understands how to find and use the facilities and services of the UMCP Libraries most appropriate for his/her subject specialty.

Other Groups of Objectives

Once we had submitted the final draft of undergraduate objectives, we were able to move through the other three groups much more quickly. The graduate objectives followed closely the outline of undergraduate objectives with the addition of what we felt were more sophisticated terminal objectives.

The faculty objectives presented some exceptions, because of the fact that faculty research and teach. Therefore, in that document of objectives we included a section titled "How faculty instructional development can be promoted and assisted," which was essentially a call for faculty to help monitor the information and library literacy of their students. We omitted the section on "How information sources are structured," because that had been covered in the previous two documents. The undergraduate objectives document was thirteen pages long; both the graduate and faculty objectives documents were three pages each.

The final category was for administration, staff, and non-UMCP library users. Our expectation was that their needs would be different from the other categories, and their backgrounds would be diverse. Therefore, we completely eliminated the format we had used for the other three groups and developed a simple statement for UMCP administration and staff: These users should understand the basic facilities and services offered by the UMCP Libraries that will be most useful to them in performing their jobs. Most often, administration and staff do not require instruction in the use of the libraries, but rather UMCP librarians will offer them greater assistance in doing research. Staff members working for administration or faculty should have enough knowledge of the libraries to enable them to carry out their responsibilities with minimal assistance from librarians. Since we recognize no official obligation to non-UMCP users, we developed a simple statement that left our commitment open for later development: Such users should have enough knowledge of the UMCP library system as to be able to accomplish the work they come to do in the libraries with minimal assistance from librarians. They should be aware of what service policies affect them (e.g., circulation, use of automated reference services, and use of special collections).

Administrative Feedback

Throughout the whole process, as I have mentioned, we were sending drafts of the various documents to the associate director for public services and then making further revisions according to her suggestions. You can imagine our sense of satisfaction when, after about fourteen months of work, we sent to her the final copy of the four documents and a general introduction. We were all very much concerned about what would happen to these documents we had labored over so intensively.

The Finished Product

In the many months since we have finished the document, it has not gotten much farther than the associate director's office. She has submitted it to the director of the libraries, who gave her some suggestions for approaching faculty with at least the undergraduate objectives. Since then, the associate director has been appointed to a university committee to implement the plans for the improvement of undergraduate education. She has presented the library instruction objectives to them, but they, at this point, are not sure how they can be implemented within the curriculum. They have suggested that we present them to individual departments, which might work, but in a way it defeats our purpose of having our objectives become part of the university's overall commitment to curricular change. However, the associate director has not yet given up. Right now we are in the proposal stage of a project that would quantifiably demonstrate the benefits of instruction in library research with regard to the students' papers and other research.

Within the libraries, we are using the objectives as our own standard for the development of programs and projects. In fact, we have already had several instances when we referred to the objectives:

1. Last spring, we began an evaluation of our junior composition program. A committee, composed of librarians, a library school faculty member, and a junior composition faculty member, was established to examine the junior composition program and make recommendations as to how it could be improved. One of the first places we started was with the library instruction objectives; from them, we developed a list of competencies that we expected students to have mastered by the time they receive library instruction in their classes. The work of this committee has led us to re-examine our priorities for freshman composition, to determine that we need to concentrate more on individual instruction projects, and to begin the development of several such individual projects.

2. We have started to write a basic workbook for use in our junior composition classes, based on the objectives we have developed for basic library users.

3. The member of the library school faculty who served on the junior composition evaluation committee is currently working with me on a CLR grant to develop a Hypercard program for teaching our users how to access periodical articles, from defining what an index is, through differentiating among the basic Wilson indexes, to using our Serials List and locating the periodicals within the various libraries. It was from this faculty member, Delia Neuman, that I got my real lesson in writing enabling or behavioral objectives. We worked from the original undergraduate objectives to the very specifics of what we wanted each student to be able to do once s/he had completed the Hypercard program. I have included these objectives in your handouts, (Appendix 3) and as you can see, they are very specific. For instance, on page eight of your handout on UMCP Objectives, (Appendix 2) you see the item 3.b. at the bottom of the page states: "The

user recognizes that most controlled vocabulary describes the subject or author of the information source. S/he can identify useful items in the subject catalog and the basic periodical indexes." In the handout for the Hypercard Project, one behavioral objective that corresponds to the above terminal objective is 2.B: "Given a particular topic, the user locates (an) appropriate subject heading(s) within an index for that topic."

4. One of our staff is working on her Ph.D. dissertation in education. Her topic is the self-directedness of adult students and how that is reflected in their library skills. We worked together on a questionnaire, which she will use as her evaluative tool in her research. The questionnaire is based solely on the library instruction objectives that I submitted to her. She has developed a chart that links each question to one or more of the objectives specified in our documents. The tool seems to be valid, and she has given me permission to use it for the libraries' purposes after she has finished her work.

These are just some of the ways we have used the objectives so far. As new projects and programs are developed (it seems every day), I find that the objectives become more and more useful to me and to others involved in the projects. I am still convinced that it was worth the effort. However, I have a few suggestions for those of you who are contemplating the same task:

1. Make sure that you have administrative support from the beginning of the project. It is a massive task to develop these objectives, as I have demonstrated, and the people involved will want to be assured that their work will not be tossed into a file drawer never to be seen again. The more support you can get, the better. Use library administrators. Use faculty that you have won over. Spread the word.

2. Choose group members from a wide range of library units. By selecting a wide range of librarians, you can get feedback from most of the departments who are involved with public services and library instruction. Additionally, each unit then feels that its interests are represented in the development of the objectives and has more of an interest in it.

3. Choose group members who have a special interest in library instruction. Our one group member who was not a library instruction fan proved

not to be very dependable in working on the objectives and contributing to the group with his own special perspective.

4. Give yourself lots of time. Each institution has its own needs, its own services and facilities, and its own special group of users. You need to fit all of them into your objectives, and that can mean much thought and discussion, writing and revising. Other responsibilities have to take priority at times, and you cannot spend all your time or your committee members' time working on this one project.

5. Be prepared for the vagueness of the model statement. Part of this vagueness is probably by design, to make the statement applicable to all libraries and users. However, when you are faced with drawing up objectives for your institution, you will probably want to clarify many of the objectives in the model statement.

6. Have your own good reasons for developing these objectives. Do not count on the faculty embracing library instruction objectives upon first reading. You may have to work more subtly to have them accepted within the institutional environment. However, keep in mind how useful these objectives can be in developing your own library instruction programs.

Conclusion

The draft of the Model Statement of Objectives was accepted by ACRL within the past year. There were no changes made to the draft in the final document. The draft of UMCP Objectives that we developed has been accepted by myself and the rest of our committee, by our associate director, and will probably be integrated into public service policy this year. We will continue to push for the objectives to be accepted by the whole university community. However, even without that acceptance, I feel a great sense of satisfaction in the completion of our document. We now have not only a basis upon which to evaluate our programs, but we also have a structure for planning for and expanding our instruction efforts.

I hope that my presentation has given you some insights into developing objectives of your own. If you have any questions or if I can be of help to you in determining what to do in your efforts, please ask me now or write to me at the University of Maryland.

Model statement of objectives for academic bibliographic instruction: Draft revision

Prepared by the ACRL/BIS Task Force on Model Statement of Objectives
Lori Arp, Chair

A proposed revision of the 1979 model statement.

The following draft document represents the efforts of a special Task Force within ACRL's Bibliographic Instruction Section to review and revise the 1979 Model Statement of Objectives for Academic Bibliographic Instruction. This revision was undertaken in the spirit of updating the original Statement so that it would more closely reflect current thinking and trends in bibliographic instruction. The original statement was intended to provide guidance in the development of instruction programs as well as to stimulate discussion about BI in the profession. Similarly, the revision seeks to achieve the same goals. While the document draws on the 1979 Statement, its scope has been expanded to encompass not only undergraduate instruction needs, but other user groups within academic libraries. It also differs from its predecessor in that its focus is on the conceptual processes of using information, rather than on tool specific or institution specific detail.

Those of us who have observed the growth of this document are excited about this new direction and we would like to share it with the profession through an open hearing in San Francisco. By holding this hearing we hope to confirm that the document represents the instructional needs of the Section so that it may then move forward in the process of becoming an official guideline of the Section. This work furthers our mission of developing policy statements that provide direction for instruction librarians. The hearing has been scheduled for Monday, June 29, 11:00 a.m.–12:30 p.m. The room location will be listed in the ALA schedule.

Readers are referred to: 1) "Towards Guidelines for Bibliographic Instruction in Academic Libraries," *C&RL News*, May 1975, pp. 137–39, 169–71; 2) "Guidelines for Bibliographic Instruction in Academic Libraries," *C&RL News*, April 1977, p. 92; and 3) *Bibliographic Instruction Handbook*, published by ACRL in 1979, for a review of the original Model Statement of Objectives and Guidelines for Bibliographic Instruction. We welcome your written comments on the revision. Please address these to: Betsy Baker, BIS Chairperson, Northwestern University Library, 1935 Sheridan Road, Evanston, IL 60201.

The Bibliographic Instruction Section would like to acknowledge the members of the Task Force: Lori Arp (chair), Barbara Beaton, Joseph Boissé, Julie Czisny, David Ginn, Roland Person, Jan Rice, and Beth Woodard.—*Betsy Baker, Chair, BIS.*

Rebecca Jackson: Appendix 1

Introduction

The primary purpose of the Model Statement is to generate thinking in the discipline of bibliographic instruction concerning the direction of existing instructional programs. It is intended to help librarians articulate and focus on what their instructional objectives should be and stimulate research into whether existing programs are achieving these objectives. As such, the Statement is not designed to introduce the new librarian to the field, nor is it designed to introduce an outside faculty member to the relevant concepts within the discipline. Rather, it is intended to serve as a statement of general direction for practicing librarians to review when examining current instructional programs or developing the keystones of new programs.

The role of bibliographic instruction is not only to provide students with the specific skills needed to complete assignments, but to prepare individuals to make effective life-long use of information, information sources, and information systems. To this end, the Model Statement attempts to outline the pertinent processes individuals use when gathering information. The Statement does not attempt to be comprehensive. The content is designed as a set of examples or points of departure and is not intended to serve as an institution's primary document.

The Model Statement is comprised of a set of general and terminal objectives which describe the general processes used when gathering information. Three objectives are normally used to describe the learning activities desired for a particular instructional unit. These objectives include: general objectives; terminal objectives; and enabling objectives. General objectives describe the overall goals of the programs and what the program is intended to achieve. Terminal objectives break down the overall objectives into specific discrete measurable results. Enabling (behavioral) objectives define the specific knowledge or skills necessary to achieve the terminal objectives. They are associated with the behavior of the person who has to master the material. Since each institution must determine their own enabling objectives, they are not included in this document, which attempts to generalize the processes used to access information.

For convenience, the series of general and terminal objectives listed in the Model Statement has been broken into four broad areas of concern with corresponding objectives listed in each of the areas. The Statement outlines how information is:

    a) identified and defined by experts;
    b) structured;
    c) intellectually accessed;
    d) physically organized and accessed.

The section headings represent significant areas or topics of concern to instruction librarians. No set order is intended.

When developing the Model Statement, the Task Force was guided by the following principles:

1. *User groups targeted by the objectives*. The Model Statement is designed to address the needs of all potential user groups within academic libraries. This was done for two reasons: 1) Experience has shown that there is no homogeneous group of "students" or even "undergraduates," but rather there exists a diverse student body whose members operate on a continuum of research sophistication; 2) Increasing sophistication in the field of bibliographic instruction has resulted in the development of many excellent programs of instruction for students, faculty and university staff alike. The revised document attempts to reflect the needs of these user groups also.

2. *Ordering of the objectives*. Depending on the information need of the individual or group in question, the librarian may find instruction in "highly sophisticated" information access skills essential for the undergraduate, while the graduate student or even the faculty member may need training in basic skills. In order to provide the greatest flexibility, the objectives are not ordered; rather, it is for the librarian to determine what objectives fulfill the needs of the specific user group in question.

3. *Institution and tool specific information*. It would be literally impossible to list all the objectives which describe institutional and tool specific differences. The Model Statement reviews the similarities within these sources and focuses on the process of using information and information sources, recorded and unrecorded, rather than focusing on library processes. The document is therefore conceptually based and does not include tool specific or institution-specific detail. The Task Force feels that tool specific or institution specific information is more appropriately placed within enabling objectives.

4. *Language used*. The Model Statement uses very specific language to describe generic processes. Since common terms used by librarians have different and often divergent meanings, it is recommended that the attached glossary be consulted when using the document.

5. *Incorporation of technological advances*. Advances in technology have been incorporated into various sections of the document where appropriate rather than examined separately. For example, the methods used to retrieve information sources from an online catalog are explained in the "Intellectually Accessed" section, and the explanation that a catalog is a holding list is detailed in the "Physically Organized and Accessed" section. By describing processes rather than tools, it is hoped that the Statement will remain effective long after the present "new" technology becomes old.

6. *Evaluation of information sources and systems*. It was felt that evaluation of information, information sources, and information systems is something that occurs throughout the search pro-

Rebecca Jackson: Appendix 1 (continued)

cess. To this end, evelution issues have been incorporated into each section of the document where appropriate.

7. *Evaluation of objectives*. Specific attention was not devoted to developing evaluation designs for the attainment of objectives in an instructional setting, as it was felt that guidance in this matter was available through *Evaluating Bibliographic Instruction: A Handbook*, published by ACRL's Bibliographic Instruction Section in 1983.

8. *Structural flexibility*. The structure of the document has been designed to permit as much flexibility as possible. It consists of four major areas of concern, each with its own general and terminal objectives. It is probable that no one library's program will include all the objectives listed; rather, each objective is suggested as an element related to the area of concern. The flexibility of the document lies in its "mix and match" nature: terminal objectives of one section may be matched with terminal objectives of another section depending upon the program being designed. In addition, the Model Statement simply lists suggested areas of interest; when designing a program, the librarian may find that additional terminal objectives must be created in order to reflect the needs of the group in question.

Using the Model Statement

The Model Statement is designed to be used in two ways. First, it is intended to serve as a checklist through which to assess and examine present programs. Second, it is intended to serve as a resource through which to develop new programs. To use the Statement effectively for the latter purpose, the following steps are recommended:

1. Define the user group and the present level of sophistication;

2. Determine the purpose of instruction;

3. Determine which overall sections of the document are relevant to the proposed program;

4. Select the relevant terminal objectives from each section;

5. If needed, create additional subpoints to the terminal objectives selected.

6. Develop enabling objectives.

Model statement of general and terminal objectives

1. How information is identified and defined by experts.

General Objective: The user understands how information is defined by experts, and recognizes how that knowledge can help determine the direction of his/her search for specific information.

T1*.The user understands that individuals or groups identify themselves as belonging to specific areas and or disciplines.

---

*T = Terminal Objective.

T2. The user recognizes that individuals within these groups may combine information from information sources with original thought, experimentation, and/or analysis to produce new information.

T3. The user recognizes that disciplines use specific methods to communicate information.

a. The user recognizes that information sources can be recorded or unrecorded sources which may appear in different physical formats.

b. The user recognizes that information sources go through various review processes to be accepted as credible by the research community.

c. The user understands the processes through which information sources are accepted and disseminated in the research community.

T4. Once a topic of interest is selected, the user understands how it can be refined and can formulate a question.

a. The user recognizes when a question is discipline-specific or interdisciplinary.

b. The user understands that the initial question may be too broad or narrow to investigate effectively and that adjustment in scope, direction, or timeframe may be needed.

T5. The user understands how to construct an approach or strategy appropriate to the scope and complexity of the question and appropriate to the anticipated result of the research process.

a. The user understands that the indentification of specific information sources will depend on the individual question and the strategy devised.

b. The user recognizes that the audience of the end product will in part determine the direction and type of search conducted.

c. The user understands that the form and the purpose of the end product will in part determine the direction and type of search conducted.

2. How information sources are structured.

General Objective: The user understands the importance of the organizational content, bibliographic structure, function, and use of information sources.

T1. The user understands how the organizational content of recorded information sources is structured and how this knowledge can help determine the usefulness of the source.

a. The user understands the importance of evaluating the author's credentials.

b. The user understands how the timeliness or the date of publication may determine the value of a source.

c. The user recognizes that the publisher's reputation may affect the usefulness of the source. The user recognizes that in periodical publications, the editorial review process is as important as the publishing information.

d. The user recognizes the importance of title, thesis, preface, introduction, table of contents, appendixes, summary, and/or abstract in evaluating the scope, limitations, and special features of the

Rebecca Jackson: Appendix 1 (continued)

information source and thereby its usefulness.

e. The user recognizes that the purpose of the author in presenting ideas, opinions, or research may in part determine the usefulness of the source.

f. The user recognizes the organization or arrangement of an information source may affect its value (hierarchical, alphabetical, chronological, tabular, regional, classified, schematic, or numerical).

g. The user recognizes that the amount and type of documentation used may affect the value of a recorded information source.

T2. The user recognizes that unrecorded information sources exist and can evaluate their potential usefulness.

a. The user recognizes the importance of the individual's or group's credentials and is able to evaluate this information to determine the source's credibility in relation to the topic.

b. The user recognizes the importance of evaluating the timeliness of the information.

c. The user recognizes the importance of correctly identifying the source's thesis and arguments to determine whether the information provided is pertinent to the topic.

T3. The user understands how information sources are bibliographically structured and how this knowledge can help determine the usefulness of the source.

a. The user recognizes that the information needed to identify information sources is manipulated into systematic sequences called citations and that the amount of information required and the form of a citation may vary from field to field.

a. 1. The user recognizes that the bibliographic structure of recorded information sources may vary among disciplines and within subject areas.

a. 2. The user recognizes the major types of citations and knows where they typically occur (documentary notes, in-text citations, bibliographic entries, etc.).

a. 3. The user recognizes that the form of a citation varies for different subjects areas and disciplines.

a. 4. The user recognizes that the amount of information required in a citation varies for different subject areas and disciplines.

b. The user understands the relationship of citations to other information sources.

b. 1. The user understands that the purpose of a citation is to enable others to identify and locate pertinent information sources.

b. 2. The user understands that some sources may indirectly refer to other sources through the use of incomplete citations (implicit vs. explicit footnotes).

b. 3. The user understands the significance of identifying information sources which are repeatedly cited by more than one source.

b. 4. The user understands the link between the information provided within a citation and the organizational structure of the source cited and recognizes the importance of the link in evaluating the usefulness of the source identified.

3. How information sources are intellectually accessed by users.

General Objective: The user can identify useful information from information sources or information systems.

T1. The user understands that although any information about an information source could be used to help identify and locate it, there are certain elements of information called access points which are accepted by the research community as the most pertinent through which to identify a source.

a. The user recognizes that the "author" entry is a commonly used access point.

b. The user recognizes that the title of a recorded information source is another commonly used access point.

c. The user recognizes that a "subject" topic, or description field is a commonly used access point.

d. The user recognizes that the use of additional access points depends on the structure and format of the source used to identify new information.

d. 1. The user recognizes that each element of information found within a citation may potentially be used as an access point.

d. 2. The user recognizes that information found within an abstract or summary may potentially be used as access points (usually through the method of key word searching where each word can be used as an access point).

d. 3. The user recognizes that additional access may be available through codes, categories, or mapping which may not be obvious in the information source or system.

e. The user understands that some sources use controlled vocabulary assigned by an indexer, cataloger, or computer programmer as access points.

e. 1. The user recognizes that most controlled vocabulary describes the subject or author of the information source.

e. 2. The user recognizes that the rules governing indexing practices may influence the process of retrieval.

e. 3. The user understands that there may be printed or online lists or thesauri which may aid in the identification of these access points.

e. 4. The user recognizes the relationship of broader, narrower, and related terms.

T2. The user understands that there are a variety of information sources called access tools whose primary purpose is to identify other information sources through the use of access points.

a. The user recognizes that access tools used vary by discipline or subject area.

b. The user recognizes that access tools used vary by the type of information source needed.

c. The user recognizes that access tools vary in format and recognizes the implications of format as it relates to the availability of access points.

d. The user recognizes the importance of the organizational content of the access tool in determin-

Rebecca Jackson: Appendix 1 (continued)

ing whether or not it is a good information source.

e. The user understands that no access tool is comprehensive in scope.

f. The user understands the importance of selecting the appropriate access tool in order to identify useful information sources.

T3. The user understands how to manipulate access points to identify useful information or information sources.

a. The user understands when it is appropriate to search for information through the use of a single access point.

b. The user understands the concept of Boolean logic and its importance in searching for information under more than one access point.

c. The user understands the importance of browsing.

d. The user understands the importance of proximity searching (looking for two or more words in the same sentence, paragraph, record or file).

e. The user understands that given insufficient information to identify a particular access point, there are steps which may help identify it.

e. 1. The user understands truncation.

e. 2. The user understands key word searching and knows when it may be appropriate and possible.

T4. The user can evaluate the citation retrieved or the accessed information and determine whether or not it is at the appropriate level of specificity.

T5. The user recognizes the absence of recorded information sources on a specific topic, realizes the implications and recognizes the alternatives.

a. The user realizes that the lack of recorded information sources does not preclude the existence of unrecorded information sources.

b. The user recognizes that the lack of recorded information may suggest the necessity of original analysis or data collection.

c. The user recognizes that he/she may have to change the direction of the search if the use of unrecorded information sources or the gathering of primary data is not feasible.

5. How information sources are physically organized and accessed.

General Objective: The user understands the way collections of information sources are physically organized and accessed.

T1. The user understands that libraries and library systems may group information sources by subject, author, format, publisher, type of material, or special audience.

a. The user recognizes that many library systems are decentralized and the materials at each location may be distinguished by subject, format, publisher, type of material, or by special audience.

b. The user recognizes that materials in like formats are usually housed together in special areas of the library or in particular units of the library system along with the appropriate equipment needed to utilize these materials.

c. The user understands that a library may choose to house materials by one publisher together in one location or disperse them throughout the library's holdings.

d. The user recognizes that types of materials may be grouped together in order to provide ease of use or because of preservation and maintenance concerns.

e. The user recognizes that some libraries provide separate collections for special user groups.

f. The user understands that materials on like subjects are usually housed together.

f. 1. The user recognizes that some branches of a library system may be designated by the subject area or discipline.

f. 2. The user understands that classification schemes are designed to enable libraries to locate materials on the same subject in the same discipline in close proximity to each other.

T2. The user understands that the library uses call numbers to assign a unique physical address to each item in the collection.

T3. The user understands that individual items within a library system's collections are listed in special holdings or location files.

a. The user understands that there is usually a central holdings or location file for the library's collection and that might be in one or more formats.

b. The user understands that various special collections in the library or library system may have special holdings file and that they may or may not be subsets of the central file.

c. The user is aware that there are special files which can be used to identify the holdings of items available from other libraries.

T4. The user understands that the library staff is comprised of individuals with varying degrees and areas of expertise, who provide certain services through departments and who may be helpful in accessing information.

T5. The user understands the policies and procedures used by library departments and recognizes that these may vary.

T6. The user understands that the campus library is not the only location through which to retrieve necessary material.

a. The user recognizes that libraries do not have comprehensive holdings and that one library may lend an item from its collection, or furnish a copy of an item from its collection to another library not under the same administration.

b. The user recognizes that in order to facilitate library cooperation in resource sharing, many libraries have developed networks and consortia.

c. The user understands that information sources may be available for purchase by individuals through publishers and or document delivery services and that some information sources are only available on a purchase basis.

d. The user recognizes that personal networks may be essential to retrieving appropriate information.

Rebecca Jackson: Appendix 1 (continued)

Glossary

Access: to retrieve information.

Access points: specific pieces of information identified as being useful to the retrieval of information.

Bibliographic structure: the framework of explicit links of footnote references and bibliographic citations or implicit links of tacit relationships.

Citation: a bibliographic record (or systematic sequence) which includes the information necessary to access an information source physically.

Communication: the transfer of information in the various media from one person, place, or device to another.

Data: the symbols or characters of a language. Examples: the letters of the alphabet; numbers; etc.

Document (Recorded Information Source): a physical entity in any medium upon which is recorded all or part of a work or multiple works. Examples: book, journal article, etc.

Information: a grouping of data which has a particular meaning within a specific context. Examples: a word, a name; etc.

Information source: a single entity from which information is retrieved. Examples: a person, a book, a journal article, an index, etc.

Information system: an organized structure of interrelated information sources. Examples: an online catalog, etc.

Intellectual access: the isolating or selecting of useful information from information sources or systems.

Physical Access: the physical retrieval of an information source.

Process: manipulating, preparing, and handling information to achieve the desired results.

Structure: the logical arrangement or organization of information.

Unrecorded information: oral communication. ■■

Approved by the ACRL Board of Directors and the ALA Standards Committee at the ALA Annual Conference, July 1988.

Reprinted with permission from College & Research Libraries News, *May 1987, a publication of the Association of College and Research Libraries, a division of the American Library Association.*

Rebecca Jackson: Appendix 1 (continued)

LIBRARY INSTRUCTION OBJECTIVES

UNDERGRADUATES

University of Maryland College Park Libraries

NOTE: It is desireable for high school graduates entering the University of Maryland, College Park, to have attained the library skills comparable to those in the curriculum plan for Montgomery county. This includes basic skills in:

> Use of the card catalog
> Use of the <u>Readers Guide to Periodical Literature</u> and
>   similar periodical indexes
> Use of basic reference books such as encyclopedias,
>   dictionaries, directories
> Ability to determine from a citation basic types of
>   publications and where to look for them
> Ability to work with a reference librarian to develop a
>   search strategy for a subject.

For the purposes of these objectives, the undergraduate student body is divided into two levels:

1. Basic students: these students are taking or will have completed the Fundamental Studies and Distributive Studies of the University Studies program and other courses in the first college years. The library and bibliographic skills at this level are rather generic, with an emphasis on the ways to use the variety of library materials and the access tools to identify and locate them. Critical evaluation of the material will largely be based on analysis of the materials themselves, with additional reference to the reputations of the authors and the comments in reviews. The use of conflicting and critical sources will be confined largely to the gathering of opposing viewpoints with a given issue literature, as in "taking sides" readings and problem-oriented collections.

2. Advanced students: these students will be taking or will have taken courses in a major field of study, courses in the Advanced Studies program (Development of Knowledge and Analysis of Human Problems, a possible departmental capstone course). In these studies the students move toward a wider perspective in analysis and use of the literature, with a focus on the use of critical and comparative resources, and efforts to integrate multiple perspectives and multi-disciplinary approaches. The hoped-for use of multiple intellectual strategies will be matched by the mastery of a variety of ways of access to published and unpublished materials, and the use of criticisms and dialectic in the literature to evaluate theories and generalizations. In the basic programs, the students learn to distinguish authorities from non-authorities in subject fields; in the advanced program

1

Rebecca Jackson: Appendix 2

they learn to distinguish between conflicting authorities in a subject field and conflicts between methods and disciplines.

When no level is indicated, it is assumed that the competencies are basic. These are general, not subject specific, objectives and should be mastered before the student can master research goals in his/her major field of study.

2

Rebecca Jackson: Appendix 2 (continued)

I. How information is identified and defined by experts

General Objective: The user understands how information is defined by experts, and recognizes how that knowledge can help determine the direction of his/her search for specific information.

A. The user recognizes that disciplines use specific methods to communicate information.

    1. The user recognizes that information sources can be recorded or unrecorded sources which may appear in different physical formats.

        a. At the basic level, the user:

            1) understands that sources may be found by using books, periodicals, microforms, computer reference sources, pamphlets, nonprint media such as films and tapes, and human resources.

            2) identifies the most valuable collections for his/her purposes and can recognize what formats each collection is comprised of, eg., government documents appear as hard copy and microforms, technical reports are mostly on microfiche.

        b. At the advanced level, the user understands the relationship between information desired and format. The student should be able to use all formats and should be more aware of how to reach the people who are experts in a given discipline.

    2. The user understands the processes through which information sources are disseminated in the research community, i.e., publications of conferences, invisible colleges.

        a. At the basic level, the user understands that books and periodicals are only two possible sources of information. He/she is aware of other types of sources and has used one or more of them.

        b. At the advanced level, the user knows the encyclopedias, indexes, associations, major journals, the main types of literature in his major.

B. Once a topic of interest is selected, the user understands how it can be refined and how to formulate a question.

    1. The user can formulate a search question.

3

Rebecca Jackson: Appendix 2 (continued)

2) understands the significance of identifying information sources which are repeatedly cited by more than one source.

b. The advanced user understands the importance of analyzing the context of any given source in order to evaluate its relevance and authority: the context in the development of the literature (theoretical approach, historical stage of revision) and in the context of specific critical discussions on the subject.

III. How information sources are intellectually accessed by users.

General objective: The user can identify useful information from information sources or information systems.

A. The user understands that although any information about an information source could be used to help identify and locate it. there are certain elements of information called access points which are accepted by the research community as the most pertinent through which to identify a source.

1. The user recognizes that commonly used access points are author, title, and subject.

2. The user recognizes that the use of additional access points depends on the structure and format of the source used to identify new information.

a. The user recognizes that each element of information found within a citation may potentially be used as an access point.

b. The user recognizes that information found within an abstract or summary may potentially be used as access points (usually through the method of key word searching where each word can be used as an access point).

3. The user understands that some sources use controlled vocabulary assigned by an indexer, cataloger, or computer programmer as access points.

a. The user recognizes the relationship of broader, narrower, and related terms.

b. The user recognizes that most controlled vocabulary describes the subject or author of the information source. S/he can identify useful items in the subject catalog and the basic periodical indexes.

8

Rebecca Jackson: Appendix 2 (continued)

OBJECTIVES FOR HYPERCARD PROJECT -- University of Maryland
College Park Libraries

1. Introduction to periodical indexes

    The user will describe the nature and purposes of indexes.

    A. The user will define a periodical index.

    B. The user will name two different types of periodical
        indexes, e.g., newspaper, magazine, mixed.

    C. The user will differentiate between a popular and a
        specialized index.

    D. The user will state the titles of three different
        periodical indexes.

    E. The user will state that print, microfilm, and
        electronic indexes are available.

2. Instruction in the use of periodical indexes

    *The user will select appropriate indexes and subject
    headings and identify the elements of a citation in a basic
    general index.*

    A. Given a particular topic, the user will select an
        appropriate general index for that topic.

    B. Given a particular topic, the user will locate
        appropriate subject heading(s) within an index for that
        topic.

    C. The user will identify all the elements in a given
        citation, i.e., article author, article title,
        periodical title, volume, date, pages.

    D. The user will match abbreviabet journal titles to the
        full titles.

    *The user will use subject headings, subheadings, citations,
    and cross references in index entries.*

    A. Given a page from an index, the user will identify the
        subject heading, a subheading, a citation, and a cross
        reference.

    B. The user will follow a cross reference to its referent.

1

Rebecca Jackson: Appendix 3

3. Instruction in the use of the University of Maryland, College Park Serials List.

The user will understand the operation of the microfiche machine

A. *The user will to turn on the microfiche machine and insert the microfiche card properly.*

The user will identify locations and holdings for any periodical within the UMCP Libraries.

A. Given a periodical index citation, the user will identify the UMCP Serials List as the source of information to locate that article.

B. Given a specific periodical title, the user will select the correct microfiche to be used.

C. The user will identify and state the purpose of the index at the top of each column of the microfiche card.

D. Given a specific periodical title, the user will use the index to locate that title on the card.

E. Given a specific periodical title, the user will determine the call number for that title.

F. Given a specific issue of a periodical, the user will determine which library/libraries holds that issue. The user will identify what format that issue is in, i.e. microfilm, microfiche, bound, current stacks. The user will identify the appropriate strategy for finding a periodical title not found on the serials list, i.e., will asking the Reference Desk for assistance.

4. Description of the arrangements of periodicals in the various UMCP libraries.

The user will determine where in the Libraries s/he can find the periodical needed.

A. The user will explain the difference in the ways periodicals are stored in McKeldin and Hornbake Libraries.

B. The user will identify the appropriate strategy for finding periodicals in the other UMCP Libraries, i.e., ask at each library how periodicals are stored.

RJ
2/23/89

2

Rebecca Jackson: Appendix 3 (continued)

Competencies for Short-Term

or Lifelong Learning?

Carolyn Kirkendall

Introduction

From time to time in our professional literature in the past, an intriguing theme has occasionally surfaced--a topic you've probably formed an informal or even subconscious opinion about. It's a subject that the LOEX office has wanted to address in pro and con format for some time, and this year's conference theme seemed an especially appropriate opportunity.

This is the topic that Patrick Wilson[1] and some British user education librarians[2] in particular first expounded upon, and about which our own Keith Stanger from Eastern Michigan University reacted to in an opinion piece published in the first issue of *Research Strategies*.[3] Keith called the problem "the limits of bibliographic instruction."

It's the argument that merely teaching library use skills and teaching search strategy does not, should not, and cannot produce lifelong learners. To paraphrase Keith's opinion, library exercises, treasure hunts, and assignments to find term paper topics--learning how to find bits of information as he puts it--won't make students better thinkers or better users of information.

On the other side of the coin is the argument that teaching search strategy can result in long-term retention and can produce library users who apply this experience to become self-sufficient, self-reliant library and information users. We've heard this philosophy delineated from the original ACRL BIS Think Tank,[4] from the current literature, and from several of our speakers at this meeting.

Both these opinions have been couched in simplistic terms, and we may end up redefining

Kirkendall is Instructional Materials Center Librarian, Eastern Michigan University, Ypsilanti, Michigan.

the issues somewhat after listening to today's speakers. Our first speaker will maintain that short-term library skill competencies are the only really achievable goals to expect;[5] in rebuttal, serving as a kind of devil's advocate, our second speaker will attempt to convince us that it is not unrealistic to expect the acquisition of lifelong library skills as a result of exposing library users to search strategy instruction.

NOTES

1.   Patrick Wilson, *Public Knowledge, Private Ignorance*. (Westport, CT: Greenwood Press, 1977.)

2.   Such as Colin Harris, "User Needs and User Education," in *Library User Education - Are New Approaches Needed?* British Library Research and Development Report no. 5503. (London: British Library Research and Development Department, 1980.)

3.   Keith J. Stanger, "On the Limits of Bibliographic Instruction in Higher Education: An Opinion Piece," *Research Strategies* 1 (Winter 1983): 31-32.

4.   "Think Tank Recommendations for Bibliographic Instruction," *College & Research Libraries News* 42 (December 1981): 394-398.

5.   Richard Feinberg and Christine King, "Short-Term Library Skill Competencies: Arguing for the Achievable," *College & Research Libraries* 49 (January 1988): 24-28.

Shorting-Out on Long-Term Goals:

A Different Perspective on Bibliographic

Instruction and Information Literacy

Richard Feinberg

I would like to interject some views about bibliographic instruction that are a bit different from some that have been offered at this conference. I know that my presentation will sound like I am being critical and disparaging of what are actually the very substantial efforts of some of the most energetic and dedicated in our field. What I really intend to do is express another opinion concerning who BI librarians are and where we should be focusing. I am speaking here especially for those of us who are committed to BI, but who desire to formulate our programs in a pragmatic style that matches our particular expertise as librarians with our students' abilities and current research needs.

To get to the point, I am not in favor of teaching students to become information literate for the long term, and for the following reasons.

First of all, I do not think that it has been convincingly demonstrated by librarians, or anyone else, that it is, or will be, necessary for most of our students to be information specialists to survive or prosper in our world.

Second, I feel that much of what we say students should learn to become information literate has little relevancy to what they really need to learn today, which still is, for most undergraduates, how to find books and articles for their term paper projects. If we think that students must now be taught about the entire information environment, we are forgetting about one of our basic tenets: that in BI, content should be relevant to immediate needs.

Third, even if a librarian has the talent and background to teach comprehensive information gathering skills in a variety of subjects, and if,

Feinberg is Coordinator, Library Instruction SUNY-Stony Brook.

by chance, the students who are being taught are bright and motivated, lack of opportunity for practice and reinforcement will make this new knowledge quickly disintegrate. Studies since the 1930s, which have measured use of academic libraries, have uniformly indicated that most undergraduates use their libraries only sporadically, if at all. And our adult population does not appear to be made up of avid, intellectually hungry researchers. Most who use public libraries do so for recreational purposes. Those in business, industry, and government who are dependent on job-related information for decision making have research specialists who gather data for them. No, talking about long-term retention implied in the phrase "information literacy" would make more sense if the opportunity, or the necessity, for repeated research activity were widespread. But since it is not for the vast majority, long-term retention does not ring true as a reasonable objective.

Fourth, because the information environment is in a state of flux, we simply cannot know which of the skills, concepts, and methods we teach today will be of importance in five or ten years. It follows that future necessary skills and concepts are unknown to us at this time. It is therefore contradictory to state that we **should** and that we **can** inculcate information access skills for life-long learning.

I think we are overreaching when we say our new mission should be "information literacy." A few years ago, we apparently agreed to give our specialty a bit more stature by advocating that our teaching yield long-term results. We souped up our language for this new goal. Teaching "bibliographic instruction" became teaching "library use competency," "competency" meaning facility with certain identified skills, and for the long term. Now, the phrase "library competency" is being replaced by "information literacy," which encompasses long-term implications not to mention a greatly increased area of subject matter. It is ironic that H.W. Wilson's *Library Literature* has finally decided to incorporate the term "bibliographic instruction" as a subject heading at a time when more and more of the BI literature is casting that term aside.

We are also overreaching with some assumptions. For instance, some of us say there is a crisis, or a coming crisis, called "information illiteracy"; it is a crisis because people, it is claimed, will have to be information literate to function in our new world. By extension, it is implied that the very future of our country depends on a citizenry whose members will know how to quickly and efficiently access a variety of data on their own; and, finally, that it is our job to teach this new curriculum.

In forwarding these views, are we being factual? Are we setting realistic goals for our students and ourselves? Or are we just being self-serving by creating an artificial crisis and then claiming for ourselves a critical role in its solution?

And, to continue with my irritability, I have yet another problem, this one having to do with the implication embedded in the "long-term retention" notion that we can and should teach our students to become junior librarians and information specialists. Are there other professions whose members believe that their prodigious skills and knowledge should be passed on to their clients, or that it is even possible to do so? Why do we so put down our particular expertise? Why do we believe that the complexity of what we practice can be so easily transferred to others through bibliographic instruction, or whatever name we happen to be calling BI at a point in time?

In fact, it is we who are the experts on how to guide students in their library-oriented academic research. And we should keep that expertise for ourselves, not because we would lose some of our power or mystique by giving it away, but because what we do as librarians just cannot be given away that easily.

Yes, I think we are overreaching, because we are concerned, and understandably, about our importance, or lack thereof, in the future. We are obviously concerned about the possibility of being put out of existence by new technology, or, at least, being reduced to an innocuous role in an area that was once largely ours. Some of us might also be concerned that BI, with all its successes, still does not give us the prestige that we had hoped it would, and so we must continue to augment the definition and scope of our mission until we get that illusive recognition (from whomever we're trying to get it). The cause of "information literacy" is an example of this augmenting. "Information literacy" as it is defined in the *Cornell Glossary of Library Terms*, encompasses a huge intellectual terrain for both librarian and student. It implies the presence of a curriculum, really an information science curriculum, not merely a BI program. The exhortation that we should embrace this curriculum takes for granted something I see little evidence for: that as a group, librarians have the credentials to teach it, and that most of our students need to know it.

I am not advocating here that we stand around with hands in pockets waiting for possible disaster. In fact, it is obvious that we are not standing around, and that we will not stand around. There is plenty of action and change in the field and momentum continues to build for awareness, vigilance, and action on our part. My position regarding BI in this context of flux is that some of us will not be motivated to base our programs on alarming conjecture regarding what is up ahead, or on statements that reflect insecurity about our importance. In this period, I think BI librarians would have a good chance of success by subscribing to a simple set of objectives. We should stick to teaching those things that are within our expertise, and we should aim our teaching to meet the immediate library research needs of our students.

We may be concerned that our profession will become less important, even obsolete, if we fail to aggressively articulate a critical role for ourselves in the new information environment, and appear instead to be reactive. However, it is probably more likely that as the information environment changes, members of society more than ever will rely on libraries and librarians to mediate between them and the bewildering array of print and nonprint information sources. In BI, we can help ensure a continued important role for libraries by focusing on teaching our students the basic research skills they need today, and through our teaching, demonstrate that we are library information specialists who can be relied on today as well as tomorrow for expert, human, and economical connections to information.

If we set goals for ourselves that realistically match our skills and expertise with our students' needs, we will be in a better position to satisfy those goals. And in meeting them, we will bolster our already significant place in the world of information, even as that world inevitably, if unpredictably, changes.

REFERENCES

Breivik, Patricia Senn. "Putting Libraries Back in the Information Society." *American Libraries* 16 (November 1985): 723.

De Gennaro, Richard. "Libraries, Technology, and the Information Marketplace." *Library Journal* 107 (1 June 1982): 1045-1054.

Hacken, Richard D. "Tomorrow's Research Library: Vigor or Rigor Mortis?" *College and Research Libraries* 49 (November 1988): 485-493.

Martell, Charles, and Jennifer D. Ware. "Hard Facts, Hard Work: Academic Libraries and *A Nation at Risk*--A Symposium." *Journal of Academic Librarianship* 14 (May 1988): 72-81.

Noble, Douglas. "The Underside of Computer Literacy." *Raritan* 3 (Spring 1984): 37-64.

Rettig, James R., and Constance R. Miller. "Reference Obsolescence." *RQ* 25 (Fall 1985): 52-81.

Shill, Harold B. "Bibliographic Instruction: Planning for the Electronic Information Environment." *College and Research Libraries* 48 (September 1987): 433-453.

Stoan, Stephen K. "Research and Library Skills: An Analysis and Interpretation." *College and Research Libraries* 45 (March 1984): 99-109.

Library Literacy and Lifelong Learning

Carolyn Dusenbury

I really do not have anything to add to the arguments for the literacy imperative made by Patricia Breivik and Jan Kennedy Olsen yesterday. They both did an outstanding job in defending the professional and philosophical arguments in favor of literacy and lifelong learning. Rather than reiterate what you have already heard, and probably not do it as well, I would like to do a really "blue-collar take" on the occupational and practical considerations of promoting the goals of literacy in bibliographic instruction programs. I do not think this suggests that BI librarians should not continue to develop programs toward the ends of fully integrated, conceptually based literacy programs--but rather what you can do tomorrow or next week until that framework is in place.

I would like to put one assumption on the table at the beginning. I do not believe that this discussion is about what we should or should not do but about what we can and cannot do. If someone came into your office and said, "I can, absolutely guaranteed, show you how to make your students into independent library users, interested and fearless lifelong information seekers and consumers, and intrepid library-philes," would you, for a moment, entertain the idea that this was not the thing to do? This is the proverbial offer that you can't refuse. Unlike a classic debate, we are not talking about good and evil. Many of the short-term skills advocates are not opposed to the theory or the principle. They just want to know how. How do we begin to meet the challenge of educating a citizenry to cope with the rapid change in the amount of information that exists and that they will need to use in order to be productive in the

Dusenbury is Director, Library Public Services, California State University-Chico.

economic, political, and social environment of the future--to become, as Carolyn Michaels has said, "information-able."[1]

Does the goal of singlehandedly making the world literate seem a bit beyond your grasp as an instruction librarian? You do not lack the will, you lack the support, the time, the money, the staff--little things like that. If your institution has a vision or a program that encouraged or even permitted an articulated program that included bibliographic instruction as a required and necessary component of education, you would say: "Where do I sign?" But to most of us this is like saying "someday my prince will come..."--more possibility than probability.

Is this town really too small for both of us? Is there a common ground so that one of us does not have to be out of town by sunset? The answers are, I think, no to the first and yes to the second. Too often we confuse lifelong learning with tremendous sophistication and enormous complexity. We think of library literacy as the ability to use all the tools, the largest collections, the bibliographic and nonbibliographic universe without batting an eye. Lifelong learners are independent (!!) and self-sufficient(!!) we are told. The few. The proud. The tough. This is very macho librarianship more suited to Robinson Crusoe or John Wayne. The measure of success in lifelong learning is not being able to use a citation index at the drop of a hat, or faster than the other guy.

Perhaps it is my simple and innocent soul --but I also think we get discouraged by the incredible dimensions of the task. As Richard Feinberg said in his recent article, what leaders in bibliographic instruction "exhort us to do, e.g., teach logic, abstract reasoning, the organization of literature, and critical evaluation of sources, are the things we seem to do least well, and those things we do best, such as teaching students library mechanics...are what the leaders disparage as having limited value."[2] It is enough to discourage a person.

I would like to pose a somewhat different --a kinder and gentler, if you will--construction of lifelong learning. I do not believe that the library literacy for lifers are touting the virtues of two chickens in every pot and Dialog in every den. When we are talking about literate people, it isn't how much stuff they know, but it is the ability to take a problem and figure it out. The retention of tool specific knowledge over a lifetime is not the point. The skills people are probably right--students won't retain the ability to manipulate *Historical Abstracts* any more than a political science professor remembers the titles of Italian cabinet members. Retention of specific skills over a lifetime seems to me to be a red herring. Since

the tools are changing so fast--knowledge of specific titles and protocols may be more of a vice than a virtue. Lifelong learning is a knowledge not of a vast number of specific skills, but the ability to use information in a way that is appropriate, salient, and, to some degree, efficient.

As often happens in life, I think we are talking past one another. Some clarification of the terms is probably in order. Three of the most confusing ones in this debate are: lifelong learning, library literacy, and self-sufficiency.

Let's tackle library literacy first. Jill Fatzer has compared library literacy to language literacy. Just as there are stages of language literacy from illiterate (or pre-literate) to semi-literate to literate to fluent, there are similar states of library literacy. In both cases, Fatzer notes:

> Literacy is not a simple unitary quality that one either possesses or does not ...literacy is gained through instruction that is articulated through one's schooling, each step building on what was previously taught, the literate person is self-sufficient in reading and writing skills...The library literate can follow a systematic path or search strategy to locate texts and evaluate the relevance of the information.[3]

The library fluent can generalize skills and knowledge to "satisfy a variety of information needs. Library literacy can thus be seen not as the presence or absence of skills, but as progressive stages...leading ultimately to self-sufficiency."[4]

Lifelong learning is not synonymous with library literacy. For most people, as Patrick Wilson says, libraries are part of a reserve system of information resources available to the literate lifelong learner.[5] Library literacy may be one of the prior conditions to successful lifelong learning, but lifelong learning is not library-dependent or library-centered. In the array of resources available, the successful lifelong learner will be library literate and, as a consumer, will be able to comfortably and confidently add libraries to the array of information resources routinely used.

Self-sufficiency is the most troublesome of the three. Self-sufficiency does not have the goal of "every person a librarian." This is an idea from the first generation of bibliographic instruction, which has lost its efficacy over the life of the instruction movement. New technologies and the exploding amount of information have, rather forcefully, deflated the myth of self-sufficiency in the traditional sense. The self-sufficient library user will not be able to use every library single-handedly anymore than the literate adult must fill his or her own teeth, grow his or her own food, or (heaven forbid) do his or her own taxes. Self-sufficiency in the sense of library literacy is the ability to make an intelligent decision about the best way to answer an articulated question, to pursue a more or less efficient, organized search for the answer, and know when the intervention of a specialist is necessary.

So, if library literacy is not an additive increasing of specific skills, and requires the ability to pose a question and have a literate's ability to pursue it...how will (and can) a BI librarian do the immediate job of getting a class through an assignment and still promote the morally correct goal of library literacy and lifelong learning? Is this or is this not a reasonable proposition?

Take, for example, the following situation. You are asked to do a one-hour stand for a class of sixty students doing a term paper. This is a class in child development taught in the Psychology Department. The teacher insists that they use "scholarly" journals and cannot use magazines like *Psychology Today*. The teacher wants them to use the "Infotrac thing for psychology" and to learn how to use the online catalog. Of the sixty students, about one-third are psychology majors, but there are a lot of sociology, education, and family studies students because the course also "counts" toward the major in those departments. After some discussion, it emerges that if you could also talk about tests, *Child Development Abstracts*, and a few other things, that would fill the bill pretty nicely. Stop me if you've heard this one. In one hour, you have been asked to elucidate, putting it mildly, numerous specific skills. Whether you are a skills or literacy enthusiast, you have either a tall or impossible order. In the immortal words of Douglas Adams..."Don't panic!!"

What is achievable in this situation toward the end of library literacy in addition to the clear need for some survival skills and mechanics? If you have been fortunate enough to land at an institution with an articulated and curriculum integrated program of library orientation and instruction, using a commonly understood theoretical construct, you don't need to sweat the small stuff --students have progressively mastered basic skills such as the catalog and serials list, an orientation to the building and basic sources like *Reader's Guide* or Infotrac. How many of you would find yourself in this situation? Most of you will be able to instruct this class using some of the ideas promulgated by the library literacy and lifelong learning school. Let's go through a few examples of how you would apply them in teaching this class.

1.   The number of sources encompassed by this assignment requires a plan of attack that can be very easily encompassed by a conceptual framework such as types of sources. I suspect you will do some of this anyway. It may actually be easier to talk about abstracts, for example, as a type --how they gather a literature together in an organized construct and how the parts work. Teaching an abstract is the logical choice when compared with explaining each of a number of specific titles. This is both a specific skill, and, just as important, a generalizable one; students will be able to apply the idea of an abstract to other library needs in the future. The interdisciplinary possibilities of this assignment is also an opportunity to provide generalizable information.

2.   The ability to evaluate texts for relevance is important. This assignment calls for the use of scholarly articles, so some way to discriminate these from others will probably be necessary. The concept is an easy one to introduce. Most people would agree that the weight loss regime touted in the current *New England Journal of Medicine* or the report of the *New England Journal* article in *Time* is more creditable than one in the *Weekly Star*. If you have a few extra pounds and are a literate consumer, you want the best source for that information. What is best? You don't need to spend a lot of time in explaining the intent of each publication, its audience, the peer review process, whether or not the publication has ads for cards or whiskey or ads for a professional or scholar, and so on, to make the point that all periodicals are not created equal. Then as you introduce the types of sources, you can relate them to the example.

3.   The sheer amount of information available in this assignment calls for synthesis and the ability to evaluate sources. This is a good place to talk about question analysis and rational data retrieval. With all of our machines we have greatly expanded the ability to find more and more stuff that is, in some sense, related. Patrick Wilson calls this "bibliographic control." What we lack, he asserts, is "exploitative control" or the ability to choose the best text for our purpose.[6] To some extent automation has given some measure of exploitative control with Boolean and proximity operators. In almost any library environment, it is relatively easy to pare down the embarrassment of riches that results from state-of-the-art bibliographic control. It is also a handy place to introduce some of the concepts of question analysis. Getting the question right as the most important part of the process is, in my experience, easier to demonstrate this way than any other. The concepts of efficiency and relevance, the advantages of finding what you need with some economy rather than wading through a morass of less useful information, is one that

students can understand and appreciate.

4. Let's consider bibliographic competence versus technical competence. Do you find as you use more computer-based tools that you spend more time talking about technical competence (which key to push) than you do bibliographic competence (the construction of the database and what it contains)? I have found myself fully able to hopelessly confuse students trying to teach the technical competency of just one tool much less two or three. In an area this detailed, retention, even as a short-term skill, is abysmal. I now tend to concentrate on bibliographic competence and rely on the user-friendliness of the system, good point of use instruction, or one-on-one instruction at the time of need rather than expecting students to remember "which key does what" from a lecture a week ago. It is my experience that the technical competence, once mastered, is to a great degree finished--the puzzling stuff is still on the "inside."

This list could go on, but I hope that these points have illustrated that, in addition to feasibility, there may be some advantage to using the concepts of lifelong learning to enhance the teaching of short-term skills. As a practical matter, the sheer number of online protocols that confront a student added to the reality that these systems are constantly changing also indicate to me that the emphasis of instruction should be on the conceptual issues rather than just mechanics.

In closing, I would like to talk about what I think is the most interesting development of all. Librarians are, for lack of a better term, being overrun by events. We are using mainstream technology. This makes a big difference. No longer are we teaching weird, arcane tools like card catalogs--an artifact found only in libraries, but not related to any broader utility. One of the nice things about computers is that, to some extent, they are all alike. Take online catalog training for example. In one class I taught, I used the analogy of an automatic teller machine. When the students outlined the steps, we found a pretty direct relationship to the steps needed to search in an online catalog. A few of these were as follows:

- Need money=Analysis of problem.
- Need my bank and my card=you have to have the appropriate (best) tool for the job.
- Choose transaction=qualifying your search to get the specific results desired, actually the bank is less forgiving because you must qualify the search to have a successful result.

What a concept...library imitates REAL LIFE!!

Related to this development is the reality that to a greater extent, our users are not in the library. Instructional skills, especially mechanics, must be taught within the system. We simply do not see these people. The challenges for instruction are very interesting and this future is more immediate than we think it is.

The upshot of this is that I do think the goals of lifelong learning and literacy are ones that we can incorporate into our short- and long-term futures as instruction librarians. Rather than mechanical skills, we should attempt to teach generalizable skills that will not atrophy as new technologies emerge. We need to concentrate not on the specific means to an end, but on the ways to use information well and wisely. We need to transmit the empowerment that literacy skills provide. Rather than the few, the proud, the tough...we need the curious, the aware, and the literate.

NOTES

1. Michaels, Carolyn, "Some Practicalities," *RQ* 25 (Spring 1986): 319-321.

2. Richard Feinberg and Christine King, "Short-Term Library Skills Competencies: Arguing for the Archievable," *College & Research Libraries* 49 (January 1988): 24-28.

3. Jill B. Fatzer, "Library Literacy," *RQ* 26 (Spring 1987): 313-314.

4. Fatzer, 314.

5. Patrick Wilson, *Public Knowledge and Private Ignorance: Toward a Library and Information Policy.* (Westport, CT: Greenwood Press, 1977.)

6. Patrick Wilson, *Two Kinds of Power: An Essay on Bibliographical Control.* (Berkeley, CA: University of California Press, 1968.)

Summary by Carolyn Kirkendall

Is there consensus that most of us can agree with points that both our panelists raised? While we may be talking apples and oranges in part, both speakers illustrate Patricia Breivik's initial premise: "library instruction encompasses too small a concept," and the concept of information literacy is broad enough to encompass both short-term and long-term instruction.

Instructive Sessions

GOING OUT ON A LIMB AND FALLING OFF

Phyllis Eisenberg, Librarian
Piedmont Virginia Community College

When I was a new librarian, our college president told the faculty that we should be innovative and not be afraid to fail. Our president had confidence in our creative potential. I felt expansive and encouraged. Then, I happened to meet the director of the Virginia state budget office, a powerful and political man, who asked me how things were going at my college. I told him about our many new projects and how our president had challenged us to be innovative and not to be afraid to fail. "I tell *my* people not to be afraid to fail," he said, "but *if* they fail, they're fired." I was shocked; I felt diminished.

But maybe it did not matter what either one said because a professional librarian is sufficiently neurotic and compulsive to ignore such outside noise and can't help trying something new, and, hopefully, better--taking a risk--climbing out on a limb and, sometimes, falling off.

Last summer I needed to develop a new, eight-session, one-credit library instruction course because the college was doing a quick turnaround from the quarter system to the semester system. The library course is one of a group of courses offered by the student services division, and a student must select and complete a student development course as one of the requirements for graduation.

Under the quarter system, I had taught a library course with the standard approach of basic skills, a pathfinder, and a tour of the University of Virginia library. After awhile, this course became very unappealing to me. I then developed a one-day intensive workshop given on a Saturday, which worked out very well especially because community college students have complicated work schedules and family responsibilities.

The course became extremely popular, which was very flattering. Registration always closed out early, and students begged to be let in after it closed. It received wonderful student evaluations. It obviously was not a failure, but I was beginning to think that it was.

I was concerned that students were not learning enough to prepare them for what I knew would lie ahead for them in the four-year institutions or in the workplace. I could not be sure that they went away from the workshop with a conceptual understanding of library organization and research. Of what value were the individual skills they learned? Would they fall back into the old preconceptions and confusions? These became important questions to me. Therefore, I was very enthusiastic about starting from scratch with a new course and a fresh chance to do better.

I decided to broaden the content and scope of the course focused on giving students a solid understanding of library and information organization and the research process. Then, they would have a basis for future confrontations with libraries: how to approach the use of an unfamiliar library with confidence, how to develop a research topic, how to figure out unfamiliar access tools. I wanted the student to achieve a mind-set for problem solving in the library. It appeared to be a straightforward goal.

But then I blurred the focus with a peripheral goal. I wanted students to come away from the course excited about the variety and wealth of information and enjoyment to be found in the library collection, to feel the pleasure of discovery, and to know the rewards of a good search. If the students could understand why libraries are valued institutions in our society, then they would be positively motivated toward reading, ideas, and education. I wanted to assert the importance of this body of knowledge and of its intrinsic value to the student's success at Piedmont Virginia Community College and beyond.

In changing the emphasis from teaching skills to teaching the underlying concepts of what happens in library research, I planned to use a systems analysis approach based on a chapter on libraries in a computer-science textbook. I had used this concept in my one-hour presentations for English composition classes already. Here, we viewed the library as being made up of many systems, and each system as a body or mass of information manipulated by an access tool. Each system had a particular kind of organization and access points. Thus, the student would have a way of thinking about how to approach any new hurdle in the library such as a complicated reference work, a computer search, or a card catalog, thinking, "It's a system. How does it work?"

I also tried to incorporate ideas from the book, *Learning the Library: Concepts and Methods for Effective Bibliographic Instruction*, by Anne Beaubien, Sharon Hogan, and Mary George. They describe part II, "Understanding the Research Process," as the heart of the book. It deals with search strategy in the research process, and the research process in the humanities and the social sciences.[1]

The authors' statement of purpose for the book is worth noting: "Our aim," they write, "...is to concentrate primarily on the theoretical underpinnings of bibliographic instruction, on the concepts, thought processes, and intellectual decisions that the efficient library researcher must make in order to function freely in the world of limitless knowledge, however deeply buried it may be."[2]

They go on to make the case for the value of cognitive learning. That is, "...using the natural human thought process as the framework for teaching new ideas and new skills to students of any age...cognitive learning draws on existing patterns of logic that students have developed to help them understand new subject matter...cognitive learning is more transferable than rote memorization...and transferability is a major object of any BI program."[3] It "...can best be achieved through a program based on concepts rather than on the presentation of titles."[4]

I called my new course "Library Literacy" hoping that the name would convey the purpose of the course to the students--that they would become literate in the use of the library. If you will look at the syllabus dated, fall 1988, (Appendix 1) you see that the first item is a required textbook costing $10, not a welcome sight for many community college students with limited funds. Why did I require a text? I wanted students to have a sourcebook to refer to afterwards--something to return to as needs arose for information in their coursework or personal lives. This was probably the first time that a textbook was required for any of the student development courses. It was written by Bruce L. Felknor and titled, *How to Look Things Up and Find Things Out.*

I liked the book. It was written by an editor, not by a librarian, and intended for a general audience, not for scholars. Published in 1988, the sources are very up-to-date. It reads well. For example, he begins, "This is a book of secrets: the secrets of making reference publications work for you. As soon as any bit of knowledge or information is written down somewhere, it is effectively hidden there and--except by accident--can be found again only by someone who knows exactly

where to look. The person who recorded it, we may hope, was following a plan or organizing principle. In the world of reference works, there are abundant clues to the plan of each particular work. It's a simple matter to follow these clues and find out the plan."[5] Aha! The systems approach to figuring things out. I should add that none of the students objected to the reading assignments --just to the over-all amount of work I assigned.

Reading through the syllabus, you can see how I was trying to flesh out my ideas for the course. I filled the cup to overflowing. In the first class, the students looked at the syllabus, listened to my list of expectations, heard about why the KGB and the FBI competed for the undercover services from, of all people, librarians, and had a self-guided tour of service points and locations in the library. And then, almost half of them dropped the course. I was crushed, especially because I was very sensitive to the vulnerabilities of community college students. They need to be nurtured and encouraged, not frightened off.

My enthusiasm had blinded me to one of the truths in higher education--the power of the syllabus to reduce the size of a class. But it follows that those students who remain are a superior group --motivated, interested, ready to work. And they worked. They read the assignments in the textbook, listened attentively to my lectures, created personal library glossaries, spent hours on an unnecessarily long reference exercise, struggled over a complicated exercise on research problem analysis, and bravely attacked other assignments that, hopefully, would help them to learn concepts as well as to find facts.

But the lectures were too long; they rambled. Each session was overloaded. I would run out of time for them to work in the library. I was unrealistic to expect that I could have a polished product the first time around. I knew that I was going in the right direction but the course needed more work and refinement. This was more complex than developing a simple skills course and I never got over the greatest hurdle of all, insufficient time for preparation, which plagued me all the way. The college embarked on a number of major projects and activities that affected the entire faculty and many of the staff. I was working eleven- and twelve-hour days. My environment was not conducive to a thoughtful preparation for the course.

But the lack of time and the burden of duties do not explain away everything that I perceived was going wrong. Here is a rough list of possibilities I am considering for next year:

1.   I need to slim down my goals for the course. They are too muddied now between concepts, skills, and attitudes.

2. I need to take the time to understand the subject matter better myself in order to communicate it more precisely, especially research problem analysis. In my regard, I need to prepare explicit examples and explanations of what I am trying to get across and not try to wing it. Things went well when I was better prepared.

3. I need to work on the exercises so that they are simple to follow, especially those dealing with concepts and process. The items should not be redundant. They should be capable of being completed in a limited time period, I need to reduce the work load.

4. Finally, as I mentioned before, I should not have expected success with the very first run-through. This was a new approach with complex ideas, which needed to be developed further before I panicked.

One happy outcome was that this class, as a group, scored the highest of any class I have taught on a standardized skills test that I gave as a final exam. I was also encouraged by the fact that in the student evaluations of the course, they all answered "yes" to the question "Would you recommend this course to other students?" Something good had happened; I am going to try again.

NOTES

1. Anne K. Beaubien, Sharon A. Hogan, and Mary W. George, *Learning the Library: Concepts and Methods for Effective Bibliographic Instruction.* (New York: R.R. Bowker Company, 1982).

2. Beaubien, Hogan, and George, 3.

3. Beaubien, Hogan, and George, 66.

4. Beaubien, Hogan, and George, 67.

5. Bruce L. Felknor, *How to Look Things Up and Find Things Out.* (New York: Morrow Press, 1988), 9.

COURSE SYLLABUS
Fall 1988

Library Literacy STD 100-40
5:30 - 6:55 p.m.
August 25 - October 13, 1988
PVCC Room 605

Instructor: Phyllis Eisenberg
PVCC Librarian
Phone: 977-3900 ext. 304
Office: Room 731 in Library

Required Text *How to Look Things Up and Find Things Out* by Bruce L. Felknor

Course Goal To become a more sophisticated library user who can determine the steps for research and make efficient and effective use of library resources.

Activities To accomplish the goal, we shall read, write, talk, work in the library, tour Alderman Library, U.Va., and write an essay/short answer exam.

Schedule

Aug. 25 The theory of information and library organization.

How the PVCC library is a microcosm of any major research library.

Why Russian KGB has targeted librarians for espionage efforts and the FBI has enlisted librarians in a counter-espionage program.

Sept. 1 The research process, problem analysis, search strategy. An overview of how research in the major academic fields differs. The difference between fact and opinion.

Sept. 8 Finding your way through the information jungle; getting started with topics and reference books.

Sept. 15 Why scholars use journals. Juggling indexes, citations, and microfilm. Why the *New York Times* is a student's goldmine.

Sept. 22 Making sense of the card catalog before it's too late, and it becomes a computer.

Sept. 29 The big time--a tour of Alderman Library, University of Virginia.

Oct. 6 The library technocrat: computers, data bases, and automation. Education Library, Ruffner Hall, U.Va.

Oct. 13 Exam. All projects and assignments due.

Attendance Students are required to attend all sessions, arrive on time, participate in class activities, and keep me informed of any difficulties you may have. It is understood that students will have their own transportation to Alderman Library.

Grading No letter grades are given in STD 100 courses. Students receive an S if all course requirements are met. Students receive a U for failure to complete course requirements and receive no course credit.

PIEDMONT VIRGINIA COMMUNITY COLLEGE
Route 6, Box 1-A, Charlottesville, Virginia, 22901-8714

Phyllis Eisenberg: Appendix 1

COURSE SYLLABUS
Spring 1989

Library Literacy STD 100-40
5:30 - 6:55 p.m.
February 6 - April 3, 1989
PVCC Room 605

Instructor: Phyllis Eisenberg
PVCC Librarian
Phone: 977-3900 ext. 304
Office: Room 731 in Library

Course Goal To become a more sophisticated library user who can determine the steps for research and make efficient and effective use of libraries and library materials.

Activities To accomplish this goal there will be short instructional sessions, work in specific areas of the library on finding information in books, indexes, microfilm, etc., and tours of University of Virginia libraries.

Schedule

Feb. 6 How libraries are organized.
How the PVCC library resembles a major research library.

In the library: Orientation to service points and materials.

Feb. 13 Getting started with topics and reference books.

In the library: Hands on search of reference materials on typical undergraduate topics.

Feb. 20 Why scholars use journals. Learning about periodical indexes, citations, and microfilm.

In the library: Finding answers using periodical indexes and microfilm.

Feb. 27 Why the *New York Times* is a student's goldmine. The *Newsbank* service.

In the library: Exploring the variety of information available in these sources.

Mar. 6 Making sense of the card catalog before it's too late, and it becomes a computer.

In the library: Finding sources for a typical undergraduate paper.

Mar. 13 Tour of Alderman Library, University of Virginia.

Mar. 20 Spring Break.

Mar. 27 Demonstration of a fully automated library. Tour of Education Library, Ruffner Hall, University of Virginia.

Apr. 3 Skill check. Catch up.

Attendance Students are required to attend all sessions, arrive on time, and participate in class activities. It is understood that students will have their own transportation to the University of Virginia tours.

Grading No letter grades are given in STD 100 courses. Students receive an S if all course requirements are met. Students receive a U for failure to complete course requirements and receive no course credit.

PIEDMONT VIRGINIA COMMUNITY COLLEGE
Route 6, Box 1-A, Charlottesville, Virginia, 22901-8714

Phyllis Eisenberg: Appendix 2

INFORMATION LITERACY THROUGH INTERACTIVE INSTRUCTION: USING THE ONLINE CATALOG TO TEACH BASIC CONCEPTS OF INFORMATION ORGANIZATION AND ACCESS

Polly Frank, Bibliographic Instruction Librarian
Mankato State University

I am going to talk to you about a method for teaching basic concepts of information organization and access with the help of the online catalog. I thought it might be wise to explain why one would use the online catalog for this purpose when it is apparent that students generally lack interest in learning about all the bells and whistles the online catalog has to offer.

Although access has vastly improved with the emergence of interactive information technology, our students have not come to value these changes as we have. (Appendix 1) We have seen that student interest and attention may be no more evident than in the old card catalog days. While we marvel at the search capabilities of interactive catalogs our students often behave as bored Alices, wandering about in a more wonderous wonderland. Students often acquire and apply what they view to be a satisfactory subset of the information they need. In pointing this out, I do not mean to belittle the intentions of our students. We all choose to learn subsets of information that could make our lives easier. Who hasn't elected to learn only "some" of the system capabilities in a word processing or database management program, for example. Christine Borgman has described this tendency as the "Einstellung effect" explaining "once people develop some basic skills at using a system, they may restrict themselves to these methods even when inefficient, rather than invest the mental energy in learning new ones."[1]

So how does the librarian deal with students' indifference to learning more about the online catalog? The idea is to get away from teaching the use of the online catalog solely as an end in itself, a tool to be understood for some unknown mystical reason. Instead, the librarian utilizes the catalog as an interactive instructional tool, working with students' real problems to teach basic concepts of information organization and access. The librarian can teach core concepts within instructional objectives and at the same time, offer "responsive" instruction working with students' actual needs. Projecting the catalog's responses on a large screen, the librarian can exploit the interactive capabilities of the online catalog, using it as a springboard to visually explain many basic concepts, like these. (Appendix 2) At a recent NEA seminar on instructional development, Harvard education Professor Richard Light noted that

learning increases dramatically when groups, rather than individual learners, use interactive technology in the instructional setting.

I am going to tell you how I have used the online catalog in the classroom, working with undergraduate students in speech and composition classes. I call this method "referencing instruction" as it responds to the real problems of students related to their speech or composition assignments. When students have an assignment their level of concern may be raised at least to the extent that they consider what they know or don't know about using the library. The librarian attempts to build on that level of concern and teach concepts that are considered worth knowing by working with students' actual problems.

This method is most effective if the librarian involves students in the instructional process. At the beginning of the class, the librarian explains the structure of the session. Students are told that the class will be a work session, that many of their individual problems will be addressed, and that they will be asked to participate in the problem solving. Clearly stating these goals sets the tone of respect for the ideas and participation of the students.

The librarian collects student topics at the beginning of class and lists them on the board. The students are given this list of questions to stimulate thinking about their research needs. The librarian explains that the students will be considering how their topics are similar in terms of the various kinds of search problems they pose. (Appendix 3)

The librarian pursues only a few basic objectives. We all know how tempting it is to throw everything at the students, especially when teaching with interactive technology. An additional concern is that responsive instruction always involves some meandering from the task at hand. With a limited number of objectives to meet, the librarian can more effectively direct class discussion and still be responsive to students' needs.

In her objectives, (Appendix 4) the librarian considers how the online catalog could be used to illustrate the concepts and makes a list of typical student problems to serve as examples. In the classroom, the librarian uses the real problems of students instead of her examples, whenever possible, and draws attention to the problems shared among classmates. This might be better explained by an example.

One objective may be to help students learn how they can recognize the scope and coverage of access tools. The librarian asks students to think about the topics on the board and consider why they would want to identify the types of materials covered as well as subjects and years of coverage. Using the online catalog, the librarian explains that one can often identify the types of materials cited in a catalog or index relating the appropriate "introductory," "beginning," or "help" screens to the prefatory and introductory notes in a printed index. Students at Mankato State find the types of materials cited in the PALS Online Catalog using a help screen. At MSU, the librarian points out the various formats, including serial publications. With some discussion and questioning, the librarian helps students recognize that periodicals are one type of serial. On examining a few records, the librarian shows the students what is indexed in a periodical record and prompts them to think about what is not searched. (Appendix 5) When students can be led to discover that the contents of periodicals are not indexed, this serves as a springboard for introducing periodical indexes as another form of access.

The librarian talks to the students to find out more about their topics on the board. She explains why she would use the online catalog to search for some of their topics based, in part, on the information they found in the "introductory" and "help" format screens. She also explains why some of the topics would be likely candidates for periodical indexes. She helps students point out related student problems and identify topics that they think could be searched in the online catalog. The students test some of their assumptions while learning about a variety of search options. When the OPAC proves to be of limited use for a student's topic, a discussion about why this is true could lead to identifying other access tools likely to meet the student's needs. The librarian introduces the idea of choosing "likely" access tools, using "help" screens and prefaces, and steers students away from thinking in terms of "always use" or "never use" when choosing an index or catalog.

Another objective might be to teach students the advantage of thinking creatively when naming concepts within a thesis statement. We all know how students can get frustrated, misdirected, or give up when they cannot find the information they need indexed under the terms they choose. Projecting this topic analysis form (Appendix 6) or using it as a worksheet might help students visualize the concepts within their topic and serve as an introduction to expansive and contractive search strategies using Boolean operators. With their own topics, students can be shown how to make informed choices in the search process, choosing keyterms or subject keyterms that badly "hit upon" entries related to their topics and then examining those entries to select appropriate subject headings. Involving the students in creative searching in the online catalog helps the librarian explain how these strategies compare with keyterm and controlled vocabulary searches in other print and computerized indexes.

The librarian may want to teach students how they can explore and focus a topic. The students explore their topics on the OPAC by reconsidering saved sets with new concepts or by browsing subject fields. The "BROWSE SUBJECT" command will be a more effective strategy when Mankato State's subject authority file comes up next year. The file will cross-reference related subject headings and give a count of the number of items traced under each heading.

When students' topics are viewed in a group, it is sometimes easier for students to distinguish topics that are very broad and that will need further work to become manageable. The librarian might explain how periodical indexes of a field and special encyclopedias can be used to explore and sometimes focus a topic. The librarian guides the class in naming disciplines that cover their topics and helps them look for indexes and encyclopedias in these fields using a keyterm search. (Appendix 7)

The librarian may want to teach students how they can choose publications that meet specific criteria rather than use anything and everything they find on their topics. This concept could be introduced using the online catalog also. The PALS Online Catalog at Mankato State first notes the number of items in a search and then lists the items. As call numbers are withheld at this point, the librarian shows students that they can begin making choices based on author, title, and date of publication. If students express an interest in choosing materials based on currency of publication, language, or format, they can experiment with limiting searches by these criteria.

When students have trouble making choices because retrieved items seem of similar value, the librarian might point out authors that appear repeatedly in their search. The librarian explains the value of looking for information that gives some indication of the authority of the author in that field. If students want to find out what else an author has written, they are shown local and systemwide author searches and introduced to *BIP Plus*. For students whose criteria includes finding contrasting points of view on their topics, the librarian explains how congressional hearings might address that need. (Appendix 8) At Mankato State, the class can look for congressional hearings with topic searches as over half of the federal government depository items we own are now online. And, of course, students' attention should be drawn to the publication information and note fields within bibliographic displays to help identify materials that meet their criteria.

With this approach to instruction, we try to help students realize that they have an information seeking problem and identify what that problem is. When the responses of the interactive catalog are projected in the classroom, students can work together to try different ways of approaching problems. Students can be shown how to evaluate their results, to choose other appropriate strategies when needed, and test those strategies. Typically, in the classroom, librarians pose well-structured problems while in our everyday experience we know that problems are often ill-structured. Students seem interested in interactive instruction, researching actual problems even when results are not "perfect" as compared to watching the librarian use preplanned "works-every-time" examples. The librarian frequently asks, "why," "how," and "what if," and always shows students the relationship between the online catalog and other access tools with regard to the problem at hand.

In addition to problems related to term paper and speech assignments, the online catalog has been used to teach a variety of other concepts interactively. Occasionally, a classroom instructor asks us to cover a specific type of source like a citation index. I have described the indexing in the permuterm section of the index comparing it to the online catalog's "keyterm within title" search. When training student workers, I have used the browse call number command to test or reinforce their understanding of call number sequence. (Appendix 9) Student workers are asked to explain why one call number precedes or follows another. And at the reference desk, when students' online searches have turned up items largely in one call number area I have directed them to the browse call number command to help them experience the advantage of browsing.

The online catalog has the capacity to illustrate how information is organized and accessed and to work with students' problems in a live and vital way. Students get involved in identifying their information needs, planning how to solve them, verbalizing the procedures they will use, drawing upon their prior knowledge, using the librarian's hints, finding information, and sorting out information they do not need.

Using the online catalog to teach interactively is risky as one can never predict exactly what will happen. I have taken this chance in an effort to connect with students and I will continue to do so as it is energizing for me and often more interesting for my students.

NOTE

1. Christine L. Borgman, "Psychological Factors in Online Catalog Use, or Why Users Fail," in *Training Users of Online Public Access Catalogs: Report of a Conference Sponsored by Trinity University and the Council of Library Resources*. (Washington, DC: Council on Library Resources, Inc., 1983), 28.

REFERENCES

"Assessment: The NEA Perspective." *Higher Education Advocate* 6 (10 April 1989): 1.

Bechtel, Joan. "Developing and Using the Online Catalog to Teach Critical Thinking." *Information Technology and Libraries* 7 (March 1988): 30-40.

Borgman, Christine L. "Psychological Factors in Online Catalog Use, or Why Users Fail." In *Training Users of Online Public Access Catalogs: Report of a Conference Sponsored by Trinity University and the Council of Library Resources*, ed. by Marsha H. McClintock, 23-34. Washington, DC: Council on Library Resources, Inc., 1983.

King, David, and Betsy Baker. "Human Aspects of Technology: Implications for Bibliographic Instruction." In *Bibliographic Instruction: The Second Generation*, ed. by Constance A. Mellon, 85-107. Littleton, CO: Libraries Unlimited, 1987.

Kobelski, Pamela, and Mary Reichel. "Conceptual Frameworks for Bibliographic Instruction." *Journal of Academic Librarianship* 7 (May 1981): 73-77.

Mellon, Constance A., and Kathryn E. Pagles. "Bibliographic Instruction and Learning Theory." In *Bibliographic Instruction: The Second Generation*, ed. by Constance A. Mellon, 134-142. Littleton, CO: Libraries Unlimited, 1987.

Nielsen, Brian, Betsy Baker, and Beth Sandore. "Educating the Online Catalog User: A Model for Instructional Development and Evaluation." Bethesda, MD: ERIC Document Reproduction Service, ED 261-679, 1985.

Ready, Sandy K. "Putting the Online Catalog in Its Place." *Research Strategies* 2 (Summer 1984): 124-125.

Rudd, Joel, and Mary Jo Rudd. "Coping with Information Load: User Strategies and Implications for Librarians." *College & Research Libraries* 47 (July 1986): 315-322.

Tobin, Carol, et al. "The Computer and Library Instruction." *Reference Services Review* 12 (Winter 1984): 71-78.

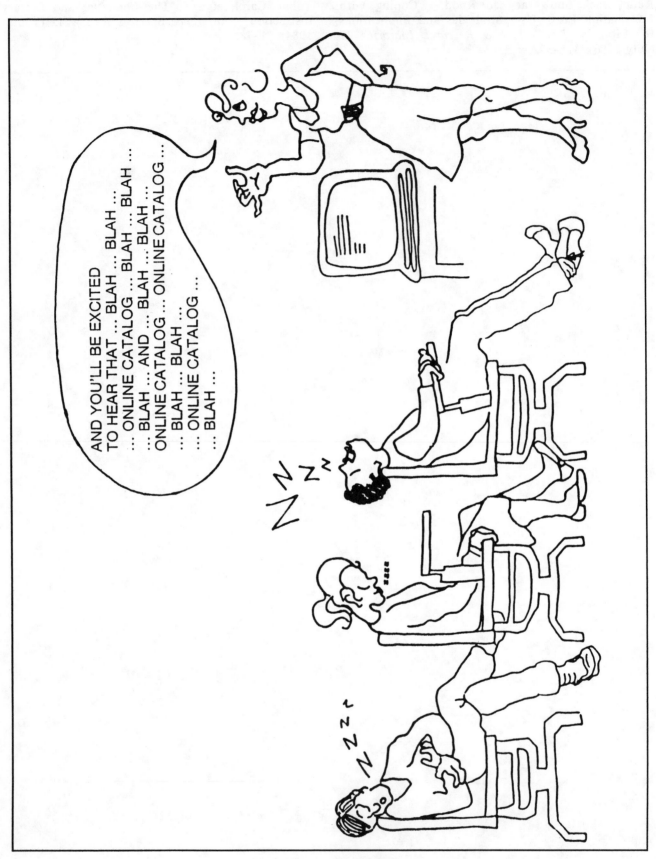

Polly Frank: Appendix 1

RECOGNIZING THE SCOPE AND ORGANIZATION OF AN INDEX

IDENTIFYING AND DESCRIBING PARTS OF A THESIS STATEMENT

SEARCHING CONTROLLED VOCABULARY AND KEYTERM INDICES

BROWSING AND READING CALL NUMBERS

EXPLORING AND FOCUSING A TOPIC

SELECTING AND EVALUATING PUBLICATIONS

Polly Frank: Appendix 2

WHAT DO I NEED THIS INFORMATION FOR?   TERM PAPER? CLASS
PRESENTATION? PERSONAL INTEREST?

HOW MUCH DO I KNOW ABOUT THIS TOPIC?   DO I NEED BACKGROUND
INFORMATION?

HOW BROAD (OR HOW NARROW) IS MY TOPIC?   DO I NEED TO FOCUS?
IS MY TOPIC QUITE SPECIALIZED WITH SEVERAL CONCEPTS
CONSIDER TOGETHER?

DO I NEED SPECIFIC KINDS OF SOURCES? (i.e. PROFESSIONAL
JOURNALS, VISUAL AIDS, ETC.)   WHAT ARE THE REQUIREMENTS
OF THE ASSIGNMENT?

IS THIS A POPULAR OR SCHOLARLY TOPIC?   WHICH DISCIPLINES ARE
INVOLVED?

HOW MUCH (OR HOW LITTLE) INFORMATION DO I NEED?

DO I NEED VERY CURRENT INFORMATION?

HOW MUCH TIME DO I HAVE TO GET THE INFORMATION I NEED?

Polly Frank: Appendix 3

OBJECTIVE 1

    WHAT ONLINE CATALOG FUNCTIONS COULD ILLUSTRATE OBJ 1?

        . . . .

        . . . .

        . . . .

    EXAMPLES OF TYPICAL STUDENTS' PROBLEMS TO USE

        . . . .

        . . . .

IN CLASSROOM

    REAL PROBLEMS REPLACE PRE-PLANNED EXAMPLES

    SIMILARITIES AMONG STUDENT PROBLEMS ARE NOTED

Polly Frank: Appendix 4

```
HELP FO                                          Screen 001 of 001
*TYPE-OF-FORMATS AVAILABLE
  BO -- Book          MI -- Microform     SE -- Serial
  FI -- Filmstrip     MO -- Motion Picture SL -- Slides
  KI -- Kit           OT -- Other         SO -- Sound Recording
  MA -- Map           SC -- Score         VI -- Video Tape
  DI -- Disc (Floppy) AV -- combination of FI KI MO OT SL SO VI




TI INTERNATIONAL JOURNAL OF SPORT PSYCHOLOGY

LOCTN: PERIODICAL GV561 .I61
TITLE: International journal of sport psychology.
PUBLR: Rome : Pozzi.
DESCR:   v. : ill. ; 25 cm.
DESCR: Began publication with v. 1, 1970.
SUBJT: Sports--Periodicals.
SUBJT: Sports medicine--Periodicals.
SUBJT: Psychology, Applied--Periodicals.
----Type DS to Display item availability Status
DS 1988
BAR-CODE-ID      LOCATION       DUE----TIME  HOLDING
30101008005399 3RD Periodcl   *ON SHELVES   v. 19 no. 1 1988
30101008147787 3RD Periodcl   *ON SHELVES   v. 19 no. 2 1988
```

Polly Frank: Appendix 5

TOPIC ANALYSIS WORKSHEET

1) WRITE DOWN YOUR RESEARCH QUESTION AS A STATEMENT

2) UNDERLINE KEY WORDS OR KEY PHRASES IN YOUR RESEARCH
   STATEMENT.

3) LIST EACH KEY WORD AT THE TOP OF ONE OF THE "CONCEPT"
   COLUMNS BELOW.

4) MAKE A LIST OF SYNONYMS OR RELATED TERMS UNDER EACH
   CONCEPT.

CONCEPT 1	CONCEPT 2	CONCEPT 3
------------	------------	------------
OR	OR	OR
------------	------------	------------
OR	OR	OR
------------	------------	------------

Polly Frank: Appendix 6

```
TE INDEX# OR ABSTRACT? AND PERIODICALS AND BUSINESS
2142 RECORD MATCHES AFTER TERM INDEX???????????????????
2977 RECORD MATCHES AFTER TERM ABSTRACT?
 537 RECORD MATCHES AFTER TERM PERIODICALS
  07 RECORDS MATCHED THE SEARCH

Screen 001 of 001
NMBR DATE  --------------------TITLE--------------------
0001 1940- Business education index.
0002 1959- Business periodicals index.
0003 1982- Business international index.
0004 1968- F & S index international: industries, countr
0005 1980- Predicasts F & S index Europe.
0006 1980- Predicasts F & S index international.
0007 1979- Predicasts F & S index.


TE CRIM# OR CORRECTION? AND ENCYCLOP#
3054 RECORD MATCHES AFTER TERM CRIM????????????????????
3468 RECORD MATCHES AFTER TERM CORRECTION?
   4 RECORDS MATCHED THE SEARCH

NMBR DATE  --------------------TITLE-----------------  ----AUTHOR--
0001 1973  Bloodletters and badmen;a narrative encyclo  Nash, Jay Ro
0002 1949  Encyclopedia of criminology,                 Branham, Ver
0003 1982  The encyclopedia of American crime /         Sifakis, Car
0004 1983  Encyclopedia of crime and justice /
```

Polly Frank: Appendix 7

```
TE TEENAGE# OR YOUTH AND RUNAWAY?
 213 RECORD MATCHES AFTER TERM TEENAGE?????????????????
1839 RECORD MATCHES AFTER TERM YOUTH
2452 RECORD MATCHES AFTER TERM ADOLESCE???????????????
  29 RECORDS MATCHED THE SEARCH

AND HEARING?
   7 RECORDS MATCHED THE SEARCH

NMBR DATE  --------------------TITLE-------------------    -------AUTHOR------
0001 1986  Exploitation of runaways :  hearing before th   United States.  Cong
0002 1984  Juvenile Justice, Runaway Youth, and Missing    United States.  Cong
0003 1978  Oversight hearing on the Runaway youth act :    United States.  Cong
0004 1982  Oversight hearing on runaway and homeless you   United States.  Cong
0005 1985  Oversight hearing on runaway and homeless you   United States.  Cong
0006 1986  Private sector initiatives regarding missing    United States.  Cong
0007 1972  Runaway youth.  Hearings, Ninety-second Congr   United States.  Cong
```

Polly Frank: Appendix 8

```
NMBR    (CA)--INDEX KEY----------    ------------TITLE-----------
0001    ND 212.J27                   Abstract & surrealist art in
0002    ND 212.N395                  Abstract painting and sculptu
0003    ND 212.N46                   Recent painting USA:
0004    ND 212.N6                    Art: USA: now.
0005    ND 212.T5                    American painting, 1900-1970,
0006    ND 212.W5                    Milestones of American painti
0007    ND 212.5.A25C69 1982         Art-as-politics :
0008    ND 212.5.A25S2 1976          triumph of American painting
0009    ND 212.5.A25S4 1983          Abstract expressionist painti
0010    ND 212.5.F5A77 1983          Art of the real :
0011    ND 212.5.R4A43               realist revival.
0012    ND 212.5.R4C4514             Hyperrealistes americains /
0013    ND 212.5.S57S6 pt1           Social art in America 1930-19
0013    ND 212.5.S57S6 pt2           Social art in America 1930-19
0014    ND 225.H6                    Five artists of the Old West:
0015    ND 235.N45L65 1971           New York school, the first ge
0016    ND 236.B3                    Three nineteenth century Amer
0017    ND 236.T44                   Three American modernist pain
0018    ND 236.T442 1969             Three American romantic paint
```

Polly Frank: Appendix 9

LIBRARY
CATALOG ACCESS SYSTEM

library
mankato state
minnesota

BASIC DIRECTIONS

1. To send all messages to the computer, you must depress the "New Line" key.

2. To correct a typing error, press the "Back Space" key and retype.

3. A space is essential after all commands (CO, AU, etc.) and between all words.

4. Do not hesitate to ask a librarian for assistance.

   NOTE: For a complete explanation of all search commands, type: HELP

* SEARCHING BY AUTHOR AND TITLE

When you know both the author and title of a work, the combination search is the best way to find out if the library has the work.

To search by author/title combination:

1. Type: CO AUTHOR'S LAST NAME, FIRST TITLE WORD

   (leave off "a", "an", or "the" at the beginning of the title

2. Depress the "New Line" key.

For example, to search for Ernest Hemingway's, **The Sun Also Rises**, type:

   CO HEMINGWAY SUN

* SEARCHING BY TITLE

To find out if the library has a book when you know only the title:

1. Type: TI TITLE OF BOOK

   Leave off "a", "an", or "the" at the beginning of the title)

2. Depress the "New Line" key.

For example, to search for the title, **The Old Man and the Sea**, type:

   TI OLD MAN AND THE SEA

* SEARCHING BY AUTHOR

To obtain a list of books that the library has by an author:

1. Type: AU LAST NAME, FIRST NAME, MIDDLE INITIAL

   (if you know only part of the name, enter as much as you know)

2. Depress the "New Line" key.

For example, to search for the author Ernest Hemingway, type:

   AU HEMINGWAY ERNEST

Polly Frank: Appendix 10

BASIC DIRECTIONS, CONTINUED

* SEARCHING BY TERMS

Searching by "term" means that you have the computer look for specific words supplied by you. You may instruct the computer to look for a single word or for several words.

SINGLE TERM SEARCH

1. Type: TE WORD YOU HAVE CHOSEN

2. Depress the "New Line" key.

For example, if you are interested in "wolves", type:

TE WOLVES

MULTIPLE TERM SEARCH (using 2 or more words)

1. Type: TE WORD AND WORD AND WORD ...

2. Depress the "New Line" key.

For example, if you are interested in "discrimination against women in employment", type:

TE DISCRIMINATION AND WOMEN AND EMPLOYMENT

It is possible to form other search combinations using Boolean operators (and, or, not) - see the Librarian.

NOTICE: Any record displayed tells you the subject heading for your topic. You may want to do a Subject Search using this subject heading.

* SEARCHING BY SUBJECT

Before conducting a subject search, it is a good idea to consult **Library of Congress Subject Headings** (a large, red two-volume set of books located near the terminal) to be sure your subject heading is used.

To get a list of books we have in our library on a subject:

1. Type:
   SU SUBJECT HEADING FOR YOUR TOPIC #

2. Depress the "New Line" key.

For example, to search for information on the topic "learning handicaps", type:

SU LEARNING DISABILITIES #

Always type the # sign after your subject heading for best results.

* DISPLAY STATUS - DS

After locating **one desired record,** type DS to determine whether the item is available for check out.

Business enterprises *(May Subd Geog)*
Here are entered works on business concerns as legal entities, regardless of form of organization.
UF Business organizations
Enterprises
Firms
Organizations, Business
BT Business
Commercial law
Universitates (Civil law)
NT Architectural firms
Architecture—Conservation and restoration—Business community participation
Black business enterprises
Branches (Business enterprises)
Business enterprises, Foreign
Corporations
Couple-owned business enterprises
East Indian business enterprises
Handicapped-owned business enterprises
International business enterprises
Landscape architectural firms
Medical policy—Business community participation
Money-making projects for children
New business enterprises
Partnership
Student-owned business enterprises
— Accounting
USE Accounting
— Finance
UF Business finance
Managerial finance
NT Accounts receivable loans
Cash management
Inventory loans

4/89

Polly Frank: Appendix 10 (continued)

LIBRARY
CATALOG ACCESS SYSTEM: INTERLIBRARY LOAN REQUESTS

HOW TO CHECK YOUR INTERLIBRARY LOAN REQUESTS

---

1. On the online catalog enter:

   DISPLAY PATRON DETAIL (DPD) command followed by your bar code number and your password. Your password is your last name unless you have changed it with the PASSWD command.

   Example: DPD 20101000000001   JOHNSON

   The online catalog will respond with information about your interlibrary loan requests. Also, it will list the MSU materials you have borrowed or are waiting for.

   Example:

   ```
   Screen 001 of 001
   NMBR  STATUS   BAR—CODE—ID      CHARGED—PLACED   DUE—EXPIRE    RN
   0001  CHARGD   30101003109691   103088   15:47   112088  16:30
   0002  CHARGD   30101006180376   110388   10:03   112488  16:30
   0003  HOLD     30101003803905   110388   10:04   010288  00:00
   0004  OVRDUE   30101006375810   110688   15:45   110688  23:45
   0005  PENDING  ILL—ID 0026885   110588   14:20   111688  00:00
   0006  HERE     ILL—ID 0025065   110288   12:25   113088  00:00
   0007  CHARGD   ILL—ID 0023247   103088   16:12   112788  00:00
   0008  PROBLM   ILL—ID 0026483   110388   11:38   120388  00:00
   0009  UNFLLD   ILL—ID 0029203   110188   09:27   120588  00:00
   ............Type DPD NMBR(s) to display specific records
   ```

   Interlibrary loan requests are identified in the display by their ILL request number.

2. Type DPD and the numbers of individual requests to identify the items you requested.

   Example: DPD 5 7

Polly Frank: Appendix 10 (continued)

Catalog responds:

```
Screen 001 of 001    Record 0005 of 0008 MSU
NMBR  STATUS  BAR—CODE—ID   CHARGED—PLACED   DUE—EXPIRE    RN
0005  PENDNG  ILL—ID 0026885    110588  14:20     111688  00:00

LOCTN: ***INTER—LIBRARY LOAN***
AUTHR: Beuchner, Frederick
TITLE:   The Magnificent Defeat
PUBLR: New York, Seabury Press
.................Type NDR to proceed thru display list

Screen 001 of 001    Record 0007 of 0008 MSU
NMBR  STATUS  BAR—CODE—ID   CHARGED—PLACED   DUE—EXPIRE    RN
0007  CHARGD  ILL—ID 0023247    103088  16:12     112788  00:00

LOCTN: ***INTER—LIBRARY LOAN***
AUTHR: Campbell, J.L.
TITLE:   Inside Apple's Prodos
EDITN:  1984
PUBLR: Reston Pub.
NOTE:   OCLC #2399560—11/30/86
```

INTERLIBRARY LOAN DEFINITIONS

CHARGD — item is checked out to you

HERE — interlibrary loan item is ready to be picked up at Reference service counter

OVRDUE — item checked out to you is overdue

PENDNG — interlibrary loan request in process

UNFLLD — interlibrary loan request is between steps in processing

CLEARD — item has been checked in today; this entry will be cleared overnight

8/88

Polly Frank: Appendix 10 (continued)

USING TABLOID LITERATURE TO
TEACH CRITICAL READING SKILLS

Dan Ream, Head, Reference Services
Virginia Commonwealth University

Background

In 1984, the University of Tennessee Undergraduate Library, in cooperation with that campus's library school, began offering a credit course for undergraduates entitled "Finding Information: Resources and Strategies." It was decided early on that the course should include a session that would teach students the critical thinking and research skills necessary to assess the quality of information sources they would be using. A lecture/discussion, assignment, and outside readings were prepared. Copies of each of these are provided, although this LOEX presentation will focus primarily upon the part of these materials dealing with tabloid literature.

The Need

Information seekers are growing increasingly independent in their acquisition of information. In part, this may be explained by the media's realization that information presented in an entertaining way (or "infotainment") can draw a large audience. In television this phenomenon can be observed in the success of programs such as "Geraldo," "Oprah Winfrey," "Donahue," "A Current Affair," "20/20," and "Sixty Minutes." In print, the products of this phenomenon include *People Magazine* and a number of tabloid publications such as the *National Enquirer, Weekly World News*, and the *National Examiner*. Readership of these publications far exceeds that of *Newsweek, U.S. News and World Report, Time*, or any scholarly journal.

On another front, electronic access to information such as full-text databases and increasingly user-friendly end-user searching access promises that this user independence may grow in the future. In both cases, information seekers are growing more independent of librarians' expertise in providing reliable information on their libraries' shelves. As information seekers leave the librarians' "protection" behind, we must teach them the critical skills necessary to evaluate the sources they use.

Using Tabloid Literature as a Teaching Tool

Holding up a tabloid newspaper in front of a classroom of college students invariably gets their attention: some students laugh, others smile,

and all of them seem surprised to see one of these in a college classroom. Asking the class if they have read one of these publications also gets a variety of reactions from embarrassment to wisecracks, but virtually all college students seem to know that such publications should be thought ridiculous. This feeling of superiority to these publications seems to boost students' confidence and makes them eager to discuss tabloid articles in a critical way.

Students are first provided copies of an article entitled "Buffalo Bill Was Not a Wild West Living Legend." The article's content can best be summarized by its opening sentence: "Legendary western tough guy Buffalo Bill Cody was in reality a mincing swish totally undeserving of his he-man reputation." After taking a few minutes to read the article, students are then asked if they believe the article is true and why or why not. Through discussion students usually come to notice the following points:

- no authors' name appears
- no sources are quoted or attributed
- the language used (such as "mincing swish") is emotional/hysterical
- the article contents do not clearly support the thesis

The process of discovering these points is described as "internal evaluation," meaning evaluation based solely on the source itself.

Students are next asked how they would verify the accuracy of this story and they easily conclude that a search for other sources about Buffalo Bill should achieve this. They are then asked to look at the article provided from the *Reader's Encyclopedia of the American West* and they contrast it with the previous article. In doing so, they find that an author's name is given, sources are attributed, and the language is more objective. Although he is described as a showman, there is no inkling in this second source that Buffalo Bill was a "mincing swish."

The use of language is then discussed using the following imaginary headline--"27 Million Turkeys Murdered in North Carolina Massacre." It is explained that this was the number of turkeys "harvested" in 1984 in that state. Students are asked how else this headline might be worded. A variety of possibilities are offered, and disagreements follow about the connotations of various words suggested. Students are then given a handout from the *Webster's Dictionary of Synonyms,* which explains variants on the verb "to kill." Unlike most thesauri, this tool explains the differences in meaning, which are often subtle. This source is recommended to students for future use in studying word-choice and connotation.

Students are next given a tabloid article entitled "Vampirism Can Be Inherited" and asked to critique it also. Although the language remains "colorful," this article does show an author's name, quotes a possibly reliable source, and does seem to support its thesis.

Discussion is next shifted to methods of "external evaluation," which is explained as using other sources to verify the authority or accuracy of an article. Students are then asked to look at biographical sketches of the expert quoted and the author. They note that the expert has worked on the subject of the story - porphyria; and the author has worked on other pieces related to this general area. A medical dictionary definition is also provided showing that the disease named does have symptoms similar to that described in the tabloid article.

Students in the class, who have already done several assignments using indexes and abstracts, are asked how they would search for more articles on this topic. Key concepts are identified as "vampirism," "lycanthropy," and "porphyria," and an online search is determined to be the best method for combining these concepts. Students are then shown the copies of two articles located through such a search. Last of all, a *Newsweek* article on the same subject and quoting the same authority is shown to the class. This article appeared several months after the tabloid article

they initially looked at.

At this point, the class has covered a variety of methods of internal and external evaluation of an information source. Lest they should think this is only necessary for tabloid articles, the class is then presented with the case of Linus Pauling and his book *Vitamin C and the Common Cold.* Anyone seeking biographical information on Pauling would be impressed with his numerous degrees, positions held, and awards, including two Nobel Prizes. Nonetheless, a literature search easily shows that Pauling's recommendations in this book were the subject of great controversy in both popular and scientific literature.

In conclusion, students are warned to be skeptical, even of "experts." On this subject, students are assigned an outside reading by Richard Feynman entitled "Most Experts Don't Know More Than the Average Person." Other sources for external evaluation are incorporated into the class's homework assignment--these include: review sources, letters to the editor, biographical reference sources, and Katz's *Magazines for Libraries.* Students are also assigned to read an article about Random House's recall of a book for factual inaccuracy.

Anyone interested in contacting me for further discussion on this topic is welcome to do so. Another librarian, Nancy Thomas Totten at Indiana University Southeast, has also done some similar work using tabloid literature, which she presented at a poster session at the 1989 ACRL Conference. She would also be glad to discuss her work with anyone interested.

Teaching materials handed out during this session will not be reproduced in the LOEX conference proceedings, but will be available for loan from the LOEX Clearinghouse.

A GRADUATE COURSE IN INFORMATION LITERACY

Linda J. Wilson, BI Coordinator
Virginia Tech

I love baseball. I love its simplicity. I love its complexity. I love its pace. I have spent many hours watching and discussing baseball with a certain friend. There is one thing for which I cannot forgive him: he played the game. Due to the circumstances of my sex, I have never known what it is to stand at the plate and experience the fastness of a fast ball. I believe I said this to him one too many times. Unbeknownst to me, he called Chuck Hartman, the Virginia Tech Hokies baseball coach and told him he had a fat, old librarian friend who wanted to know what a fast ball felt like. So Coach Hartman told him to bring the librarian by during batting practice. "But," Coach Hartman said, "he'll need to wear a batting helmet for safety's sake." To which my friend replied, "Then you better get a chest protector out too, because he's a she." Anyway, next Friday I'll be standing at the plate, facing the pitcher, poised for that fast ball.

When a colleague of mine in the College of Education asked if I would be interested in teaching a doctoral level course on information technology, I jumped at the chance. After all, the library already existed as a laboratory and librarians already possessed the expertise to teach the course. As I proceeded to recruit my team of teachers, one underlying idea dominated my perception of how the course should be taught: I wanted the students to experience the fast ball; I wanted them to be in the game. A powerful characteristic of information technology is its ability to enthuse. The medium is truly the message.

A definition of information literacy emerged as we planned the content and sequence of the course. We wanted students to understand, first of all, the journey of ideas from a scholar's brain to the various print and electronic indexes where these ideas became accessible to the scholarly community as a whole. Second, we wanted them to recognize the roles of the actors along the way: scholars, publishers, vendors, libraries, computing centers, utilities, users. Throughout the course we explored the role of the academic library as one of the actors in this journey.

The syllabus that follows outlines the topics covered by the course. (Appendix 1) The first class period involved a panel discussion among the director of the libraries, the director of the campus computing center, and their mutual boss, the vice president for information services at Virginia Tech. Several of the major issues were presented

initially with the help of a videotape. The ensuing panel discussion naturally evolved into a lively discussion involving the students. With characteristic directness, students asked questions of a university vice president that librarians had been dying to ask for years.

Subsequent class sessions were a combination of discussion, lecture, demonstration, and student experimentation with a variety of technologies. Believe it or not, our head of cataloging gave a fascinating lecture on the history of OCLC, much of which she had witnessed firsthand. The head of acquisitions and the assistant director for technical services covered areas relating to the changing role of the library as a preserver of the past and controller of information, the changing meaning of "authorship," and the problems with reproduction and piracy of information.

One particularly entertaining class period was spent with a professor at Virginia Tech who has built an "Idea Salon" in an old garage. It is this professor's belief that new technologies can converge to generate innovative solutions to persistent problems. For example, a group of staff members from the Virginia Department of Corrections visited the Idea Salon to study the problem of prison overcrowding. Strange combinations of visual, auditory, olfactory, and tactile stimuli were introduced to the group through the use of new technologies in an attempt to start them thinking about the problem in new ways.

Another guest lecturer from the Communication Network Services Department on campus spoke about telecommunications. His department had just finished wiring the campus, making it possible to access the university's mainframe and the library's catalog from any dorm room or office on campus. An interesting discussion followed about decentralized access to information. In the class session on microcomputer applications in the library, we used two examples we were currently working on: a Pro-Cite local newspaper index and a HyperCard library directory. The final class session covered research trends in the area of information technology.

One of the potential pitfalls of the course, which we definitely wanted to avoid, was the perception by the students that each session was complete unto itself. Probably the easiest way to teach this course would be to say, "Now, class, today we are going to cover ERIC on CD-ROM," and then never mention it again in the course. We also wanted to avoid a parochial approach to the information--that the course was just another orientation to the library.

We hope we were able to unify the course into a coherent whole by introducing readings in which the underlying legal, ethical, economic, and organizational issues were presented to the students from a variety of viewpoints. Our reading list follows. While we did emphasize the role of academic libraries in the journey of ideas--after all, this is the area we know best--we tried to point out the constantly occurring changes that are forcing academic libraries to reconsider their role in information literacy. Another unifying theme was how the nature of information differs from other commodities, and how this difference affects us.

"Information Technology" is now an established part of the curriculum for students working toward their doctorates in the field of instructional technology. It will be offered biennially. Several future projects may also result from the existence of this course. I have adapted the course for an undergraduate honors class, entitling it, "The Information Revolution," and have submitted an abstract of it for acceptance. Parts of the course will be featured in an "Information Systems" course being offered via satellite through the Office of Distance Learning. One of the students in the course, a high school English teacher, has brought her classes to the Virginia Tech Library and asked that I teach them (in an hour and a half) everything we taught her in the semester-long Information Technology class.

Lots of positive things have resulted from teaching this course. Certainly, the librarians who helped teach it have enhanced their roles and the role of the library on campus. We learned a tremendous amount. Teaching it forced us to read about the major issues and to organize our thinking about how information is organized, stored, and managed. We learned both that we are experts qualified to teach at a doctoral level and that we need to learn a lot more about how we fit into the journey of ideas. The feedback the students provided was invaluable, both to us and to the library administrators who participated in the classes. We are happy with our first attempt at a comprehensive course on information literacy. As they say in baseball: "Sometimes you win; sometimes you lose. But sometimes you win."

EDCI 5780: Seminar in Education (Information Literacy)

Spring Quarter, 1988
Wednesday, 4-6:50 pm
Newman Library Resources Room
Virginia Polytechnic Institute & State University

Course Overview

Peter Drucker has defined information as organized data, refined into knowledge and combined into wisdom. If, as he proposes, information is our "crucial resource," then institutions of higher education must learn to manage and use evolving information technologies in productive ways. This course examines: (1) the nature of information as a resource; (2) the impact on information of emerging and converging technologies; (3) the legal, ethical, economic and organizational issues involved in using and managing new information technologies; and (4) the trends and future uses of information technology on university campuses. Special emphasis is placed on the role of the academic library in the "informatization" of society. The orientation of the course is toward the practical applications of new technologies through on-site demonstrations.

Proposed Syllabus

Mar. 9   Panel Discussion: Information, Technology and the Changing Role of Libraries in Higher Education

Mar. 16   Lecture/Demonstration: Utilities: OCLC

Mar. 23   Lecture/Demonstration: Online Library Systems

Mar. 30   Lecture/Demonstration: Publishers/Vendors

Apr. 6   Lecture/Demonstration: Idea Salon--The Beginning of Information (4:00-5:30) Telecommunications (5:45-6:50)

Apr. 13   Lecture/Demonstration: Microcomputer Applications in Libraries

Apr. 20   Lecture/Demonstration: Online Databases

Apr. 27   Lecture/Demonstration: Emerging Technologies--CD-ROM, Interactive Video

May 4   Lecture/Demonstation: Specialized Applications of Technologies: Ready Reference, Special Services to the Handicapped

May 11   Lecture: Information Technology and Research Trends

May 18   Exam Period--Paper Due

Linda J. Wilson: Appendix 1

Evaluation

Students' grades will depend on:

    a) discussion and participation, based partially on ability to integrate readings with class activities;
    b) brief written reactions to two reserve readings per week;
    c) assignment based on ERIC print, online and CD-ROM searches;
    d) research paper or project due May 18.

Examples of topics for papers or projects will be distributed in class. There is no final examination.

Linda J. Wilson: Appendix 1 (continued)

EDCI 5780: Seminar in Education (Information Literacy)

Examples of topics for research papers:

How paperless will our society become?

Present and future trends in the management of information in higher education institutions

Equal access to information in the Information Age

Electronic publishing and copyright law

How electronic publishing has affected fields of research, such as medicine, law, physical sciences, etc., and vice versa

How electronic publishing has affected the way scholars do research

A comparison of the use of online databases vs printed sources for library research

An overview of online database technology--history, present development, future trends

How the impact of standards on publishing and retrieval of information have benefitted research

Publisher/vendor practices that encourage/discourage access to information by the scholar

Alternative to a research paper:

A research proposal for a project on anything within the scope of the course. The project need not be feasible with the student's present resources, but it should be realistic and doable. The proposal would involve: problem definition, literature review (not necessarily comprehensive but certainly relevant), proposed measures, other methodological issues and their proposed solutions, anticipated implications for practice and/or further research.

Linda J. Wilson: Appendix 1 (continued)

EDCI 5780: Seminar in Education (Information Literacy)

Topics for Assignment

1. Cognitive assessment or educatinal testing of severely handicapped students.

2. Use of learning contracts or self-directed learning in adult education.

3. Reasons public school teachers leave teaching.

4. Relationship of spatial visualization to math ability and achievement.

5. Role of the principal in microcomputer use for management purposes.

6. Family involvement in early intervention programs or preschool handicapped programs.

7. Preschool guidance counseling.

8. Evaluation of public school principals.

9. Counseling gifted students in public schools.

10. Gifted underachievers in public schools.

Assignment

I. Select one topic from the list above and use the ERIC print indexes (CIJE and RIE) to compile a bibliography of at least 10 titles.

II. Develop a strategy for searching the same topic in the ERIC online database. Make an appointment with one of your instructors to run the online search. Print out a bibliography of at least 10 titles.

III. Using the same online search strategy, run a search in the ERIC database on CD-ROM and print out at least 10 titles.

Linda J. Wilson: Appendix 1 (continued)

EDCI 5780: Seminar in Education (Information Literacy)

<u>Selected Readings on Reserve</u>

There is no required text for this course. Assigned readings
listed below are on reserve in Newman Library. Readings are to
be completed by the dates preceding them. Select at least two
readings from the list assigned for each date.

Mar. 16   Battin, Patricia. "The electronic library--a vision
          for the future." <u>EDUCOM Bulletin</u> 19 (Summer 1984):
          12-17, 34.

          Cleveland, Harlan. "Educating for the information
          society." <u>Change</u> 17 (July/August 1985): 13-21.

          Evans, G. Edward. "Teaching new technologies: Whose
          role is it?" <u>IFLA Journal</u> 10 no. 2 (1984): 151-
          157.

          Heterick, R. C., Jr. <u>Information Systems: A Planning
          Prospectus</u>. Blacksburg, VA: Virginia Polytechnic
          Institute and State University, 1988.

Mar. 30   Crawford, David. "Meeting scholarly information needs
          in an automated environment: A humanist's perspective."
          <u>College & Research Libraries</u> 47 (November 1986): 569-
          574.

          Greenberger, Martin (ed.). <u>Electronic Publishing Plus:
          Media for a technological future</u>. White Plains, NY:
          Knowledge Industry Publications, 1985.

          Neavill, Gordon B. "Electronic publishing, libraries,
          and the survival of information." <u>Library Resources &
          Technical Services</u> 47 (January/March 1984): 76-89.

          <u>Campus of the Future: Conference on Information
          Resources</u>. Dublin, OH: OCLC Online Computer Library
          Center, 1987.

Apr. 13   Brooks, Daniel T. "Copyright and the educational uses
          of computer software." <u>EDUCOM Bulletin</u> 20
          (Summer 1985): 6-13.

          Carlson, David. "Software piracy: A look at legal
          issues." <u>Wilson Library Bulletin</u> 60 (June 1986):
          36-38.

          Walch, David B. "The circulation of microcomputer soft-
          ware in academic libraries and copyright implications."
          <u>Journal of Academic Librarianship</u> 10   (November

Linda J. Wilson: Appendix 1 (continued)

1984): 262-266.

Apr. 20 Co, Francisca. "CD-ROM and the library: Problems and prospects." <u>Small Computers in Libraries</u> 7 (November 1987): 42-49.

Davies, David H. "The CD-ROM medium." <u>Journal of the American Society for Information Science</u> 39 (January 1988): 34-42.

Drake, Miriam A. "Library 2000--Georgia Tech: A glimpse of information delivery now and in the year 2000." <u>ONLINE</u> 11 (November 1987): 45-48.

Herther, Nancy K. "CDROM and information dissemination: An update." <u>ONLINE</u> 11 (March 1987): 56-64.

May 11   Council on Library Resources, Inc. <u>Annual Report 1985</u>. Washington, DC: CLR, 1985.

Council on Library Resources, Inc. <u>Annual Report 1987</u>. Washington, DC: CLR, 1987.

Johnson, Herbert F., (President of Association of Research Libraries). Personal correspondence to Mary Jo Lynch, Director of the ALA Office of Research. Washington, DC, August 19, 1987, (regarding research questions of interest to ARL).

Metz, Paul. "Thinking big: A commentary on the research agenda in academic librarianship." <u>College & Research Libraries</u> 46 (September 1985): 390-394.

Linda J. Wilson: Appendix 1 (continued)

EDCI 5780: Seminar in Education (Information Literacy)

   Lecture/Discussion: Specialized Applications of
   Technologies in Libraries--Ready Reference

The following technologies are currently available at the Newman
Library Reference Desk(s):

NAME	FORMAT	UPDATE	DESCRIPTION
VTLS	online local	daily	(content, access, time period, comprehensiveness, limitations)
OCLC	online remote	daily	
InfoTrac	CD-ROM	monthly	
Dow Jones	online remote	daily	
AutoGraphics	CD-ROM	monthly	
BIP Plus	CD-ROM	quarterly	
Ulrichs	CD-ROM	quarterly	
Local Newspaper File	pc file local	daily	
Mainframe	online local	daily	
DIALOG, NTIS, Wilsonline, etc	online remote	depends on d.b.	
Westlaw	online remote	daily	

Linda J. Wilson: Appendix 1 (continued)

Poster Session Abstracts

Active Library Learning For Political Science Students: Several In-Class Exercises

Libbie Brooks
University of Georgia
Athens, Georgia

Members of the University of Georgia Main Library Reference Department have developed a good working relationship with the University's Political Science Department. Each quarter, students in several sections of POL 101 attend instructional sessions in the library. Although there is no formal and consistent information literacy program at Georgia for freshmen, or undergraduates in general, many freshmen and sophomores are introduced to a large, research library through POL 101. In order to take advantage of this opportunity to speak to underclassmen (and -women!), the author has devised several in-class exercises to promote thinking, keep the students' attention, add some variety to library sessions, and include some much-needed humor. These exercises can easily be adapted for use in other subject areas.

Exercises include the following: a comparison of articles and advertisements from a conservative news magazine and a more liberal publication; a small group exercise in which each group has to answer questions about one part of a typical library search strategy and make a presentation to the class; and a library case study with questions. One other exercise is taken from a term paper workshop, offered in the Main Library several times each quarter. This exercise, which has a political science theme, involves a comparison of information found in a news magazine article with that in a scholarly journal article on a similar topic.

There has been no formal evaluation of results after using these in-class exercises, but the author has noted that students take more interest in the sessions, many of them actively participating in discussions promoted by the exercises. There has also been more laughter, which almost always encourages learning by allowing the students to drop some of their defenses. In summary, students are exposed to evaluation of information sources, their organization and retrieval in a library, all of which combine to make the students more information literate. Last but not least, the author enjoys these sessions, because they are varied, usually fun, and allow much more interaction with the students.

University of Georgia

CLASS EXERCISE #1: INFORMATION EVALUATION (POINTS OF VIEW)

This exercise grew out of a library instruction request for a Political Science 101 section with a research assignment on the Iran-Contra hearings. The teaching assistant wanted his class to be able to distinguish between different perspectives expressed in writing. I had the students first read descriptions of The New Republic and National Review from Magazines for Libraries, then read unlabeled excerpts of editorials on Iran-Contra from the two magazines, trying to determine which editorial came from which magazine. They were to cite which phrases, sentences, or passages served as clues.

In looking for editorials from these two magazines, I also found advertisements in both publications for the same documentary on conservatives, one for the show on PBS and one for the resultant video. It was interesting to see how the advertisements seemed to differ according to the intended audience, and by showing the students these two ads, I was able to emphasize even more strongly the importance of distinguishing different points of view while reading.

Note that advertisements for Absolut Vodka were the same in both magazines (that brought a laugh from the students!).

ACTIVE LIBRARY LEARNING: FOUR POLITICAL SCIENCE CLASS EXERCISES

*LIBBIE BROOKS, UNIV. OF GEORGIA
LOEX CONFERENCE 1989, ANN ARBOR

University of Georgia

CLASS EXERCISE #2: SMALL GROUP DISCUSSIONS OF SEARCH STRATEGY

How to introduce freshmen to the library in their own classroom and without a specific research assignment?

That's how this class exercise came into being. I didn't want to stand in front of the class and ramble on about search strategies. I wanted to engage the students and have them think through the essentials of using a library. I came up with four sets of questions, each set representing one step in a generic library search strategy. The questions were meant to provoke BOTH thought and laughter. After the students worked together to answer the questions, each group reported their conclusions to the rest of the class. I tried to cover what they missed and pull everything together coherently.

University of Georgia Libraries
Athens, Georgia 30602

I. CHOOSING A TOPIC/FINDING BACKGROUND INFORMATION

1. What are the best ways you have used to choose a topic?

2. What makes a lousy topic?

3. Why is it important to find and read background information on a topic?

4. What are 3 myths about librarians?

II. FINDING BOOKS

1. How are books arranged in libraries?

2. Identify the steps you would take to locate a book in the UGA Libraries (HINT: approximately 4 steps).

3. If you had to explain the meaning or concept of "call numbers" to a visitor from Mars, what would you say?

4. What does a reference librarian do all day?

III. FINDING PERIODICALS

1. What are 2 ways the periodicals could be arranged in libraries?

2. How are periodicals arranged in the UGA Libraries?

3. What are "periodicals" anyway?

4. List the steps you would take to locate a periodical article in the UGA Libraries (HINT: approximately 5 steps).

5. What are the most effective ways to ask a reference librarian your most burning reference questions?

IV. OTHER SOURCES

1. What are some other sources of information (besides books and periodicals) in the library?

2. What are some other sources of information outside the library?

3. If you were going to do a paper on the civil rights movement and marches with a particular focus on the recent Forsyth County march, what kind of strategy for finding information would you use in the library? (Be as specific as possible.)

4. List 3 complaints, compliments, questions, or suggestions you have about the UGA Libraries?

An Equal Opportunity / Affirmative Action Institution

University of Georgia

CLASS EXERCISE #3:   CASE STUDY ON STUDENT LIBRARY USE

By devising this case study, I was trying to renew <u>my</u> enthusiasm for teaching countless Political Science 101 sessions and simultaneously test the case study method, a hot topic on the University of Georgia campus at that point, for library sessions. It worked well on both counts! It also promoted better class discussion. This exercise works either by first breaking up the class into small groups or by having everyone work individually. The student in the case study had the same assignment as the group of students I was addressing.

THE CASE OF OTIS

Otis decided to do his paper on Cyprus and its relations with the U.S. It sounded like a cool country, but he really didn't know a thing about it - he didn't even know exactly where it was. He proceeded to the basement of the Main Library to look at the most recent issues of <u>Newsweek</u>, hoping to find an article or two. Not finding anything at all, he remembered that his TA had suggested using the journal <u>Foreign Affairs</u>. He talked a friend into finding the call number for it, so he could find the earlier issues. (The most recent issues in Current Periodicals had plenty of articles on U.S.-Soviet relations, but nothing on Cyprus.) He spent 2 hours looking through back issues of <u>Foreign Affairs</u> on the 4th floor, not finding anything at all, before he got hungry and left for The Grill.

After lunch Otis returned to the library, passed the smiling reference librarians in the reference room, and headed for the subject card catalog. Surely he could find a book on Cyprus! Yes, this one looked good: <u>The Economy of Cyprus</u> by A.J. Meyer, Harvard University Press, 1962. Best news yet - it had a bibliography! Maybe he could get some information sources from the bibliography.

Before going upstairs for the book, Otis decided to stop by <u>World Book</u>, the encyclopedia. He knew he could probably rely on it for a lot of information about Cyprus.

<u>Questions</u> - 1) Did Otis make a glaring error in trying to find information? If so, what?

2) What are the good points of his search?

3) Evaluate the information sources Otis used or tried to use?

University of Georgia

CLASS EXERCISE #4: INFORMATION EVALUATION (MAGAZINE VS. JOURNAL)

Term Paper Workshops at the University of Georgia Libraries include several segments, the last one of which is evaluating information. I developed this segment, using a political science topic. I wanted the students to become actively involved in learning how to distinguish a popular magazine from a scholarly journal. The students looked at photocopies of a <u>Newsweek</u> article on Jesse Jackson and a scholarly journal article also on Jackson. I then had them describe the two periodicals, comparing and contrasting them, while I wrote the comments on the board.

A candidate on a roll: After Super Tuesday, he's not just running a civil rights crusade and flailing around...

The Power Broker

The 'new' Jesse Jackson has expanded his appeal and seems likely to swing the Democratic race. What is the price for his support?

Jesse Jackson and the Symbolic Politics of Black Christendom

By JAMES MELVIN WASHINGTON

ABSTRACT: This article examines the significance of the Reverend Jesse Jackson's bid for the Democratic party's presidential nomination. Jackson's candidacy represents a new use of political revivalism, an old evangelical political praxis recast in the modalities of African American Christian culture. This praxis is an aspect of American political culture that has often been overlooked because of past misunderstandings of American folk religion in general, and black Christianity in particular, as captives of an otherworldly and privatized spirituality. This article contends that black Christianity has an identifiable and coherent political style with both passive and active moods. The dominant manifestations of these moods are, respectively, political cynicism and political revivalism, which are the consequence of the correct folk perception that it is impossible to reason with the purveyors of the absurdities of racial injustice. A critical assessment of black Christianity's political symbolic capital seems appropriate.

James Melvin Washington, Ph.D., is associate professor of church history at Union Theological Seminary and adjunct associate professor of religion at Columbia University in New York City. His forthcoming books include Frustrated Fellowship: A Critical History of the Black Baptist Quest for Social Power, 1773-1953 and two anthologies, Afro-American Protestant Spirituality and Martin Luther King, Jr.: A Prophet for Our Time.

The Annals, The American Academy of Political and Social Science, Vol. 480, July 1985, pp. 89-105.

Librarian's Guide

Evaluation Exercise

Use of two articles on the same subject, Jesse Jackson in this case:

1) Students practice evaluation of sources by scanning and analyzing information in both articles.
2) Students begin to understand the differences between scholarly and popular writing.

In having students characterize/describe each of the articles, you should be looking for such words/phrases as the following:

Newsweek	Annals
Pictures	No pictures
Color	Relatively long
Flashy title	Analytical
"Newsy"/Facts	Large words
Relatively short	Written by professor
Written by reporters	Footnotes
Current	Abstract
Etc.	Descriptive title
	Etc.

You may want to break up the workshop participants into a number of smaller groups, depending on time and total number of people, and have them describe each article. Then have them report findings to the large group with you perhaps jotting down the descriptive words and phrases on the blackboard. Summarize findings and process at the end of the exercise.

The University of Georgia

Libraries

Athens, Georgia 30602

AN EQUAL OPPORTUNITY/AFFIRMATIVE ACTION INSTITUTION

University of Georgia

Introducing Information Literacy In the
Northwestern Michigan College Experience

Douglas Campbell
Northwestern Michigan College
Traverse City, Michigan

In 1986, Northwestern Michigan College received a Title III grant to create programs directed toward student retention. One of the results was a self-paced computer driven college orientation program. Entitled "The NMC Experience," it contains modules on a wide variety of campus functions and services -- including the library. All students are required to complete the NMC Experience during their first term. The first version of the library module emphasized rules, hours, and procedures for locating things. A total revision was accomplished in 1987. The new module was designed to introduce students to the need for information literacy and to show the library's function as a part of the information network. Graphics and animation were added in order to compete with the health services, financial aids, and parking modules, among others, for the students' attention.

Terminals for the NMC Experience are located in the library. As a result, every new student must come to the library during his or her first term. The program may be entered at any point and reviewed as often as desired. There is a short test at the end which gives immediate feedback.

Northwestern Michigan College

Starting Out Right: Teaching Information Literacy Skills to New College Students

Bob Diaz and Darlene Nichols
University of Michigan
Ann Arbor, Michigan

Every summer at the University of Michigan, the Comprehensive Studies Program offers a summer course to a select group of incoming students. These are students in good academic standing who have, in general, graduated from high schools with weak college preparatory prorams. This transitional program "Summer Bridge" is designed to acquaint students with college life and equip them with the skills they need to succeed.

The staff of the Comprehensive Studies Program have always considered information literacy a critical element in the students' preparation for academic success. Comprehensive Studies Program faculty rely on librarians at the University of Michigan Undergraduate Library to provide instruction in information-handling skills. Although the *UGL Workbook* has been the major component of the library instruction segment of the Summer Bridge program for several years, in the summer of 1988, the faculty and librarians chose to try a new approach. Working together, we developed an instructional session intended to provide students with some basic concepts of information literacy. Instructors anticipated that, in learning these concepts, students would begin to develop the ability to evaluate both information and information sources. A ninety-minute session covered the following:

-- natural vs. controlled vocabulary and how vocabulary influences search
      strategy; including the use of thesauri and subject headings
-- critical thinking: evaluating the research topic in light of available
      sources; the role of automated research tools
-- how information is generated: a discussion of primary vs. secondary
      sources; the place of "tertiary" or "finding" sources; when to use
      automated sources

Students consolidated the classroom instruction by completing an exercise on each of these concepts. The exercises were designed to enable them to begin synthesizing information for their assigned research topic.

Although only a beginning, this instructional program gave students a solid base for developing skills to succeed in an information-rich society.

University of Michigan

CLASS OUTLINE

I. **INTRODUCTION**: Students are greeted and librarian instructors are introduced. The purpose and goals of the class are briefly described. Students are encouraged to take notes.

II. **NATURAL LANGUAGE VS. CONTROLLED VOCABULARY**: Getting the most out of subject searching

Coverage: The differences between natural language and controlled vocabulary; the importance and use of subject thesauri, such as the Library of Congress Subject Headings (LCSH).

Activity: Students are given a one page article on marihuana to read and after breaking up into small groups, are asked by the instructor to come up with three to eight terms which best describe the article. The instructor writes all the terms on the black board.

Discussion: Using marihuana as an example, the instructor presents the fact that there are often many words or terms used to describe the same phenomena and asks the students how they would solve the dilemma of not knowing which term to use when doing a subject search. After discussing possible solutions with the class, the instructor then introduces the concept of controlled vocabulary. LCSH is introduced as an example of a controlled vocabulary thesaurus and a transparency of the entry on marihuana in LCSH is shown and discussed with the class. The discussion concludes with an overview of the benefits of using a subject thesaurus when doing subject searching.

III. **CRITICAL THINKING**: Becoming educated information consumers

EVALUATING YOUR TOPIC

Coverage: The role of constant evaluation in focusing a research topic and making the topic more interesting. The importance of using the information as opposed to merely collecting information.

Activity: Students are presented with a set of questions to consider in the process of doing research. These questions are discussed and they are asked to add more questions to the list. New questions are written out on the blackboard:

Are there any terms that need to be defined?
What are the main issues?
Where is this important? What is the context of the topic? (historical, social, etc.)
What are the critical timelines?
How has this been viewed historically? How is it viewed now?
What are the varying points of view that are relevant? (political, social, economic, etc.)
What discipline(s) has/have the most relevance?

University of Michigan

EVALUATING YOUR SOURCES

Coverage: Why all sources are not created equal. Some of the problems researchers should look for as they conduct research (e.g. bias, age, inadequate coverage of the topic). Considering the value of a source's contribution to the research.

Activity: Students receive copies of two articles on the same topic (e.g. the psychology of twins) -- one from a psychology journal and one from a popular magazine. Students discuss how these differ and when one might be a better source of information than the other. Students also discuss how books differ from articles in general and how the different sources complement each other.

Activity: Students are given an "assignment" to do a research paper on the Reagan Presidency. They then see a list of made-up titles and are asked to evaluate these sources based on the brief information given.

IV. THE GENERATION OF INFORMATION: Understanding the development of information

Coverage: Using a timeline approach, how information develops and matures and builds on itself. How today's news may become tomorrow's scholarship. The contribution of working backward along the timeline from general background, primary resources to specific, primary sources.

Activity: Students are told that it is now 1964 and President Kennedy has just been shot. They trace the progress of information about the event from word-of-mouth to television, daily news sources, magazines, books and journals, reference and research sources.

University of Michigan

V. TIPS ON DOING RESEARCH

Coverage: Using reference sources to find background and factual information; how to find books in the University of Michigan(U of M) Undergraduate Library; using indexes to find periodical literature; how to locate periodical literature at the U of M Undergraduate Library; getting help at the reference desk.

Discussion:

1) Using the reference collection: The librarian discusses the various types of tools found in a typical reference collection and explains that it is a good idea to begin one's research there, particularly if one needs to find definitions, facts or a broad overview of a topic.

2) Finding books at the U of M Undergraduate Library: The instructor explains how the U of M's library cataloging system, including the newly implemented online catalog MIRLYN, works, and how to locate books in the Undergraduate Library.

3) Finding periodical literature: The major differences between magazines and journals are reviewed. The instructor explains that such literature is found by using periodical indexes, and that there exist different indexes for different disciplines. The mechanics of how to find periodical literature at the U of M are reviewed.

4) Getting help: The instructor briefly explains the role of the reference librarian in the research process and encourages the students to keep in mind that the reference staff is always eager to help the students with their research questions.

VI. CONCLUSION

Review of major concepts covered in class

1) Natural vs. controlled vocabulary
2) Critical thinking
3) The generation of information
4) Tips on doing research

Explanation of class assignment

University of Michigan

Summer Bridge Library Research Skills Program
July 1988

Name_____

Date_____

Article #_____

Review exercise #1

a. You have received an article from a popular periodical. Read the article and give it one or more subject headings using *your own* terms. Write these subject headings below.

_____

_____

_____

_____

b. Look in *Readers' Guide to Periodical Literature* (either the original paper index or the computerized version) for your article. Under what subject(s) did you find it? Below write the *assigned* subject headings for your article.

_____

_____

_____

c. If you wanted to find articles related to your topic in scholarly journals, what index(es) would you use?

_____

_____

University of Michigan

d. Look in an index to scholarly journals. Find an article related to your assigned article. Under what subject heading did you find it?

_____

e. Write down the *citation* (author, title, journal name, volume, pages, and date of publication) to a scholarly article related to your assigned article.

_____

_____

Name_____

Date_____

Review exercise #2

a. On a separate piece of paper, list the important questions you need to ask yourself when evaluating your paper topic. For example, one important question is what disciplines are involved. Attach that sheet to your exercise pages.

b. Write down your *paper topic* for class (not the article in exercise #1). Then evaluate your topic using the questions in part a. Write out the answers in brief below.

University of Michigan

Review exercise #3

a. Imagine that you have access to all the information in the world. If you wanted to locate primary sources on your paper topic, what kind of information would you use (for example, data from scientific studies)? List these below.

b. Find two of the following on your paper topic: a book, a scholarly journal article, or a popular magazine article. Below briefly compare the two types of sources.

University of Michigan

Evaluating sources of information

- What kind of source is it? Is it a book, a magazine or a journal? Is it appropriate for the paper?

- Who is the author? What is his/her bias?

- When and where was this published? Is the timeframe appropriate for the paper?

- Who is the publisher?

University of Michigan

Primary sources *vs.* Secondary sources
(a partial list)

Primary sources	*Secondary Sources*
manuscripts	books
documents	articles
eyewitness accounts	essays
diaries	newspapers
letters	
transcripts	
newspapers	

University of Michigan

Evaluating sources of information

The Role of the Presidency in the United States by Ronald Reagan

Reagan as President by Opie Que, Chair, U.S. Communist Party

Ronald Reagan : A Biography published in 1974

The American Presidency published in Libya

University of Michigan

Marihuana

    sa   Cookery (Marihuana)

    x   Ganja

          Marijuana

    xx   Cannabis

          Drug Abuse

-- Law and Legislation

Marijuana

    See   Marihuana

****

sa = this is a related term which you can try

x = this term is not used

xx = this is a broader term; it is used

University of Michigan

Some differences between scholarly journals and popular magazines

magazine

- general audience

- journalist or generalist author

- usually no bibliography

- often written like a story

journal

- scholarly reader (professor, student, etc.)

- written by person in the field

- has bibliography or references

- usually has specific structure

University of Michigan

PREPARING RESEARCH PAPERS

The research paper presents the results of careful investigation of a subject. To be successful, it must clearly express facts and ideas and must accurately document sources used. Preparation is the key to writing a good research paper. This includes finding information, selecting and interpreting data, and evaluating source materials. This guide suggests a research strategy which will help you fully exploit UGL resources.

CHOOSE A TOPIC

Select a general topic which interests you and which falls within the scope of your assignment.

Obtain background information.
- Familiarize yourself with facts, trends, concepts, and terminology by consulting a GENERAL ENCYCLOPEDIA for an introduction to your subject, a SUBJECT ENCYCLOPEDIA for specialized information, or an INTRODUCTORY BOOK (or an article or chapter in a textbook, a history, or a survey) for an overview of your topic.
- Look at the BIBLIOGRAPHIES which may accompany these background sources to identify likely titles.

Limit your topic.
- Briefly outline the facts and concepts you already know and write out questions which might be asked about the subject.
- Select as your research topic the questions or ideas which seem most interesting and significant to you.
- Decide on the purpose of your paper. Is it to persuade, to explain, to inform?
- Write a tentative thesis statement which clearly indicates the purpose of your paper.

COMPILE A TENTATIVE BIBLIOGRAPHY

Make a list of books and journal articles you think will be useful in your research.

Finding books.
- Check the MIRLYN ON-LINE CATALOG and the CARD CATALOG by author and title to see if the UGL has the materials which were listed in the background sources. Copy down the call numbers of the ones you find.
- Look in the CATALOGS for lists of subject-related materials under an appropriate subject heading followed by BIBLIOGRAPHY.
  Example: ARCHITECTURE--BIBLIOGRAPHY
  If you find a suitable bibliography, look in it for books which are pertinent to your topic. Copy down the author and title of any books you think could be useful and then check the CATALOGS to see if the UGL has them.
- Identify subject headings which you might use to find books on your topic. There are two ways of doing this:
  - Consult the *Library of Congress Subject Headings* for a list of headings. These are the red books located on a dictionary stand near the CARD CATALOG.
  - Look at the "tracings" along the bottom of cards in the CARD CATALOG. If you know a work appropriate to your topic, look it up by the author. Its subject tracings, also listed in the MIRLYN record, can be used to find other likely books.

University of Michigan

Finding periodical articles.
- Periodical INDEXES and ABSTRACTS are used to find newspaper and journal articles by looking up either subjects or authors. Use them to select articles which appear to bear on your topic.
- Copy down the author, title, name of journal, page numbers, and date for each article which you select.

BEGIN PRELIMINARY RESEARCH

Skim the books and articles in your tentative bibliography.
- Evaluate them for usefulness, eliminating obviously unsuitable items.
- Check the bibliographies of these books and articles for additional sources.
- Compile a working bibliography.

EVALUATE YOUR PROGRESS

- Is there enough material?
- Can you complete your research in the time available?
- Can you adequately cover the topic in the paper's prescribed length?
- Revise the topic as necessary.

BEGIN IN-DEPTH RESEARCH

- Study the material in your working bibliography.
- Take notes. Be sure to include full bibliographic information for each source used (author, title, publisher, place and date of publication).

SOURCES OF FURTHER ASSISTANCE

- REFERENCE STAFF.
- Guides to research and writing papers:

    MLA Style Sheet (UGL Reserve Z 253 .M68 1984 and available at Reference Desk)
    Manual for Writers of Term Papers, Theses, and Dissertations (LB 2369 .T93 1987 and available at Reference Desk)
    Student Guide for Writing College Papers (LB 2369 .T94 1969a)
    American Psychological Association Publication Manual (UGL Reserve Z 253 .A55 1983 and available at Reference Desk)
    MLA Handbook for Writers of Research Papers (available at Reference Desk)
    Chicago Manual of Style (UGL Reference shelves Z 253 .C532 1982)

11/87

University of Michigan

RESEARCH HINTS

Nothing will guarantee that any paper you write will get an "A" rather than a "B", but the points listed below may give your research a special edge. When you think you've finished all of your research, stop and ask yourself these questions. Then feel free to drop by the Undergraduate Library's Reference Desk for assistance in digging a little deeper into your research topic.

* BACKGROUND. Do you fully understand the background of your topic? Are you relying solely on what you have learned in class and from your textbook? Take the extra step of going beyond the obvious information that everyone else will have too by locating some broad outlines of the subject. For example, the *Encyclopedia of the History of Ideas* can help you get a more rounded perspective on many basic concepts in philosophy and history. The staff of the UGL Reference Desk can help you find material for your background research.

* DEFINITIONS. Have you defined your terms? Even if you have a basic understanding of the meaning of a word or phrase, it would be helpful to find a precise definition. Everyone knows what an "attitude" is, but psychologists have a very precise definition in mind when they use that word. Specialized dictionaries in fields from art to math can help you nail down a term.

* CONTEXT OF CURRENT TOPICS. Have you fully explored the context of your topic? Even the most current topic will have something of a background. Look at the recent history of the people involved. What issues are central to the event?

* CONTEXT OF OLDER TOPICS. Have you carefully covered the more recent information on a well established topic? Water pollution has been written about in journals, books and magazines for decades. You can write about the problems everyone discusses or you can go beyond that by analyzing recent events.

* PERSPECTIVE. Have you objectively considered every side of the issue you are discussing? Even in a position paper, where you are required to support one side or the other of an argument, it pays to understand all of the issues. In political science, for example, we tend to think of the presidential race as Democrat versus Republican. But there are other parties and even splinters within the two major parties. Consider the advantages of keeping your perspective as broad as possible when completing your research.

University of Michigan

* FORMAT. Have you obtained information in as many appropriate formats as possible? Many people do not consider any research sources beyond books, magazines, journals, and newspapers. The libraries on this campus are rich in manuscripts, letters, diaries, statistics, maps, charts, and graphs. At least reflect on the possible value of other formats in your presentation.

* QUALITY. Have you analyzed the quality of your research material? Surrogate motherhood, for example, can be found as a topic in both the *New York Times* and the *National Enquirer*. Which would you choose as a reliable, authoritative source? Much subtler distinctions can be made in almost every field. Do you need scholarly journal articles written by professionals in the field for the education of their colleagues or do you need popular magazine articles which report news written by journalists for the information of the general public? Each has an appropriate place. Have you chosen the right one for your paper? Is the author of the book you quote so frequently a member of the organization she is analyzing? Is the publishing company owned by a political organization? Is the literary critic you are citing known in his field as an advocate of a particular school of criticism?

* COVERAGE. Have you indeed found most of the material it is possible for you to find on your topic? Even the most sophisticated researcher, can remain unaware of new sources. The good senior astronomy major will know about the *General Science Index*. The great senior astronomy major will know about new books such as *Patrick Moore's A to Z of Astronomy*. If you feel that you have covered everything completely, take one more minute to ask at the Reference Desk for any further sources.

9/88 LW

University of Michigan

FINDING PERIODICAL ARTICLES

Popular magazines - for the layperson, uses non-technical language; provides <u>general</u> information on a wide variety of subjects.

Scholarly journal - usually reports current research on a specific topic; some jargon/technical language used; use for writing scholarly research papers.

HOW DO I GET TO AN ARTICLE ON MY SUBJECT?

USE AN INDEX OR AN ABSTRACT!

For magazines: *Readers' Guide to Periodical Literature, Infotrac*

For journals: subject specialty indexes such as *Psychological Abstracts, Social Sciences Index, Education Index, Biology Digest,* etc. Ask at the Reference Desk for ideas on which indexes might be most helpful for your topic.

USING THE INDEXES

Indexes are arranged, for the most part, alphabetically by subject. You'll probably want to think of several items under which your topic might be listed. Again, ask at the Reference Desk for suggestions. Under many subject headings in the indexes are "see also" references, which can give you additional places to look for information on your topic.

> **Disarmament and arms control**
> *See also*
> Reagan-Gorbachev summit conference, 1987
> Arms control and human rights. K.L. Adelman.*World*
> *Aff* 149:157-62 Wint '86/'87

> **Title of periodical:**
> *World Affairs,* **Volume: 149**
> **Pages:157-162**
> **Date: Winter, 1986-87**

When you find the title of an article that sounds like it might be important to your work, write down the entire <u>citation</u>. The citation consists of the name and author of the article, the name of the periodical (which will probably be abbreviated - there will be a key in the front of the index to give you the full title - <u>this</u> is what you write down), the volume number, page numbers and date (month, day if given and year).

> **West Polit Q** - The Western Political Quarterly
> **World Aff** - World Affairs (Washington, D.C.)
> **World Dev** - World Development
> **World Marx Rev** - World Marxist Review

University of Michigan

FINDING THE PERIODICAL

The Kardex file, located directly in front of the Reference Desk, lists, alphabetically by title, all periodicals to which the UGL subscribes. Each card includes information on, among other things, how far back our subscription goes (in the upper left corner), and the status of recent issues (bound or unbound). All bound volumes are shelved in the rear of the main floor of the UGL, arranged alphabetically by title of the periodical. Recent issues which have not yet been bound are on reserve on the 3rd floor. Ask for them by title and date at the Reserve Desk.

Use MIRLYN, the UM computerized catalog, to find which library on campus owns the journal you need. For example, type:

t=world affairs

The system reponds with a **guide screen**:

```
MIRLYN SEARCH REQUEST;  T=WORLD AFFAIRS
 AUTHOR/TITLE GUIDE -- 38 ENTRIES FOUND
     1    WORLD AFFAIRS  <LOND
     2    WORLD AFFAIRS  <WASH
     4    WORLD AFFAIRS AND TH
     26   WORLD AFFAIRS DIGEST
```

Type **1** and the first 18 titles (the number 1 screen can hold) will be displayed on an **index screen**:

```
MIRLYN SEARCH REQUEST;  T=WORLD AFFAIRS
 AUTHOR/TITLE INDEX -- 38 ENTRIES FOUND, 1 - 18 DISPLAYED
      1 UL:WORLD AFFAIRS  <LOND
      2 UL:WORLD AFFAIRS  <WASH
      3 UL:WORLD AFFAIRS  <WASH
      4 UL:WORLD AFFAIRS AND THE COLLEGE CURRICULUM *SWIFT RIC<1959
```

Type the number on the left to display information about a title. For the example given on the other side, enter **2** (number 1 is published in London). You will see an entry with catalog information and location:

```
LOCATION;  GRADUATE LIBRARY
CALL NUMBER;  JX1901 .W93
LIBRARY HAS:
    95-99, 105-      (Library holdings begin with volume 95, 1932. Volumes 100 to 104 are not
    1932-            available  The dash means we currently receive it.)
    CURRENT ISSUES IN SSR   (SSR is the serials room on the 2nd floor of the Grad Lib)
```

Many magazine/journal records do not have locations on the first screen but say:
CONTINUED ON NEXT SCREEN; press ENTER

If several libraries own a title, you may see this prompt:
FOR ANOTHER COPY AT THIS OR ANOTHER LOCATION, press ENTER

Rev 5/89

University of Michigan

HOW TO FIND BOOKS AT THE UNDERGRADUATE LIBRARY

FINDING THE CALL NUMBER

1. Decide on how you want to look for the book - by author, title or subject.

    a. Author - get the full name.
    b. Title - get the correct title, including any available subtitle.
    c. Subject - get the correct subject heading from the *Library of Congress Subject Headings*. These large red books are tables by the MIRLYN terminals. Ask at the reference desk for help if you have not used these books before.

2. Look up your entry in the MIRLYN catalog first, then the card catalog if you do not find it in MIRLYN. Authors, titles and subjects are filed together in one alphabet in the card catalog.

    a. If you find what you want, write down the call number from the screen or the upper-left corner of the card. Some MIRLYN workstations have printers.
    b. If you **cannot** find what you want, ask at the reference desk for help. You may also want to go directly to the Graduate Library next door. Since their card catalog, on the second floor, contains cards for most of the books in other libraries on campus up to mid-1988, you might find what you want there. The staff at the Information Desk will help you further.

FINDING THE BOOK

3. Using the signs on the top of the catalogs in the Undergraduate Library, determine which floor contains your book. Books marked "Reference" are on the first floor and books marked "Reserve" are on the third floor at the University Library Reserve Service Desk.

4. If you get to the correct place and the book is not on the shelf, decide if it is worth a little more hunting. If it is, try some of the following steps.

    a. Ask a reference librarian to help you use the Geac to find out if the book has been borrowed by someone else. If so, you might still get it back in time to be of use to you.
    b. Ask the circulation staff to help you by searching for the book if it is listed on Geac as an Undergraduate Library book that is IN LIBRARY. They will then try to find it and hold it for you within about 48 hours of your request.

5. If you still cannot find or get what you want, see a reference staff member. It might be possible to find a substitute for you.

University of Michigan

WHERE ARE THE BOOKS?
a UGL location chart

Look at the call number for your book. (Remember that magazines and journals do not need a call number in the UGL as they are, for the most part, arranged alphabetically by title on the first floor.) Take the first letter and go to the floor indicated by the chart below. Also included is a brief notation as to the subject area most often covered by the Library of Congress's subject classification system for each letter.

CALL NUMBER	LOCATION	GENERAL LC SUBJECT AREA
A	Second floor	General works
B		Psychology, philosophy, religion
C	Basement	Biography
D		History, area studies
E		U.S. history
F		Popular culture
G		Geography, folk-lore
H		Social sciences
J	Second floor	Political science
K		Law
L		Education
M		Music
N		Art, architecture
P	First floor	Literature, language, communications
Q	Second floor	Sciences
R		Medicine
S		Agriculture
T		Photography, Technology
U		Military Science
V		Naval Science
Z		Bibliographies
999	Main floor lobby	PRONTO collection

I, O, W, X, Y not used

University of Michigan

Teaching the Wise Use of Information:
Evaluation Skills for Nursing Students

Lynne Fox
University of Northern Colorado
Greeley, Colorado

The exercise presented in this poster session presents   presents strategies for facilitating development of skills included in Objectives 2T1-T2, and T3B2-3 of the Model Statement of Objectives for Academic Bibliographic Instruction.   These Objectives focus on the development of skills to evaluate accuracy, currency and credibility of resources and strategies to resolve discrepancies between information sources when they occur.

BIBLIOGRAPHY
TEACHING THE WISE USE OF INFORMATION:
EVALUATION SKILLS FOR NURSING STUDENTS

Cameron-Clarke, D. A. (1988, August 17).   Rubens suffered, but not from pigments: Letter. New York Times, 1:22:4.

Conway, J. F. (1988). Renoir and Monet: Letter. Lancet, 2 (8606), 337.

Kahn, M. F. (1988). Renoir and Monet: Letter. Lancet, 2 (8606), 337.

Milling-Pedersen, L. and Permin, H. (1988). Renoir and Monet: Response to letter. Lancet, 2 (8606), 337.

_____. (1988). Rheumatic disease, heavy-metal pigments, and the great masters. Lancet, 2 (8597), 1267-1269.

Phillips, J. (1988, July 15). For artists, the choice of color can be fateful: Letter. New York Times, 1:30:4.

Schmenck, H. M. (1988, June 23). Did masters pay a price for the boldness of their art? New York Times, 2:11:6.

Staggs, S. (1988, December). Poisonous muse. Artnews, p. 18.

University of Northern Colorado

DISCUSSION QUESTIONS:
ANATOMY OF A DISAGREEMENT:
WHAT CAN BE DONE WHEN EXPERTS DISAGREE?

1. In what types of publications do theses articles appear? (Research, professional, popular?)

2. Which source would be considered most reliable based on the author's credentials, documentation of information, and the publication's credentials and reputation?

3. What steps would you take to determine which "expert" gave the most reliable and accurate information?

4. What length of time passed between the appearance of the first article and the appearance of the last article discussing this topic? When were the articles written? When were they published?

5. What was the source of the information that appeared in the first _Lancet_ article? What was the source of information in the _New York Times_ article printed 6/23? How are these sources documented?

6. What methods are used to convey ideas in the discussion following the original article? (Anecdote, interview, opinion, original research or others?) Is information conveyed using one method more scholarly and reliable than the others?

7. Do all the writers provide references or quote other sources? (References can be implicit or explicit: Which articles use these methods?)

8. Did the letter writers in the _New York Times_ read the original _Lancet_ article? Did the _Artnews_ writer read the original _Lancet_ article? Did the authors in the _New York Times_ and _Artnews_ completely understand the researcher's methods and conclusions as expressed in the report of their research which appeared in the _Lancet_?

9. Does the discussion in the _New York Times_ mention the response letters which appeared in the _Lancet_? Do the response letters in the _Lancet_ ever mention the discussion in the _New York Times_? How would a researcher locate all the documents relevant to a scholarly disagreement between experts?

University of Northern Colorado

HOW TO EVALUATE INFORMATION SOURCES

I.   BOOKS
     A. Consider the Author

Questions: Is s/he an <u>authority</u> on the topic?
                  -- Does the author's academic or work background relate
                     to the book's topic?
                  -- Is the author cited by other writers?
                  -- What else has this author written on this or related
                     topics?
Answers: Use a <u>biographical directory</u> or encyclopedia to find out
                  more about the author's background and writings. For
                  example:
                  <u>Biography and Geneaology Master Index</u> (REF Biog: CT
                     214 B564)
                  Use <u>bibliographies</u> of other books or articles on the
                  topic. Is this author's work cited? For example:
                  <u>Bibliographic Index</u> (REF Indexes) or CARL PAC w (word)
                     search to find bibliographies
                  Use CARL PAC to find other books by this author in UNC
                  Libraries.

     B. Consider the Book's Content

Questions: Was the book <u>reviewed</u> favorably?
                  -- Does the review compare/contrast the book with others
                     on the same topic?
                  -- Where does the review appear? What is the reputation
                     of the journal?
                  -- Is the reviewer an expert on the topic?
Answers: Use an <u>index to book reviews</u>. Look at several reviews
                  in various journals to determine whether the reactions
                  were consistent. For example:
                  <u>Book Review Digest</u> (REF Indexes)
                  <u>Combined Retrospective Index to Book Reviews in
                     Scholarly Journals</u> (REF Indexes)
                  Book review sections in indexes such as <u>Social
                  Sciences Index</u> or <u>Humanities Index</u>
                  Use a <u>periodical directory</u> to find out more about the
                  journals or magazines in which reviews appear. For
                  example:
                  <u>Magazines for Libraries</u> (Ready REF)
                  Use a <u>biographical directory</u> to find out more about the
                  reviewer. (See I.A.)

     C. Consider the Publication Date

Question: Is the information in the book still accurate?
Answer: Older works should not be ignored since they often
                     provide valuable insights. Careful comparison of an
                     older work with more recent writings is needed to
                     assess accuracy. To avoid reliance on dated or
                     inaccurate sources, choose a mix of "vintage" and

University of Northern Colorado

current books on social science or humanities research topics. In science research use only current materials.

II. MAGAZINE OR JOURNAL ARTICLES

These are usually more difficult to evaluate since articles are not reviewed and since biographical information may not always be available on authors.

A. Consider the Author

Question: Is s/he an <u>authority</u> on the topic?
Answer: Use a <u>biographical directory</u> to find out more about the author. (See I.A.)

B. Consider the Article's Contents

Questions: Does the author present <u>facts or opinions</u>?
Does s/he cite or quote <u>authorities</u> on the topic?
Is a <u>discussion</u> of the article by another writer available?
Is the article <u>cited</u> by other writers?

Answers: Use a <u>periodical index</u> to find other articles on the topic. Compare viewpoints.
Use a <u>biographical directory</u> to find out more about cited or quoted authorities. (See I.A.)
Use a <u>periodical index</u> to determine whether a discussion of a specific article is available. The citation for a discussion will follow the index entry for the article discussed.
Use a <u>citation index</u> to determine whether other writers have cited the article. For example:
<u>Arts and Humanities Citation Index</u> (REF Indexes)
<u>Science Citation Index</u> (REF Indexes)
<u>Social Sciences Citation Index</u> (REF Indexes)

C. Consider the Journal

Questions: Where is the journal <u>indexed</u>?
What is the <u>reputation</u> of the journal?
Answers: Use a <u>periodical directory</u> to locate information on specific journals. For example:
<u>Magazines for Libraries</u> (Ready REF)

D. Consider the Publication Date

Questions: Is the information still <u>accurate</u>?
Answer: For topics where ideas are rapidly changing, such as science, focus on recent articles. For other topics, a mix of classic and current articles may be useful, especially if primary sources (published at the time of an event) are needed.

FROM: O'Hanion. (1987). How to evaluate information sources. Columbus, Ohio: Ohio State University Undergraduate Library.

University of Northern Colorado

More Than a Push-Button *Readers' Guide*: Using Infotrac's *Magazine Index Plus* to Teach Concepts in Information Literacy

Nancy Niles
SUNY-College of Agriculture and Technology
Cobleskill, New York

Infotrac's *Magazine Index Plus* has great appeal for students, but many of them use it without considering the underlying system of organizing/ classifying the information written about their topics. A short in-house produced video shows students how to exploit Infotrac's capabilities and helps them gain a better understandig of the nature of information and the index's relationship to the "organic" structure of a topic.

Discussion Group Handouts

and Sample Materials

No other change in American society has offered greater challenges than the emergence of the Information Age. Information is expanding at an unprecendented rate, and enormously rapid strides are being made in the technology for storing, organizing, and accessing the ever growing tidal wave of information. The combined effect of these factors is an increasingly fragmented information base—large components of which are only available to people with money and/or acceptable institutional affiliations.

Yet in an information society all people should have the right to information which can enhance their lives. Out of the super-abundance of available information, people need to be able to obtain specific information to meet a wide range of personal and business needs. These needs are largely driven either by the desire for personal growth and advancement or by the rapidly changing social, political, and economic environments of American society. What is true today is often outdated tomorrow. A good job today may be obsolete next year. To promote economic independence and quality of existence, there is a lifelong need for being informed and up-to-date.

How our country deals with the realities of the Information Age will have enormous impact on our democratic way of life and on our nation's ability to compete internationally. Within America's information society, there also exists the potential of addressing many long-standing social and economic inequities. To reap such benefits, people—as individuals and as a nation—must be information literate. To be information literate, a person must be able to recognize when information is needed and have the ability to locate, evaluate, and use effectively the needed information. Producing such a citizenry will require that schools and colleges appreciate and integrate the concept of information literacy into their learning programs and that they play a leadership role in equipping individuals and institutions to take advantage of the opportunities inherent within the information society.

Ultimately, information literate people are those who have learned how to learn. They know how to learn because they know how knowledge is organized, how to find information, and how to use information in such a way that others can learn from them. They are people prepared for lifelong learning, because they can always find the information needed for any task or decision at hand.

American Library Association: Presidential Committee on Information Literacy Final Report

The Importance of Information Literacy to Individuals, Business, and Citizenship

In Individuals' Lives

Americans have traditionally valued quality of life and the pursuit of happiness; however, these goals are increasingly difficult to achieve because of the complexities of life in today's information and technology dependent society. The cultural and educational opportunities available in an average community, for example, are often missed by people who lack the ability to keep informed of such activities, and lives of information illiterates are more likely than others to be narrowly focused on second-hand experiences of life through television. On the other hand, life is more interesting when one knows what is going on, what opportunities exist, and where alternatives to current practices can be discovered.

On a daily basis, problems are more difficult to solve when people lack access to meaningful information vital to good decision making. Many people are vulnerable to poorly informed people or opportunists when selecting nursing care for a parent or facing a major expense such as purchasing, financing or insuring a new home or car. Other information-dependent decisions can affect one's entire lifetime. For example, what information do young people have available to them when they consider which college to attend or whether to become sexually active? Even in areas where one can achieve an expertise, constantly changing and expanding information bases necessitate an ongoing struggle for individuals to keep up-to-date and in control of their daily information environment as well as with information from other fields which can affect the outcomes of their decisions.

In an attempt to reduce information to easily manageable segments, most people have become dependent on others for their information. Information prepackaging in schools and through broadcast and print news media, in fact, encourages people to accept the opinions of others without much thought. When opinions are biased, negative, or inadequate for the needs at hand, many people are left helpless to improve the situation confronting them. Imagine, for example, a family which is being evicted by a landlord who claims he is within his legal rights. Usually they will have to accept the landlord's "expert" opinion, because they do not know how to seek information to confirm or disprove his claim.

Information literacy, therefore, is a means of personal empowerment. It allows people to verify or refute expert opinion and to become independent seekers of truth. It provides them with the ability to build their own arguments and to experience the excitement of the search for knowledge. It not only prepares them for lifelong learning; but, by experiencing the excitement of their own successful quests for knowledge, it also creates in young people the motivation for pursuing learning throughout their lives.

-2-

American Library Association: Presidential Committee on Information Literacy Final Report

Moreover, the process of searching and interacting with the ideas and values of their own and others' cultures deepens people's capacities to understand and position themselves within larger communities of time and place. By drawing on the arts, history, and literature of previous generations, individuals and communities can affirm the best in their cultures and determine future goals.

It is unfortunate that the very people who most need the empowerment inherent in being information literate are the least likely to have learning experiences which will promote these abilities. Minority and at-risk students, illiterate adults, people with English as a second language, and economically disadvantaged people are among those most likely to lack access to the information that can improve their situations. Most are not even aware of the potential help that is available to them. Libraries, which provide the best access point to information for most U.S. citizens, are left untapped by those who most need help to improve their quality of life. As former U.S. Secretary of Education Terrell Bell once wrote, "There is a danger of a new elite developing in our country: the information elite."[1]

In Business

Herbert E. Meyer, who has served as an editor for Fortune magazine and as vice-chairman of the National Intelligence Council, underscores the importance of access to and use of good information for business in an age characterized by rapid change, a global environment, and unprecedented access to information. In his 1988 book, Real World Intelligence,[2] he describes the astonishment and growing distress of executives who "are discovering that the only thing as difficult and dangerous as managing a large enterprise with too little information is managing one with too much (p.29)."

While Meyer emphasizes that companies should rely on public sources that are available to anyone for much of their information (p.36), it is clear that many companies do not know how to find and use such information effectively. Every day lack of timely and accurate information is costly to American businesses. The following examples document cases of such losses or near losses.

- A manufacturing company had a research team of three scientists and four technicians working on a project, and at the end of a year the team felt it had a patentable invention in addition to a new product. Prior to filing the patent application, the company's patent attorney requested a literature search. While doing the search, the librarian found that the proposed application duplicated some of the work claimed in a patent that had been issued about a year before the team had begun its work. During the course of the project, the company had spent almost $500,000 on the project, an outlay that could have been avoided if it had spent the approximately $300 required to have a review of the literature completed before beginning the project.

-3-

American Library Association: Presidential Committee on Information Literacy Final Report

- A manufacturing company was sued by an individual who claimed that the company had stolen his "secret formula" for a product that the company had just marketed. An information scientist on the staff of the company's technical library found a reference in the technical literature that this formula was generally known to the trade long before the litigant developed his "secret formula." When he was presented with this information, the litigant dropped his $7 million claim.
- When the technical librarian for an electronics firm was asked to do a literature search for one of its engineers, four people had already been working to resolve a problem for more than a year. The literature search found an article that contained the answer the engineer needed to solve his problem. The article had been published several years before the project team had begun its work. Had the literature search been conducted when the problem was first identified, the company could have saved four man-years of labor and its resulting direct monetary costs.[3]

The need for people in business, who are competent managers of information, is important at all levels, and the realities of the Information Age require serious rethinking of how businesses should be conducted. Harlan Cleveland, explores this theme in his book, The Knowledge Executive.

> Information (organized data, the raw material for specialized knowledge, and generalist wisdom) is now our most important, and pervasive resource. Information workers now compose more than half the U.S. labor force. But this newly dominant resource is quite unlike the tangible resources we have heretofore thought of as valuable. The differences help explain why we get into so much trouble trying to use for the management of information concepts that worked all right in understanding the management of things—concepts such as control, secrecy, ownership, privilege and geopolitics.

> Because the old pyramids of influence and control were based on just these ideas, they are now crumbling. Their weakening is not always obvious, just as a wooden structure may look solid when you can't see what termites have done to its insides. Whether this "crumble effect" will result in a fairer shake for the world's disadvantaged majority is not yet clear. But there is ample evidence that those who learn how to achieve access to the bath of knowledge that already envelops the world will be the future's aristocrats of achievement, and that they will be far more numerous than any aristocracy in history.[4]

In Citizenship

American democracy has led to the evolution of many thousands of organized citizen groups that seek to influence public policy, issues, and community problems. Following are just a few examples.

-4-

American Library Association: Presidential Committee on Information Literacy Final Report

- A local League of Women Voters has been chosen to study housing patterns for low-income individuals in its community. It must inform its members of the options for low-income housing and, in the process, comment publicly on the city's long-range, low-income housing plans.

- In an upper Midwestern city, one with the highest unemployment rate in 50 years, a major automobile company offers to build a new assembly plant in the central city. The only stipulation is that the city condemn property in a poor ethnic neighborhood of 3,500 residents for use as the site of its plant. In addition, the company seeks a twelve-year tax abatement. Residents of the neighborhood frantically seek to find out how they might save their community from the wrecker's ball but still improve their tax base.

- A group of upper middle-class women in the Junior League has read about increased incidences of child abuse. They want to become better informed about the elements of child abuse: What brings it on? What incidents have occurred in their own community? What services are available in their community? What actions might they take?[5]

To address these problems successfully, each of these groups will have to secure access to a wide range of information, much of which--if they know how to find it--can be obtained without any cost to their organizations.

Citizenship in a modern democracy involves more than knowledge of how to access vital information. It also involves a capacity to recognize propaganda, distortion, and other misuses and abuses of information. People are daily subjected to statistics about health, the economy, national defense, and countless products. One person arranges the information to prove his point, another arranges it to prove hers. One political party says the social indicators are encouraging, another calls them frightening. One drug company states most doctors prefer its product, another "proves" doctors favor its product. In such an environment, information literacy provides insight into the manifold ways in which people can all be deceived and misled. Information literate citizens are able to spot and expose chicanery, disinformation, and lies.

To say that information literacy is crucial to effective citizenship is simply to say it is central to the practice of democracy. Any society committed to individual freedom and democratic government must insure the free flow of information to all its citizens in order to protect personal liberties and to guard its future. As U.S. Representative Major R. Owens has said:

Information literacy is needed to guarantee the survival of democratic institutions. All men are created equal but voters with information resources are in a position to make more intelligent decisions than citizens who are information illiterates. The application of

American Library Association: Presidential Committee on Information Literacy Final Report

information resources to the process of decision-making to fulfill civic responsibilities is a vital necessity.[6]

Opportunities to Develop Information Literacy

Information literacy is a survival skill in the Information Age. Instead of drowning in the abundance of information that floods their lives, information literate people know how to find, evaluate, and use information effectively to solve a particular problem or make a decision--whether the information they select comes from a computer, a book, a government agency, a film, or any number of other possible resources. Libraries, which provide a significant public access point to such information and usually at no cost, must play a key role in preparing people for the demands of today's information society. Just as public libraries were once a means of education and a better life for many of the over 20 million immigrants of the late 1800s and early 1900s, they remain today as the potentially strongest and most far-reaching community resource for lifelong learning. Public libraries not only provide access to information, but they also remain crucial to providing people with the knowledge necessary to make meaningful use of existing resources. They remain one of the few safeguards against information control by a minority.

Although libraries historically have provided a meaningful structure for relating information in ways that facilitate the development of knowledge, they have been all but ignored in the literature about the information society. Even national education reform reports, starting with a Nation at Risk[7] in 1983, largely exclude libraries. No K-12 report has explored the potential role of libraries or the need for information literacy. In the higher education reform literature, Education Commission of the States President Frank Newman's 1985 report, Higher Education and the American Resurgence,[8] only addresses the instructional potential of libraries in passing, but it does raise the concern for the accessibility of materials within the knowledge explosion. In fact, no reform report until College,[9] the 1986 Carnegie Foundation Report, gave substantive consideration to the role of libraries in addressing the challenges facing higher education. In the initial release of the study's recommendations, it was noted that

> The quality of a college is measured by the resources for learning on the campus and the extent to which students become independent, self-directed learners. And yet we found that today, about one out of every four undergraduates spends no time in the library during a normal week, and 65 percent use the library four hours or less each week. The gap between the classroom and the library, reported on almost a half-century ago, still exists today.[10]

Statistics such as these document the general passivity of most academic learning today and the divorce of the impact of the Information Age from prevailing teaching styles.

-6-

The first step in reducing this gap is making sure that the issue of information literacy is an integral part of current efforts at cultural literacy, the development of critical thinking abilities, and school restructuring. Due to the relative newness of the information society, however, information literacy is often completely overlooked in relevant dialogues, research, and experimentations. Moreover, most current educational and communication endeavors--with their long-standing history of prepackaging information--mitigate against the development of even an awareness of the need to master information management skills.

The effects of such prepackaging of information are most obvious in the school and academic settings. Students, for example, receive predigested information from lectures and textbooks, and little in their environment fosters active thinking or problem solving. What problem solving does occur is within artificially constructed and limited information environments that allow for single "correct" answers. Such exercises bear little resemblance to problem solving in the real world where multiple solutions of varying degrees of usefulness must be pieced together--often from many disciplines and from multiple information sources such as online databases, videotapes, government documents, and journals.

Education needs a new model of learning--learning that is based on the information resources of the real world and learning that is active and integrated, not passive and fragmented. On an intellectual level, many teachers and school administrators recognize that lectures, textbooks, materials put on reserve, and tests that ask students to regurgitate data from these sources do not create an active, much less a quality, learning experience. Moreover, studies at the higher education level have proven that students fail to retain most information they are "given."

> The curve for forgetting course content is fairly steep: a generous estimate is that students forget 50% of the content within a few months. . . . A more devastating finding comes from a study that concluded that even under the most favorable conditions, "students carry away in their heads and in their notebooks not more than 42% of the lecture content." Those were the results when students were told that they would be tested immediately following the lecture; they were permitted to use their notes; and they were given a prepared summary of the lecture. These results were bad enough, but when students were tested a week later, without the use of their notes, they could recall only 17% of the lecture material.[11]

Because of the rapidly shrinking half-life of information, even the value of that 17 percent, which students do remember, must be questioned. To any thoughtful person, it must be clear that teaching facts is a poor substitute for teaching people how to learn, i.e., giving them the skills to be able to locate, evaluate, and effectively use information for any given need.

American Library Association: Presidential Committee on Information Literacy Final Report

What is called for is not a new information studies curriculum but, rather, a restructuring of the learning process. Textbooks, workbooks, and lectures must yield to a learning process based on the information resources available for learning and problem solving throughout people's lifetimes--to learning experiences that build a lifelong habit of library use. Such a learning process would actively involve students in the process of

- knowing when they have a need for information.
- identifying information needed to address a given problem or issue.
- finding needed information.
- evaluating the information.
- organizing the information.
- using the information effectively to address the problem or issue at hand.

Such a restructuring of the learning process will not only enhance the critical thinking skills of students, but will also empower them for lifelong learning and the effective performance of professional and civic responsibilities.

An Information Age School

An increased emphasis on information literacy and resource-based learning would manifest itself in a variety of ways at both the academic and school levels, depending upon the role and mission of the individual institution and the information environment of its community. However, the following description of what a school might be like if information literacy were a central, not a peripheral, concern reveals some of the possibilities. (While focused on K-12, outcomes could be quite similar at the college level.)

The school would be more interactive, because students, pursuing questions of personal interest, would be interacting with other students, with teachers, with a vast array of information resources, and the community at large to a far greater degree than they presently do today. One would expect to find every student engaged in at least one open-ended, long-term quest for an answer to a serious social, scientific, aesthetic, or political problem. Students' quests would involve not only searching print, electronic and video data, but also interviewing people inside and outside of school. As a result, learning would be more self-initiated. There would be more reading of original sources and more extended writing. Both students and teachers would be familiar with the intellectual and emotional demands of asking productive questions, gathering data of all kinds, reducing and synthesizing information, analyzing, interpreting, and evaluating information in all its forms.

In such an environment, teachers would be coaching and guiding students more and lecturing less. They would have long since discovered that the classroom computer, with its access to the libraries and databases of the world, is a better source of facts than they could ever hope to be. They

-8-

would have come to see that their major importance lies in their capacity to arouse curiosity and guide it to a satisfactory conclusion, to ask the right questions at the right time, to stir debate and serious discussion, and to be models themselves of thoughtful inquiry.

Teachers would work consistently with librarians, media resource people, and instructional designers both within their schools and in their communities to ensure that student projects and explorations are challenging, interesting and productive learning experiences in which they can all take pride. It would not be surprising in such a school to find a student task force exploring an important community issue with a view toward making a public presentation of its findings on cable television or at a news conference. Nor would it be unusual to see the librarian guiding the task force through its initial questions and its multi-disciplinary, multi-media search—all the way through to its cable or satellite presentation. In such a role, librarians would be valued for their information expertise and their technological know-how. They would lead frequent in-service teacher workshops and ensure that the school was getting the most out of its investment in information technology.

Because evaluation in such a school would also be far more interactive than it is today, it would also be a much better learning experience. Interactive tutoring software that guides students through their own and other knowledge bases would provide more useful diagnostic information than is available today. Evaluation would be based upon a broad range of literacy indicators, including some that assess the quality and appropriateness of information sources or the quality and efficiency of the information searches themselves. Assessments would attend to ways in which students are using their minds and achieving success as information consumers, analyzers, interpreters, evaluators, and communicators of ideas.

Finally, one would expect such a school to look and sound different from today's schools. One would see more information technology than is evident today, and it would be important to people not only in itself but also in regard to its capacity to help them solve problems and create knowledge. One would see the fruits of many student projects prominently displayed on the walls and on bookshelves, and one would hear more discussions and debate about substantive, relevant issues. On the playground, in the halls, in the cafeteria, and certainly in the classroom, one would hear fundamental questions that make information literacy so important: "How do you know that?," and "What evidence do you have for that?," "Who says?," and "How can we find out?"

Conclusion

This call for more attention to information literacy comes at a time when many other learning deficiencies are being expressed by educators, business leaders, and parents. Many workers, for example, appear unprepared to deal effectively with the challenges of high tech equipment. There exists a need for better thinkers, problem solvers, and inquirers. There are calls for

-9-

American Library Association: Presidential Committee on Information Literacy Final Report

computer literacy, civic literacy, global literacy and cultural literacy. Because we have been hit by a tidal wave of information, what used to suffice as literacy, no longer suffices; what used to count as effective knowledge, no longer meets our needs; what used to pass as a good education, no longer is adequate.

The one common ingredient in all of these concerns is an awareness of the rapidly changing requirements for a productive, healthy, and satisfying life. To respond effectively to an ever-changing environment, people need more than just a knowledge base, they also need techniques for exploring it, connecting it to other knowledge bases, and making practical use of it. In other words, the landscape upon which we used to stand has been transformed, and we are being forced to establish a new foundation called information literacy. Now knowledge—not minerals or agricultural products or manufactured goods—is this country's most precious commodity, and people who are information literate—who know how to acquire knowledge and use it—are America's most valuable resource.

Committee Recommendations

To reap the benefits from the Information Age by our country, its citizens, and its businesses, the American Library Association Presidential Committee on Information Literacy makes the following recommendations:

1. <u>We all must reconsider the ways we have organized information institutionally, structured information access, and defined information's role in our lives at home, in the community, and in the work place.</u> To the extent that our concepts about knowledge and information are out of touch with the realities of a new, dynamic information environment, we must reconceptualize them. The degrees and directions of reconceptualization will vary, but the aims should always be the same: to communicate the power of knowledge; to develop in each citizen a sense of his or her responsibility to acquire knowledge and deepen insight through better use of information and related technologies; to instill a love of learning, a thrill in searching and a joy in discovering; and to teach young and old alike how to know when they have an information need and how to gather, synthesize, analyze, interpret, and evaluate the information around them. All of these abilities are equally important for the enhancement of life experiences and for business pursuits.

   Colleges, schools, and businesses should pay special attention to the potential role of their libraries or information centers. These should be central, not peripheral; organizational redesigns should seek to empower students and adults through new kinds of access to information and new ways of creating, discovering, and sharing it.

American Library Association: Presidential Committee on Information Literacy Final Report

2. **A Coalition for Information Literacy should be formed under the leadership of the American Library Association, in coordination with other national organizations and agencies, to promote information literacy.** The major obstacle to promoting information literacy is a lack of public awareness of the problems created by information illiteracy. Tne need for increased information literacy levels in all aspects of people's lives—in business, in family matters, and civic responsibilities—must be brought to the public's attention in a forceful way. To accomplish this, the Coalition should serve as an educational network for communications, coalescing related educational efforts, developing leadership, and effecting change. The Coalition should monitor and report on state efforts to promote information literacy and resource-based learning and provide recognition of individuals and programs for their exemplary information literacy efforts.

   The Coalition should be organized with an advisory committee made up of nationally prominent public figures from librarianship, education, business, and government. The responsibilities of the advisory committee should include support for Coalition efforts in the areas of capturing media attention, raising public awareness, and fostering a climate favorable for information literacy. In addition, the advisory committee should actively seek funding to promote research and demonstration projects.

3. **Research and demonstration projects related to information and its use need to be undertaken.** To date, remarkably little research has been done to understand how information can be more effectively managed to meet educational and societal objectives or to explore how information management skills impact on overall school and academic performance. What research does exist appears primarily in library literature, which is seldom read by educators or state decision makers.

   For future efforts to be successful, a national research agenda should be developed and implemented. The number of issues needing to be addressed are significant and should include the following:

   - What are the social effects of reading?
   - With electronic media eclipsing reading for many people, what will be the new place of the printed word?
   - How do the characteristics of information resourses (format, length, age) affect their usefulness?
   - How does the use of information vary by discipline?
   - How does access to information impact on the effectiveness of citizen action groups?
   - How do information management skills affect student performance and retention?
   - What role can information management skills play in the economic and social advancement of minorities?

-11-

American Library Association: Presidential Committee on Information Literacy Final Report

Also needed is research that will promote a "sophisticated understanding of the full range of the issues and processes related to the generation, distribution, and use of information so that libraries can fulfill their obligations to their users and potential users and so that research and scholarship in all fields can flourish."[12]

The Coalition can play a major role in obtaining funding for such research and for fostering demonstration projects that can provide fertile ground for controlled experiments that can contrast benefits from traditional versus resource-based learning opportunities for students.

4. <u>State Departments of Education, Commissions on Higher Education, and Academic Governing Boards should be responsible to ensure that a climate conducive to students' becoming information literate exists in their states and on their campuses</u>. Of importance are two complementary issues: the development of an information literate citizenry and the move from textbook and lecture-style learning to resource-based learning. The latter is, in fact, the means to the former as well as to producing lifelong, independent, and self-directed learners. As is appropriate within their stated missions, such bodies are urged to do the following:

- to incorporate the spirit and intent of information literacy into curricular requirements, recommendations, and instructional materials. (Two excellent models for state school guidelines are Washington's "Information Skills Curriculum Guide: Process Scope and Sequence" and "Library Information Skills: Guide for Oregon Schools K-12.")

- to incorporate in professional preparation and in-service training 'for teachers an appreciation for the importance of resource-based learning, to encourage implementation of it in their subject areas, and to provide opportunities to master implementation techniques.

- to encourage and support coordination of school/campus and public library resources/services with classroom instruction in offering resource-based learning.

- to include coverage of information literacy competencies in state assessment examinations.

- to establish recognition programs of exemplary projects for learning information management skills in elementary and secondary schools, in higher education institutions, and in professional preparation programs.

-12-

American Library Association: Presidential Committee on Information Literacy Final Report

5. **Teacher education and performance expectations should be modified to include information literacy concerns.** Inherent in the concepts of information literacy and resource-based learning is the complementary concept of the teacher as a facilitator of student learning rather than as presenter of ready-made information. To be successful in such roles, teachers should make use of an expansive array of information resources. They should be familiar with and able to use selected databases, learning networks, reference materials, textbooks, journals, newspapers, magazines, and other resources. They also should place a premium on problem solving and see that their classrooms are extended outward to encompass the learning resources of the library media centers and the community. They also should expect their students to become information literate.

To encourage the development of teachers who are facilitators of learning, the following recommendations are made to schools of teacher education. Those responsible for in-service teacher training should also evaluate current capabilities of teaching professionals and incorporate the following recommendations into their programs as needed.

- New knowledge from cognitive research on thinking skills should be incorporated into pedagogical skills development.

- Integral to all programs should be instruction in managing the classroom, individualizing instruction, setting problems, questioning, promoting cooperative learning—all of which should rely on case studies and information resources of the entire school and community.

- Instruction within the disciplines needs to emphasize a problem-solving approach and the development of a sophisticated level of information management skills appropriate to the individual disciplines.

- School library media specialists need to view the instructional goals of their schools as an integral part of their own concern and responsibilities and should actively contribute toward the ongoing professional development of teachers and principles. They should be members of curriculum and instructional teams and provide leadership in integrating appropriate information and educational technologies into school programming. (For further recommendations regarding the role of library media specialists, consult Information Power: Guidelines for School Media Programs prepared by the American Association of School Librarians and the Association for Educational Communications and Technology, 1988.)

-13-

American Library Association: Presidential Committee on Information Literacy Final Report

- Exit requirements from teacher education programs should include each candidate's ability to use selected databases, networks, reference materials, administrative and instructional software packages, and new forms of learning technologies.

- A portion of the practicum, or teaching experience of beginning teachers should be spent with library media specialists. These opportunities should be based in the school library media center to promote an understanding of resources available in both that facility and other community libraries and to emphasize the concepts and skills necessary to become a learning facilitator.

- Cooperative, or supervising, teachers who can demonstrate their commitment to thinking skills instruction and information literacy should be matched with student teachers, and teachers who see themselves as learning facilitators should be relied upon to serve as role models. Student teachers should also have the opportunity to observe and practice with a variety of models for the teaching of critical thinking.

6. <u>An understanding of the relationship of information literacy to the themes of the White House Conference on Library and Information Services should be promoted.</u> The White House conference themes of literacy, productivity, and democracy will provide a unique opportunity to foster public awareness of the importance of information literacy. (The conference will be held sometime between September 1989 and September 1991.) The American Library Association and the Coalition on Information Literacy should aggressively promote consideration of information literacy within state deliberations as well as within the White House Conference itself.

Background to Report

The American Library Association's Presidential Committee on Information Literacy was appointed in 1987 by ALA President Margaret Chisholm with three expressed purposes: (1) to define information literacy within the higher literacies and its importance to student performance, lifelong learning, and active citizenship; (2) to design one or more models for information literacy development appropriate to formal and informal learning environments throughout people's lifetimes; and (3) to determine implications for the continuing education and development of teachers. The Committee, which consists of leaders in education and librarianship, has worked actively to accomplish its mission since its establishment. Members of the committee include the following:

Gordon M. Ambach, Executive Director
Council of Chief State School Officers

-14-

American Library Association: Presidential Committee on Information Literacy Final Report

William L. Bainbridge, President
School Match

Patricia Senn Breivik, Director, Chair
Auraria Library, University of Colorado at Denver

Rexford Brown, Director
Policies and the Higher Literacies Project
Education Commission of the States

Judith S. Eaton, President
Community College of Philadelphia

David Imig, Executive Director
American Association of Colleges for Teacher Education

Sally Kilgore, Professor
Emory University
(former Director of the Office of Research, U.S. Department of Education)

Carol Kuhlthau, Director
Educational Media Services Programs
Rutgers University

Joseph Mika, Director
Library Science Program
Wayne State University

Richard D. Miller, Executive Director
American Association of School Administrators

Roy D. Miller, Executive Assistant to the Director
Brooklyn Public Library

Sharon J. Rogers, University Librarian
George Washington University

Robert Wedgeworth, Dean
School of Library Service
Columbia University

This report was released on January 10, 1989, in Washington, D.C.

Further Information

Further information on information literacy can be obtained by contacting:

Information Literacy and K-12
c/o American Association of School Librarians

-15-

American Library Association: Presidential Committee on Information Literacy Final Report

American Library Association
50 East Huron Street
Chicago, IL 60611

Information Literacy and Higher Education
c/o Association of College and Research Libraries
American Library Association
50 East Huron Street
Chicago, IL 60611

REFERENCES

1. Terrel H. Bell, Communication to CU Président E. Gordon Gee, September
   1986.

2. Herbert E. Meyer, Real-World Intelligence: Organized Information for
   Executives (New York: Weidenfeld & Nicholson, 1987), 24.

3. James B. Tchobanoff, "The Impact Approach: Value as measured by the
   Benefit of the Information Professional to the Parent Organization," in
   President's Task Force on the Value of the Information Professional
   (Anaheim, Calif.: Special Libraries Assoc., June 10, 1987), 47.

4. Harlan   Cleveland, The Knowledge Executive: Leadership in an
   Information Society (New York: Dutton, 1985), xviii.

5. Joan C. Durrance, Armed for Action: Library Response to Citizen
   Information Needs (New York: Neal-Schuman Publishers, 1984), ix.

6. Major Owens, "State Government and Libraries," Library Journal 101 (1
   January 1976): 27.

7. United States National Commission on Excellence in Education, A Nation
   At Risk: the Imperative for Educational Reform (Washington, D.C.: U.S.
   Government Printing Office, 1983).

8. Frank Newman, Higher Education and the American Resurgence (Princeton,
   N.J.: Princeton University Press, 1985), 152.

9. Ernest L. Boyer, College: The Undergraduate Experience in America
   (New York: Harper & Row, 1987).

10. "Prologue and major Recommendations of Carneigie Foundation's Report on
    Colleges" Chronicle of Higher Education 33 (5 November 1986): 10-11.

11. K. Patricia Cross, "A Proposal to Improve Teaching or What Taking
    Teaching Seriously Should Mean," AAHE Bulletin 39 (September 1986):
    10-11.

12. Edward Connery Lathem, Ed., American Libraries as Centers of
    Scholarship (Hanover, N.H.: Dartmouth College, 1978), 58.

-17-

American Library Association: Presidential Committee on Information Literacy Final Report

COMPUTERS IN THE UMCP LIBRARIES

As you notice when you walk through any of the UMCP
libraries, computers are a part of the new technology to aid in
your research. In some libraries on campus, there are several
types of computers or computer terminals and in others you may
only notice one. However, in any of the libraries it is
important to understand which computers do what and which ones
will be helpful for your particular needs.

Online Catalog Terminals

Each of the libraries has at least one online catalog
terminal for the public to use. In Hornbake, there are several
terminals in the lobby to your right as you walk in the building.
In McKeldin Library, the Online Catalog terminals are on the
second floor, by the Catalog Assistance/Information Desk and the
card catalog. Other libraries on campus, and other service sites
within those libraries, will locate these terminals in other
spots--ask at the reference desk in any library.

The Online Catalog terminals are strictly limited to doing
searches of the books that are held by the University of Maryland
Libraries, on College Park campus, and at UMBC, UMES, and UMAB-
Law. They contain only those books that can be found in one of
the above library systems. Periodicals are not yet included, nor
are articles from periodicals included. Many materials in
special collections, such as Government Documents, cannot be
found by using the Online Catalog. For periodicals, use the
Serials Lists on microfiche in any of the libraries; for
periodical articles, use the appropriate indexes; for special
collections, go to the room that houses that collection.

IF YOU ARE LOOKING FOR A BOOK IN THE UNIVERSITY OF MARYLAND
LIBRARIES, CHECK THE ONLINE CATALOG.

For more information on the Online Catalog, see section ?

Online Circulation File

At the desks where you check out and return books
(Circulation Desks) in most UMCP Libraries, you will find
computer terminals for your use that can be searched to find out
what books you have checked out, what fines you owe, and the
status of books that are supposed to be in the Libraries (whether
they should be in the Libraries or have been checked out or are

University of Maryland, College Park

missing or on reserve). This type of information is also available on the Online Catalog terminals.

IF YOU WANT TO KNOW THE STATUS OF A BOOK THAT SHOULD BE IN THE LIBRARIES OR YOU WANT TO KNOW WHAT BOOKS YOU HAVE CHECKED OUT, LOOK AT THE ONLINE CIRCULATION FILES AT THE CIRCULATION DESKS.

Microcomputer Workstations for Special Research Needs

As you wander around the reference areas in several of the UMCP libraries, you might find a microcomputer workstation or several of them. Hornbake Library has one in the Reference Area, by the Reference Desk. McKeldin Library has several located across from the Reference Desk on the second floor. Other libraries have some in different places. These are regular microcomputers that you might have in your home or office. However, these are not to be used for the standard purposes of word processing or running other applications programs.

These microcomputer workstations are to be used for special kinds of database searches. The libraries have access to special CD´s (Compact Disks) that are essentially reference sources, like indexes, statistical sources or directories. For example, the ERIC indexes (see section?) are on CD´s, as are annual reports in Hornbake Library. There are also some online databases that can be used at the workstations, such as Dow Jones News Retrieval System and the HSL(Health Sciences Library) Current Contents database. You can get more information on these databases by asking at any Reference Desk in any library. Most of these workstations are not available on a first-come, first-served basis. You must reserve times to use them by calling the reference desks in the appropriate libraries. When you come in to use the workstations at the time you have reserved, check with the librarian at the Reference Desk.

Some of these databases are somewhat difficult to use. Many of them come with tutorials on the disks. For others, there are regularly scheduled workshops in the Libraries. For all of them there are manuals and guide sheets you can use by either asking at the Reference Desk or picking one up at the workstation area.

Many of these databases contain indexes to periodical articles and can be used in place of some of the printed indexes. Remember, though, that not all articles in any of the indexes will necessarily be found in the UMCP Libraries. From these database indexes, you must go to the Serials List on microfiche to determine whether that magazine is held by the Libraries, and in which library you can find it.

2

University of Maryland, College Park

MICROCOMPUTERS IN THE REFERENCE AREAS OF THE LIBRARIES ARE ONLY
TO BE USED ON A RESERVATION BASIS. ASK AT THE REFERENCE DESK OF
ANY LIBRARY.

InfoTrac

In Hornbake Library's reference area, next to the one
microcomputer workstation you can reserve for database searches,
are four more microcomputer workstations dedicated to searching
the InfoTrac databases. These databases include a general
periodical index, similar to <u>Readers' Guide to Periodical
Literature</u>, and a government publications database. Thus, using
these workstations, you can search for magazine articles on
subjects of general interest or for items published by the
government.

These terminals are to be used only for InfoTrac searching.
They are much easier to search on than some of the databases
mentioned above and usually no instruction is needed. Since
there are four of them and since usually the searching on these
workstations goes fairly quickly, these workstations cannot be
reserved, but are used on a first-come, first-served basis.

Hornbake Library is the only UMCP library that offers
searching on InfoTrac. It is very popular with undergraduate
students because of its general information. Again, remember
that every item listed on InfoTrac is not necessarily held in the
UMCP Libraries. You still have to use the Serials List on
microfiche to find which periodicals the Libraries will have.

FOR MAGAZINE ARTICLES OR GOVERNMENT PUBLICATIONS ON GENERAL
SUBJECT AREAS OF POPULAR INTEREST, USE INFOTRAC WORKSTATIONS IN
HORNBAKE LIBRARY.

Lexis

Just as InfoTrac is only available in Hornbake, Lexis, a
legal database, can only be searched via a workstation in
McKeldin Library, across from the Reference Desk on the second
floor. Lexis requires a special workstation, one which does not
look like a regular microcomputer.

Lexis contains several databases that can be used when
researching legal subjects. These databases are full-text, which
means they contain the actual material you are looking for, not
simply a citation to a print source. Lexis is somewhat difficult
to use, but there is a tutorial available for it online. Ask a
Reference Librarian how to use the tutorial.

3

University of Maryland, College Park

Lexis can only be used on a reserve basis. Call the Reference Desk at McKeldin Library to reserve a time to use Lexis.

IF YOU ARE RESEARCHING LEGAL QUESTIONS, TRY USING LEXIS IN MCKELDIN REFERENCE.

OCLC (Online Computer Library Center)

Sometimes a particular book or magazine article you need is not in the Libraries. There is a way to solve this problem. When you are in need of material the Libraries does not have, talk to a Reference Librarian. At the Reference Desk in most libraries there is a computer terminal, used only by the Libraries staff, that connects the UMCP Libraries with a huge network of libraries all over the country. The Librarian can look up the title of the book or magazine you are looking for and tell you immediately whether that title can be found in any of the many libraries in this area, e.g., the Library of Congress, George Washington University Library, the National Agriculture Library.

If that book or magazine can be found in any area library, you can go to that library and use the item. It would be a good idea to call that library a) to make sure that they do indeed have the item you want to use, and b) to find out their policies for use of their library by UMCP students.

If that book or magazine cannot be found in any area library, you may want to do more research to find other sources that are available, or you can use the Libraries´ Interlibrary Loan services. Ask at the reference desk for information about this service.

AIM (Access to Information about Maryland)

In both McKeldin and Hornbake Libraries (as well as the Stamp Union) there is a computer terminal that can be used to get information about the University--services (including the Libraries), a calendar of events, class schedules. The system is very easy to use.

In Hornbake Library, the AIM terminal is just ahead and to the left of the Information Desk as you enter the Library. In McKeldin, the AIM terminal is located in the main lobby as you walk into the Library on the first floor.

AIM TERMINALS IN BOTH HORNBAKE AND MCKELDIN LIBRARIES GIVE INFORMATION ABOUT THE UMCP CAMPUS.

4

University of Maryland, College Park

Microcomputers

Three libraries--Hornbake, McKeldin, and Engineering and Physical Sciences (EPSL)--provide computer workstations that you can use just simply as microcomputers. They are not associated with any particular databases and can be used for your class-related or personal needs.

In Hornbake and McKeldin Libraries there are both IBM-compatible Sperry micros, as well as Macintosh microcomputers. Hornbake's microcomputer facilities are located on the ground floor, by the reserve desk, which makes them accessible 24 hours a day during fall and spring semesters. In McKeldin Library, the microcomputers are by the graduate reserve desk on the fourth floor. You will need your ID card and current registration card to use the microcomputers. The only software provided in these two facilities is the software that comes with the micros, such as DOS.

EPSL also has IBM and Macintosh microcomputers. Ask at the Reference Desk for more information.

IF YOU WANT TO USE A MICROCOMPUTER FOR PERSONAL OR CLASS-RELATED PURPOSES, HORNBAKE, MCKELDIN AND ENGINEERING AND PHYSICAL SCIENCES LIBRARIES PROVIDE MICROCOMPUTERS FOR YOUR USE.

Computer Science Center Terminals

On the ground floor of Hornbake Library there are terminals linked directly to the Computer Science Center computers. To use these terminals, you must have an account with the Computer Science Center.

EPSL also has microcomputers which can connect with the Computer Science Center's computers. Again, you must have an account with the Computer Science Center to use their computers.

Most of the computers in the UMCP Libraries are equipped with printing capabilities. Some, such as the microcomputer workstations in McKeldin and Hornbake Reference Areas for database searching, have one printer per microcomputer. Other computer workstations, such as the micocomputers for personal or class-related use in Horbake and McKeldin Libraries, share one printer for one or two computers.

5

University of Maryland, College Park

QUESTIONS

1. If you are looking for general periodical articles and you want to search quickly on a computer database, which system would be the best to use?

2. Can you use the Online Catalog terminals to find out what magazines the UMCP Libraries has?

3. If you want to type your paper using a microcomputer and your own word processing program, how can the Libraries help you?

Which computer systems in the UMCP Libraries might be of help to you in researching your topic for your research paper? List the systems below and beside each one, write what kinds of help you might get from each.

C:\GUIDES\LIBINSTR.WKB

6

University of Maryland, College Park

Microcomputer Learning Center
Health Sciences Library
University of North Carolina

Purpose The primary purpose of the Microcomputer Learning Center is to provide support for curriculum related microcomputing. Priority is given to courseware use and software placed on reserve. Microcomputer resources can be used only for University related business.

Access University of North Carolina - Chapel Hill students, faculty, and staff are eligible to use the Microcomputer Learning Center. Valid UNC identification is required to register for a microcomputer workstation. A Health Sciences Library card must be presented to check out materials. Exceptions are made for people using the Macintosh and IBM public domain software collections.

Sign-up All users must first register at the Microcomputer Learning Center desk and record their name, campus ID number or affiliation, time, and workstation. Users are guaranteed the use of a workstation for two hours and can continue working for an unlimited period, unless there is a waiting list. The lab assistant will enforce the two hour time limit when other users are signed up on the waiting list.

Reservations Equipment reservations are accepted for laser printers and for computers when users are required to study courseware placed on reserve. Reservations can be made in person or by phone. The maximum amount of time that can be reserved in one day is one hour for the laser printers and two hours for courseware.

Software All microcomputer software is for in-house use only. Microcomputer software is available on a first come first served basis and cannot be reserved. Users may access any of the software loaded on the network or may check out software from the Learning Resources Services desk. Four different software lists are updated regularily and posted for free distribution, describing the software available from 1) the Health Sciences Library , 2) the UNC Macintosh User Group, 3) the UNC IBM PC User Group, and 4) the Undergraduate Library . Personal software can be used if it does not require technical assistance from the staff.

University of North Carolina at Chapel Hill

Technical Support	The library provides technical support for software placed on reserve, loaded on the network and owned by the Health Sciences Library. Questions pertaining to equipment operations, network software, word processing, and general purpose applications should first be referred to the lab assistant. Questions pertaining to the availability of software and those which cannot be answered by the lab assistant should be directed to the Learning Resources Services Desk. Some questions may need be directed to MSC's User Services at 962-3601.
Manuals	Computer, printer, and software manuals for DOS, BASIC, and some network software are shelved in the bookcases adjacent to the lab assistant's desk. Other software manuals and tutorial disks may be checked out for in-house use from the Learning Resources Services Desk. Manuals are copyrighted and cannot be duplicated.
Duplication	Commercial software is copyright protected. Software is loaned with the understanding that it will not be duplicated. Public domain software from the campus user groups can be duplicated under the conditions specified by the producer.
Paper & Ribbons	Computer paper and ribbons are supplied by the Microcomputing Support Center for dot matrix printers. Users must supply their own paper for laser printing.
Laser Printing	IBM and Macintosh laser printers can be reserved for one hour per day in one half hour increments. One original laser copy can be printed for each document and up to five copies of a resume can be printed.
Transferring Disks	IBM disks can be converted from 5 1/4" to 3 1/2" formats and vice versa at the lab assistant's desk.

June 23, 1988

mlcpol2

University of North Carolina at Chapel Hill

Information Management Education
Health Sciences Library
University of North Carolina at Chapel Hill

QUALITY FILTERING THE LITERATURE

Guidelines For Conquering the Information Explosion

1. Try to use refereed journals, i.e. those journals that are selective about what they print. Manuscripts are reviewed and evaluated by an independent expert panel before being accepted. It is difficult to tell which journals are refeered and it is sometimes necessary to write the publisher to determine this. These journals are more <u>likely</u> to contain quality information.

2. Peer review journals <u>tend</u> to be more reliable.

3. Journals that are official publications of recognized societies <u>generally</u> reflect higher standards.

4. An article that is heavily cited by other authors is very likely to be of importance. Highly cited articles or books will often become "classic" works on the topic.

5. A book that is a synthesis of existing knowledge or gives new insights is more desirable than a book that claims to be up to date. This is because it takes approximately two years for a book to be published after the manuscript is received.

6. Students would do well to concentrate on a limited number of journals and books that cover a variety of areas with an eye toward reputable critical approaches by the authors.

7. New technology allows retrieval of information as quickly as it is generated. Use of review articles and critical books is necessary to reduce the amount of information to a comprehendible size.

8. Read with a "critical eye." Don't use everything that you see - be selective when determining what to incorporate into your research paper.

9. Learn how to identify valid studies. Take a look at a book entitled <u>Studying a Study and Testing a Test: How to Read the Medical Literature</u> by Richard K. Riegelman (1st ed., Boston: Little, Brown, 1981). Look for quality versus quantity.

University of North Carolina at Chapel Hill

10. Remember new technologies, online catalogs, personal computers, video-discs, knowledge bases, etc. will constantly be influencing and improving your ability to access and use information and literature. Take the time to acquaint yourself with these new technologies.

11. Develop good life-long learning habits such as regular perusal of key journals in your field and similar current awareness techniques.

MED40006
08/87

University of North Carolina at Chapel Hill

Maryville College-- 1986

INQUIRY: LIBRARY COMPONENT

The bibliographic instruction(BI) component of the Inquiry course addresses the need for a range of information skills involving the selection, analysis, organization, and presentation of valid data. Objectives are:

1. To review salient characteristics of information--complexity, organization, fragmentary nature, dynamic quality, et al.

2. To provide an overview of the commercial and scholarly publication process--formats, rates of publication, authorship, and authority

3. To present a basic strategy for library research that encompasses definition of topic, summary or background, use of the Library of Congress Subject Headings and card catalog for locating books, and Periodicals

4. To introduce reference resources, notably subject encyclopedias

5. To increase student awareness and understanding of periodical literature and indexes.

6. To orient students to facilities, resources, and services of the Lamar Memorial Library

Unstated objectives of BI presentations are to develop student ease and familiarity with the library, to encourage library use, and to increase reference service. If students feel welcome in the library and have learned when and where to seek assistance, these byproducts of instruction will follow.

Presentations will be made during four or more class periods by library faculty, in the main, in the library. Inquiry instructors will be present for all BI presentations, and they are encouraged to participate in class discussion. Teaching methods may include lecture-discussions, oral presentations by students, and hands-on practice with reference sources. Assignments made by library faculty will be a part of the course grade.

Bibliographic instruction will be general and non-specific to subject disciplines, in the main; however, one class period may be devoted to reference materials of special course-related interest, or the librarian-instructor may choose subject-related sources as examples, as appropriate. Instruction will be built around the Inquiry research assignment and fashioned to enhance student understanding of course content. The librarian and the course instructor will work together to plan complementary instruction and to reinforce material presented in class or BI, where possible. Passing reference will be made to the organization of the literature within a given discipline, but such considerations will not be emphasized, as it is expected that freshment will be conducting information searches in several subject areas and disciplines during their first two or three years.

SUBJECT ENCYCLOPEDIAS - A CRITICAL REVIEW

Assignment   Write a critical review of the encyclopedia you have been assigned. Your review should be approximately 500 words in length. It should describe the encyclopedia, inside and out, for someone who has never seen it. The introductory material at the front of the first volume should be especially helpful. Read it with care. Spend at least 20 minutes browsing through the volumes, using the criteria below for ideas of what to look for.

- What is the purpose of the encyclopedia? What is it trying to do? Is it successful?

- What is the range of subject matter, or what does is cover? What are its limitations?

- Look up at least two or three topics or subjects that you know something about, and comment on the comprehensiveness, accuracy, and currency of the articles. Use examples from the text to document your criticism and comments.

- When was it published? Is the date important? Why or why not? How is it kept up to date?

- How is it arranged? (In sections by subject? Alphabetically? Geographically? Chronologically?)

- Is there an index? Could you find what you were looking for by using the index?

- Are there references to related articles in the text? Do (all/some) articles include bibliographies? Are the works listed reasonably current?

- Are the articles signed?

- Does the information presented seem accurate and objective?

- Is the physical book attractive? Do the binding, paper, and type seem adequate? Can you use it or read it without problems?

- Is it illustrated? Are the illustrations in color or black-and-white? Are they appropriate and helpful? Do they appear on the same page as the text that goes with them? Are there special graphic features (maps or graphs, for example) that add or detract from the text?

If you wish, you may compare your encyclopedia's coverage of a particular topic with coverage in a general encyclopedia, such as Encyclopedia Americana or Encyclopaedia Britannica. You may also use published reviews of the encyclopedia and "Sheehy" (Guide to Reference Books, 9th ed., by Eugene P. Sheehy, shelved on Ready Reference).

Maryville College

Subject dictionaries and encyclopedias are shelved in the Reference department. The following list is not inclusive; there are others you will want to use for special purposes.

Dictionary of American Biography R920 D55

Dictionary of the History of Ideas R909 D554

Dictionary of the Middle Ages R909.07 D554

Encyclopedia of American Economic History R330.973 E56

Encyclopedia of American Forest and Conservation History R333.75 E56

Encyclopedia of American Political History R320.973 E56

Encyclopedia of American Religions R200.973 M52e

Encyclopedia of Bioethics R174.2 E56

Encyclopedia of Crime and Justice R364.03 E56

Encyclopedia of Educational Research R370.3 E56 1982

Encyclopedia of Philosophy R103 E56

Encyclopedia of Psychology R150.3 E563 1984

Encyclopedia of Religion and Ethics R203 E56

Encyclopedia of the Third World R909.0972 K96e 1982

Encyclopedia of World Art R703 E56

Grzimek's Animal Life Encyclopedia R591 G89b

Guide to American Law R348.736 G946

International Encyclopedia of Social Science R303 I61

McGraw Hill Encyclopedia of Science and Technology R503 M14 1982

New Catholic Encyclopedia R282.03 N53

New English Dictionary (popular title, "the OED") - on dictionary table

New Grove Dictionary of Music and Musicians R780.3 G883 1980

Tennessee Code Annotated R348.768 T2970t

World Encyclopedia of Political Systems & Parties R324.202 W9277

Maryville College

Name _____

Topic _____

1. DEFINITIONS. Name dictionaries used. _____

2. BACKGROUND. Name encyclopedia(s) used. _____

3. BOOKS. What subject headings were useful in finding books in the card catalog? _____

   How many books on your topic did you find listed in the card catalog? _____

   Give author, title, and date of publication of one that looks helpful. _____

4. PERIODICALS. What indexes did you use to find articles? _____

   Give author, title, periodical title, vol. number, page number, and date of issue for one article you found. _____

5. OTHER. Have you found other information--i.e., statistical compilations, biographical data, et al.--helpful? If so, list one or two sources. _____

Bibliographies

Library Orientation and Instruction--1988

Hannelore B. Rader

The following is an annotated list of materials dealing with orientation to library facilities and services, instruction in the use of information resources, and research and computer skills related to retrieving, using, and evaluating information. This review, the fifteenth to be published in *Reference Services Review*, includes items in English published in 1988. A few are not annotated because the compiler could not obtain copies of them for this review.

The list includes publications on user instruction in all types of libraries and for all levels of users, from small children to senior citizens and from beginning levels to the most advanced. The items are arranged by type of library and are in alphabetical order by author (or by title if there is no author) within those categories.

Overall, as shown in the example below the number of publications related to user education increased by fifteen percent between 1987 and 1988.

These figures are approximate and based on the published information that was available to the reviewer. However, since the availability of this information does not vary greatly from year to year, these figures should be reliable.

Publications dealing with user instruction in academic libraries were the most numerous, yet the number of publications in this category decreased by five percent. The number of publications in public school and special library categories increased while those in the all-level category decreased.

User education publications in academic libraries continue to deal with teaching users how to access and organize information, including online searching, online system use, and bibliographic

Rader is director, University Library, Cleveland State University, Cleveland, OH.

Type of Library	# of 1987 Publications	# of 1988 Publications	% Change
Academic	91	101	+11%
Public	01	04	+300%
School	17	22	+29%
Special	06	14	+133%
<u>All Types</u>	<u>15</u>	<u>08</u>	<u>-47%</u>
TOTAL	130	149	+15%

computer applications. A small percentage deal with evaluative research of user education.

This year's publications are beginning to note references to "information literacy" in a technological society. It is anticipated that next year's publications will begin to focus on information literacy as a much more comprehensive library education issue compared to bibliographic instruction.

ACADEMIC LIBRARIES

Allen, Mary Beth, and Joyce Wright. "Subject Seminars: Another Step in Library Use Instruction." *Illinois Libraries* 70 (December 1988): 652-655.

Amodeo, Anthony J. "A Debt Unpaid: The Bibliography Instruction Librarian and Library Conservation." *College and Research Libraries News* 49 (October 1988): 601-603.

Advocates that instruction librarians teach all students how to take care of library materials so that materials will continue to be preserved for future use.

Baker, Betsy. "Educating the Online Catalog User." In *Teaching the Online Catalog User*, ed. by Carolyn Kirkendall, 1-8. Ann Arbor, MI: Pierian Press, 1988.

Provides a complete outline and script for librarians to teach the online catalog based on teaching the NOTIS library automation system at Northwestern University.

Balius, Sharon A. "Changing Perspectives Evolving from Diverse End-User Applications." In *Bibliographic Instruction and Computer Database Searching*, 75-78. Ann Arbor, MI: Pierian Press, 1988.

Describes an end-user searching instruction program for engineering students at the University of Michigan.

Beasley, David. *How to Use a Research Library.* New York: Oxford, 1988.

The purpose of this monograph is to instruct college students, researchers, and writers in the use of research libraries. Specific library services are described. Information is provided about card catalogs, research tools, and types of library research needs. An appendix lists major research libraries in the United States.

Bechtel, Joan. "Developing and Using the Online Catalog to Teach Critical Thinking." *Information Technologies and Libraries* (March 1988): 30-40.

AutoCat, the online catalog developed at Dickinson College, teaches students critical thinking processes for formulating and researching topics.

Bodi, Sonia. "Critical Thinking and Bibliographical Instruction: The Relationship." *Journal of Academic Librarianship* 14 (July 1988): 150-153.

Argues that there is no uniformly accepted definition of critical thinking. The ability to think critically may involve four developmental stages. Discusses implications for user education and teacher training.

Bowen, Dorothy. "Learning Styles-Based Bibliographic Instruction." *International Library Review* 20 (July 1988): 405-413.

Discusses research on strategies for bibliographic instruction for African students. Provides teaching strategies based on the study.

Breivik, Patricia. "Information Literacy: A Colorado History." *Colorado Libraries* 14 (September 1988): 28-29.

Discusses library literacy as one of the academic skills outcomes of students in Colorado. Explains that this places responsibility for learning on students rather than professors.

Callison, Daniel, and Ann Daniels. "Introducing End-User Software for Enhancing Student Online Searching." *School Library Media Quarterly* 16 (Spring 1988): 173-181.

Describes a project at Carmel (Indiana) High School to teach students end-user searching on WilSearch. Includes student worksheets and logs.

"Caught in the Web--Scholars, Scientific Journals,

and Libraries." Editorial. *Research Strategies* 6 (Spring 1988): 50-51.

Discusses librarians' roles in dealing with the proliferation of scientific journal literature.

"Coincidence." Editorial. *Research Strategies* 6 (Fall 1988): 146-147.

Discusses the problems associated with identifying and disseminating "common" knowledge in a society accommodating many special interests. Library instruction can help people explore many views and approaches to knowledge.

Coleman, James R., and Edmund G. Hamann. "Self-Instructed Use of Microcomputers in the Library." *College and Research Libraries News* 49 (October 1988): 603-604.

Describes a self-instruction module used at Suffolk University to teach the use of microcomputers.

Collins, Mary E. "Teaching Research in Children's Literature to Graduate Education Students Using ERIC." *Research Strategies* 6 (Summer 1988): 127-132.

Describes a bibliographic instruction program for graduate education students in children's literature using printed and electronic indexes.

Currie, Margaret, and Dallas McLean-Howe. "Bibliographic Instruction for the Print-Handicapped." *College & Research Libraries News* (November 1988): 672-674.

Reports on the successful outcome at the University of Toronto Libraries in setting up library visits and instructional sessions for the print-handicapped.

Dale, Doris. "The Learning Resource Center's Role in the Community College System." *College and Research Libraries* 49 (May 1988): 232-238.

Advocates a teaching role for community college libraries to move the library into the center of the educational process and to stimulate more library use.

Davis, Scott, and Marsha Miller. "New Projection Technology for Online Instruction." *Technicalities* 8 (February 1988): 3-6.

Explains the availability and use of video projection devices and LCD equipment for use in teaching online catalog use interactively.

Davis, H. Scott, et al. *Library Staff Training for LUIS (Online Catalog) Keyword/Boolean Searching at Indiana State University Libraries.* ERIC Reproduction Service, 1988. ED 295681.

Summarizes a staff training program on LUIS

keyword and Boolean searching. Gives content of lessons, including practice exercises.

Dess, Howard M. "Coping with Chemical Nomenclature in the Age of Computers." *Research Strategies* 6 (Spring 1988): 65-76.

Provides methodologies to teach online searching for complex chemical substances to graduates and undergraduates.

Dykstra, Mary. *Subject Access and Bibliographic Information: Two Sides of the OPAC Problem.* Halifax, Nova Scotia: Dalhousie University, 1988.

Discusses the problems of subject access and bibliographic instruction in relationship to using an OPAC for access to library information in order to overcome present access constraints.

Engeldinger, Eugene A. "Bibliographic Instruction and Critical Thinking: The Contribution of the Annotated Bibliography." *RQ* 28 (Winter 1988): 195-202.

Discusses teaching skills to students to help them evaluate and interpret information by developing critical thinking skills. The University of Wisconsin-Eau Claire serves as an example.

Engeldinger, Eugene A. "Teaching Only the Essentials--The Thirty Minute Stand." *Reference Services Review* 16, no. 4 (1988): 47-50, 96.

Describes the approach to BI at the University of Wisconsin-Eau Claire: a thirty-minute lecture followed by a twenty-minute exercise. Content emphasis is on searching the catalog and periodical indexes by keyword and controlled vocabulary.

Questions the need for high-performance standards for library use education to educate life long learners. Simpler, more easily achievable goals are proposed.

Engeldinger, Eugene A., et al. "Bibliographic Instruction for Social Work Students." *Research Strategies* 6 (Summer 1988): 118-126.

Provides details about a library instruction program in the undergraduate social work curriculum at the University of Wisconsin-Eau Claire. Students are taught to locate and evaluate various types of information.

Feinberg, Richard, and Christine King. "Short-Term Library Skill Competencies: Arguing for the Achievable." *College and Research Libraries* 49 (January 1988): 24-28.

Questions the practical nature of high performance library instruction standards and advocates simpler, more achievable goals.

Fjallbrant, Nancy. "Recent Trends in Online User

Education." *IATUL Quarterly* 2 (December 1988): 228-236.

There are now 3,500 online databases and 500 search services and the International Association of Technological University Libraries (IATUL) plays an important role in online user education. Describes types of online education, methods for teaching online information retrieval, and relevant software packages.

Frank, Roza. "User Education at the Technical University of Budapest." *IATUL Quarterly* 2 (December 1988): 223-227.

Describes a user education program mandated since 1966 by the Hungarian Ministry of Education for technical universities. User education occurs in various disciplines and is handled by librarians. Instruction includes information retrieval, alphabetical catalogs, abstracts, and online services.

French, Nancy, and H. Julene Butler. "Quiet on the Set! Library Instruction Goes Video." *Wilson Library Bulletin* (December 1988): 42-44.

Describes Brigham Young University's experience with using video for instructing 5,000 freshmen in library use. Provides planning and details for implementation.

Fry, Thomas K., and Joan Kaplowitz. "The English 3 Library Instruction Program at UCLA: A Follow-Up Study." *Research Strategies* 6 (Summer 1988): 100-108.

Reports on a follow-up survey of students at UCLA after three years in a library instruction program. Results compared favorably with the earlier survey regarding library use, attitudes, and skills.

Gratch, Bonnie G. "Rethinking Instructional Assumptions in an Age of Computerized Information Access." *Research Strategies* 6 (Winter 1988): 4-7.

Discusses users' information seeking behavior and the effect of automatic systems on that behavior. Analysis of user information needs continues to be a key issue to guide them in filling these needs with appropriate resources as found in a study at Bowling Green State University Libraries.

Graves, Gail T., and Barbara K. Adams. "Bibliographic Instruction Workbooks: Assessing Two Models Used in a Freshman English Program." *Research Strategies* 6 (Winter 1988): 18-24.

Reports on a study at the University of Mississippi library to assess the usefulness of two types of workbooks in a freshman library instruction program.

Gremmels, Jill S. "Information Management Education--Beyond BI." *Indiana Libraries* 7 (1988): 6-12.

Griffin, Mary L. "BI, Reference, and the Teaching/Learning Process." *Reference Services Review* 16, nos. 1-2 (1988): 93-94.

Discusses the need for interaction between teaching and library faculty to design undergraduate assignments that demand effective library use and research skills. Examples of appropriate assignments are given.

Hawbaker, A. Craig, and Alice A. Littlejohn. "Improving Library Instruction in Marketing Research: A Model." *Journal of Marketing Education* (Summer 1988): 52-61.

Describes a course-integrated library instruction program for graduate students in a marketing research course at the University of Arizona.

Heller, Paul, and Betsy Brennemah. "A Checklist for Evaluating Your Library's Handbook." *College and Research Libraries News* 49 (February 1988): 78-79.

Describes an instrument developed at Worcester State College's Learning Resources Center to evaluate the effectiveness of library handbooks as public relations tools.

Huong, Joyce L., and Scott Mandernack. *Minimum Library Use Skills Survey*. ERIC Reproduction Service, 1988. ED 263926.

Summarizes a survey to assess the use and effectiveness of the "Minimum Library Use Skills" proposed by the Wisconsin Association of Academic Librarians in 1985. More standardization and cooperation is needed between academic and high school librarians to educate students more effectively in library use.

Isbell, Dennis. "Freshman Library Instruction at the University of South Carolina." *South Carolina Librarian* 31-32 (Spring 1988): 12-13.

Describes the new focus of freshman orientation at the University of South Carolina, emphasizing focus on the second semester of English composition.

Jacobson, Frances F. "Teachers and Library Awareness: Using Bibliographic Instruction in Teacher Preparation Programs." *Reference Services Review* 16, no. 4 (1988): 51-55. Discusses the role librarians should play in the teacher-education process to ensure that future teachers will help in teaching information literacy on all levels.

Jacobson, F.F. "Bibliographic Instruction and International Students." *Illinois Libraries* 70 (December

1988): 628-633.

Karetzky, Stephen. "Videocassette Kits for Instruction in Online Searching." *College and Research Libraries News* 49 (June 1988): 361-364.
Analyzes and evaluates three videos for online searching instruction. It was found that their quality greatly varied. Other learning methods include attending workshops and using printed training manuals.

Kautz, Barbara A., et al. "The Evolution of a New Library Instruction Concept: Interactive Video." *Research Strategies* 6 (Summer 1988): 109-117.
Describes an interactive video library instruction course at the University of Minnesota using computer-based instruction instead of traditional lecture/laboratory instruction.

Kesselman, Martin. "Hypercard and CAI." *LIRT News* 10 (June 1988): 6-7.
Describes the use of Hypercard in a CAI program to teach engineering undergraduates use of library resources at Rutgers University.

King, David N., and B. Baker. "Teaching End-Users to Search: Issues and Problems." In *Bibliographic Instruction and Computer Database Searching*, ed. by Teresa Mensching, 27-33. Ann Arbor, MI: Pierian Press, 1988.
Discusses issues related to online searching such as technology, human-machine relationships, and user-friendly software.

Koehler, Boyd, and Kathryn Swanson. "ESL Students and Bibliographic Instruction: Learning Yet Another Language." *Research Strategies* 6 (Fall 1988): 148-160.
Describes a library instruction program for ESL students at Augsburg College in Minnesota, using a four-phase approach: presearched examples, ability grouping, the online catalog, and sensitivity to various communication problems and learning styles.

Kupersmith, John. "Reducing Visual Clutter." *Research Strategies* 6 (Spring 1988): 83-84.
Provides guidelines for clear, uncluttered signage, placement, color, and maintenance.

Kupersmith, John. "Starter Kit for a Sign System." *Research Strategies* 6 (Summer 1988): 133-135.
Provides basic guidelines for starting a sign system in the library.

Kupersmith, John. "Tradeoffs in Designing Library Graphics." *Research Strategies* 6 (Winter 1988): 33-35.
Discusses issues in designing sign systems such as creativity versus order, consistency versus flexibility, structure versus detail, literal accuracy versus desired behavior, and cost versus quality.

Lawton, Bethany, and Ann Pederson. "Cue Card Clues: A New Approach to Library Orientation." *Research Strategies* 6 (Spring 1988): 77-79.
Describes a redesign of library orientation for freshmen at the University of North Dakota using cue cards.

Lanning, John A. "The Library-Faculty Partnership in Curriculum Development." *College and Research Libraries News* 49 (January 1988): 7-10.
This paper was given at the ACRL President's Program in San Francisco in 1987 by a chemistry faculty member from the University of Colorado at Denver. Discusses the importance of information literacy in curriculum development.

Lippincott, Joan K. "Taking a Leadership Role in End-User Instruction." In *Bibliographic Instruction and Computer Database Searching*, ed. by Teresa Mensching, 1-6. Ann Arbor, MI: Pierian Press, 1988.
Explains end-user instruction, gives goals and objectives for it, and provides future directions.

Lutzker, Marilyn. *Research Projects for College Students: What to Write across the Curriculum.* Westport, CT: Greenwood Press, 1988.
Explores designing writing assignments directly tied to library-based research to bridge the gap between librarians and teachers. Its purpose is to help college instructors design library research projects.

MacDonald, Gina, and Elizabeth Sarkodie-Mensah. "ESL Students and American Libraries." *College and Research Libraries* 49 (September 1988): 425-431.
Discusses the need on the part of librarians to work with ESL personnel to help foreign students become effective library users. Provides specific examples of teaching foreign students library use.

Mader, Sharon, and B. Park. "End-User Searching for the Undergraduate Business Student: A Course-Integrated Approach." In *Bibliographic Instruction and Computer Database Searching*, ed. by Teresa Mensching, 35-36. Ann Arbor, MI: Pierian Press, 1988.
Describes the development and implementation of an integrated end-user searching instruction module for undergraduate business students at Memphis State University. Sample handouts are included.

Madland, Denise, and Marion A. Smith. "Computer-Assisted Information for Teaching Conceptual Library Skills to Remedial Students." *Research Strategies* 6 (Spring 1988): 52-64.

Describes an assessment of a CAI program to teach conceptual thinking skills to remedial students at the University of Wisconsin-Stout. Although students in a class session scored higher than in a CAI session, all groups preferred CAI programs.

Malley, Ian. *Education Information Users in Colleges of Further and Higher Education.* London: British Library, 1988.

Review of the literature on educating students in colleges of higher education in information handling and library use. A bibliography of seventy-eight references dating from the early 1960s through 1986 is included.

Malley, Ian. *A Survey of Information Skills Teaching in Colleges of Further and Higher Education.* London: British Library, 1988.

Describes the results of a questionnaire survey of colleges of higher education in Scottish central institutions. The overall finding was that information skills teaching by librarians was confined mainly to traditional library skills like library orientation and bibliographic competence.

Masters, Deborah. "Library Users and Online Systems: Suggested Objectives for Library Instruction." In *Teaching the Online Catalog Users*, ed. by Carolyn Kirkendall, 29-32. Ann Arbor, MI: Pierian Press, 1988.

Gives the online catalog instruction objectives developed by ALA's Reference and Adult Services Division in 1985.

Max, Patrick. "Dealing with the New Technology: An Instructional Primer." *Indiana Libraries* 7 (1988): 13-17.

Mensching, Teresa B. "Dialog and Debate." *Research Strategies* 6 (Winter 1988): 36-38.

This column addresses the topic of former library instruction librarians as library administrators and whether or not they miss bibliographic instruction activities. Respondents include Jacqueline Morris from Occidental College, William Miller from Florida Atlantic University, Carla Stoffle from the University of Michigan, Mignon Adams from the Philadelphia College of Pharmacy and Science, and Hannelore Rader from Cleveland State University.

Mensching, Teresa. "The Importance of an Appropriate Milieu." *Research Strategies* 6 (Spring 1988): 85-87.

This column discusses the use of audio-visual materials in bibliographic instruction.

Mensching, Teresa. "Personal Favorites." *Research Strategies* 6 (Fall 1988): 185-188.

Lists several basic and intriguing guidelines to help BI librarians get started from Mary Popp at Indiana University, Sandra Yee at Eastern Michigan University, Susan Varca at Arizona State University, and Teresa Manthey at the University of Southern California.

Mensching, Teresa. "Resistance, Empathy, and Technical Expertise." *Research Strategies* 6 (Summer 1988): 136-139.

Responses are given to statements dealing with incorporating new techniques into bibliographic instruction by Jacqueline Gavryck, SUNY-Albany; Sandy Ward, Stanford University; Jean Smith, University of California-San Diego; and H. Scott Davis, Indiana State University.

Miller, Marian I., and Barry D. Bratton. "Instructional Design: Increasing the Effectiveness of Bibliographic Instruction." *College and Research Libraries* 49 (November 1988): 545-549.

Provides guidelines to help librarians incorporate instructional designs into planning bibliographic instruction while focusing on five main areas.

Miller, Marsha A. "Course-Integrated Library Instruction: Earlham College Revisited." *Indiana Libraries* 7 (1988): 24-33.

"The Mind of the New Machines." Editorial. *Research Strategies* 6 (Winter 1988): 2-3.

Explores the use of new computer technology in the information-communication-control process and the role of good teachers/librarians in this process.

Nahl-Jacobovits, Diane, and Leon A. Jacobovits. "Problem Solving, Creative Librarianship, and Search Behavior." *College and Research Libraries* 49 (September 1988): 400-408.

Explores the function of knowledge in society, in part, as people processing information to solve problems, and how librarians can become involved in these challenges.

O'Hanlon, Nancyanne. "Up the Down Staircase: Establishing Library Instruction Programs for Teachers." *RQ* 27 (Summer 1988): 528-529.

Discusses library instruction programs for future teachers so that they develop as future promoters of library literacy in K-12.

Osiobe, Stephen A. "Information Seeking Behavior." *International Library Review* 20 (July 1988): 337-346.

Reports on a study undertaken at Port Harcourt University Library, Nigeria, that investigated student information-seeking behavior. Results of the study show that browsing is the prevalent source of reference to the literature among undergraduates, followed by use of faculty staff and the library card catalog, with solicitation of the subject librarian in third place. Abstracts and indexes are poorly used and ranked sixth in the study.

Pask, Judith M. "Computer-Assisted Instruction for Basic Library Skills." *Library Software Review* 7 (January-February 1988): 6-11.

Describes the award-winning undergraduate library research skills program at Purdue University based on computer-assisted instructions.

Penchansky, Mimi B., et al. *International Students and the Library. An Annotated Selective Bibliography on the Theme of the LACUNY 1988 Institute.* ERIC Reproduction Service, 1988. ED 295679.

This list includes information on assisting foreign and immigrant students in adjusting to an academic campus in the United States including library instruction.

Peterson, Lorna. "Ask a Silly Question: Responses from Library Instruction Quizzes." *Research Strategies* 6 (Winter 1988): 25-28.

Library staff at Iowa State University share amusing and disconcerting answers to library quizzes.

Peterson, Lorna. "Teaching Academic Integrity: Opportunities in Bibliographic Instruction." *Research Strategies* 6 (Fall 1988): 168-176.

Gives an opinion piece on the need for librarians to instruct students in the principles of independent scholarship and proper documentation in order to teach academic integrity.

"Pitching Lessons." Editorial. *Research Strategies* 6 (Summer 1988): 98-99.

Discusses the problem of determining the appropriate level for library instruction in an academic setting. Advocates teaching from principles rather than from a variety of reference tools.

Popa, Opritsa D., et al. "Teaching Search Techniques on the Computerized Catalog and on the Traditional Card Catalog: A Comparative Study." *College and Research Libraries* 49 (May 1988): 263-274.

Reports on a research project at the University of California-Davis that measures students' grasp of library concepts using both an online and card catalog. The former is preferred and more successful. No difference in performance was found for American versus international students.

Porter, Elizabeth S. "There's More to the World Than World Book." *American Biology Teacher* 50 (May 1988): 290-291.

Discusses a search strategy to teach biology students for doing research papers. This strategy parallels closely the information research process used by scientists and helps students in understanding the structure of scientific literature.

Powell, Patricia J., and L.O. Rein. "OPAC Training for Patrons and Staff: A Case Study." *Southeastern Librarian* 39 (Spring 1988): 12-18.

Describes a four-part instructional program designed to teach online catalog use of the LS 2000 system at the University of Kentucky.

Ready, Sandra K. "Teaching the Online Catalog: Mankato State University." In *Teaching the Online Catalog User*, ed. by Carolyn Kirkendall, 19-28. Ann Arbor, MI: Pierian Press, 1988.

Describes an instructional program for teaching the use of the PALS online catalog. Provides sample handouts.

Reichel, Mary. "Library Literacy." *RQ* 28 (Fall 1988): 29-32.

Discusses librarians' interaction with students in library instruction sessions and the need for librarians to be knowledgeable about students' needs, abilities, and interests.

Reichel, Mary. "Library Literacy." *RQ* 28 (Winter 1988): 162-168.

This column features an article by Ellen Broidy on "Organizational Structure: Politics, Problems and Challenges." It discusses the challenges instruction librarians face in their particular library setting.

Rockman, Ilene F. "End-User Search Services in Academic Libraries: Results from a National Study." In *Bibliographic Instruction and Computer Database Searching*, ed. by Teresa Mensching, 7-11. Ann Arbor, MI: Pierian Press, 1988.

Summarizes a study of end-user search services for thirty libraries. Findings varied greatly from regularly available end-user search services to on-demand ad-hoc ones.

Schub, Sue. "Teaching Bibliographic Instruction." *Library Journal* 113 (1 February 1988): 39-40.

Provides some guidelines for first-time teachers of bibliographic instruction credit courses.

Selin, Helen. "Teaching Research Methods to Undergraduates." *College Teaching* 36 (Spring 1988): 54-56.

Describes a vigorous user instruction program for undergraduates at Hampshire College as part of a revamped curriculum for first-year students.

Skinner, Edward, and J.K. Bracken. "Teaching Students to Locate and Use Statistics on International Telecommunication Systems." *Research Strategies* 6 (Winter 1988): 29-32.

Describes a graduate course on comparative telecommunication systems and appropriate library instruction at Purdue University.

Smith, Dana E. "The Purdue Undergraduate Library Research Skills Instruction Program." *Indiana Libraries* 7 (1988): 39-48.

Smith, Jean. "Teaching Research Skills Using Video: An Undergraduate Library Approach." *Reference Services Review* 16, nos. 1-2 (1988): 109-114.

Describes the use of videotapes for undergraduate library instruction at the University of California-San Diego. Guidelines for producing tapes, a cost breakdown, and a list of additional readings are provided.

Soifer, Libby P. "Guide to Sources: Sociology. Revised." ERIC Reproduction Service, 1988. ED 291410.

This guide and annotated bibliography is designed to introduce sociology students to the basic research tools in their field that are available in the Fogler Library at the University of Maine.

Sorensen, Virginia P. "Bibliographic Instruction in a Developmental Studies Program; A Paired Course Approach." *Research Strategies* 6 (Fall 1988): 161-167.

Provides information on a library skills course paired with an English composition course in a developmental studies program at St. Cloud State University, in St. Cloud, Minnesota. Particular attention is given to scheduling the final project and learning styles of high-risk students.

Stanley, Mary. "Preparation for Undergraduate Bibliographic Instruction: A Personal Experience." *Indiana Libraries* 7 (1988): 34-38.

Stark, Marcella, and M.A. Walz. "Thumbing the Cards: The Online Catalog the Faculty and Instruction." In *Teaching the Online Catalog Users*, ed. by Carolyn Kirkendall, 35-69. Ann Arbor, MI: Pierian Press, 1988.

Describes an instructional program for the online catalog for faculty at Syracuse University. Includes a variety of sample materials.

Stebelman, Scott. "Integrating Online Searching into Traditional Bibliographic Instruction." In *Bibliographic Instruction and Computer Database Searching*, ed. by Teresa Mensching, 23-26. Ann Arbor, MI: Pierian Press, 1988.

Describes the library instruction program at the University of Nebraska-Lincoln, which features online literature searching as an integrated part of that program.

Steffen, Susan Swords. "Designing Bibliographic Instruction Programs for Adult Students: The Schaffner Library Experience." *Illinois Libraries* 70 (December 1988): 644-649.

Steffen, Susan S. "Faculty as End-Users: Strategies, Challenges, and Rewards." In *Bibliographic Instruction and Computer Database Searching*, ed. by Teresa Mensching, 17-22. Ann Arbor, MI: Pierian Press.

Provides rationale for end-user searching, parameters for teaching it, and possible benefits for faculty and librarians.

Svinicki, Marilla D., and Barbara Schwartz. *Designing Instruction for Library Users: A Practical Guide.* New York: Marcel Dekker, 1988.

This book, written for academic librarians faced with teaching students library skills, provides guidelines for instruction methods, a framework for instructional design and frequency, and learning theory. Eight case studies and an evaluation section are also given.

Taylor, Nancy, and S. Penhale. "End-User Searching and Bibliographic Instruction." In *Bibliographic Instruction and Computer Database Searching*, 57-74. Ann Arbor, MI: Pierian Press, 1988.

Describes how Earlham College, in Richmond, Indiana has integrated online searching instruction into the library instruction program for undergraduates. Handout samples are included.

"Teaching Library and Information Retrieval Skills to Academic Administrators and Support Staff." *College & Research Libraries News* 49 (April 1988): 217-223.

Describes a document drawn up by the ACRL and EBSS Bibliographic Instruction Committee on teaching library and information retrieval skills to academic administrators and support staff, in response to a request by librarians for information on what to include in such sessions and how to teach them. The document has four sections: instructional strategies; library departments and services; access to and retrieval of information; and reference tools.

Thomas, Joy. "Bibliographic Instructors in the Sciences; A Profile." *College and Research Libraries* 49 (May 1988): 252-262.

Summarizes a survey of California science librarians involved in library instruction to determine how they had been trained. Findings suggest that training and education for bibliographic instruction is still problematic.

Tims, Betty J. "Interactive Team Teaching of Government Documents Data Sources: A Case Study." *Reference Services Review* 16, no. 3 (1988): 69-72.

Describes an interactive team teaching project with a librarian and an industrial marketing professor at Auburn University. The resulting workshop taught juniors and seniors library skills for their class projects using government document sources.

VanPulis, Noelle. "Planning an Online Catalog Workshop: The Experience of the Ohio State University Libraries." In *Teaching the Online Catalog User*, ed. by Carolyn Kirkendall, 71-100. Ann Arbor, MI: Pierian Press, 1988.

Describes an online catalog workshop taught at Ohio State University to explain the Library Control System (LCS) online catalog. Includes sample handouts.

Westbrook, Lynn. "Getting in Gear: A Short-Term Program to Revitalize Your BI Staff." *Research Strategies* 6 (Fall 1988): 177-184.

Describes a workshop at the University of Michigan for bibliographic instructors to combat burnout and nervousness.

Wheeler, Helen R. *The Bibliographic Instruction-Course Handbook.* Metuchen, NJ: Scarecrow, 1988.

This work provides a skills and concepts approach to an undergraduate, research methodology credit course. It should be useful to librarians, library educators, and other academic personnel. It is based on the UCLA model where undergraduates have access to a credit course on bibliographic instruction. It provides information on BI in general, various methodologies, and details on teaching BI credit courses.

Wilson, Linda. "Preconditions to Teaching the On-line Catalog User." In *Teaching the Online Catalog User*, ed. by Carolyn Kirkendall, 9-18. Ann Arbor, MI: Pierian Press, 1988.

Provides valuable information related to setting up and maintaining the online catalog based on the VTLS System at Virginia Polytechnic Uni-

versity. Includes sample handouts.

Windsor, Laura. "The Current Status of Bibliographic Instruction in Academic Libraries: A Survey." *Colorado Libraries* 14 (March 1988): 22-24.

Summarizes a survey of fifty-two academic libraries in Colorado to find out about current trends in bibliographic instruction.

Wozny, Lucy A. "College Students as End User Searchers: One University's Experience." *RQ* 28 (Fall 1988): 54-61.

Reports on a study to assess freshman students' use of database and library searching for a research paper. Students obtained a working knowledge of online searching but had problems with search strategies.

York, Charlene, et al. "Computerized Reference Sources: One-Step Shopping or Part of a Search Strategy?" *Research Strategies* 6 (Winter 1988): 8-17.

Summarizes a study at Bowling Green State University Libraries to assess the effect of computerized reference sources on users' information-seeking behavior.

PUBLIC LIBRARIES

McWilliam, Deborah, and Jill B. Fatzer. "The Problem Assignment and the Public Library." *RQ* 27 (Spring 1988): 333-336.

Describes a library instruction program in a public library setting in Columbus, Ohio, where public librarians not only instruct college students to do their library assignments, but are working with the faculty to structure better assignments.

Schange, George. "A View from a Library Phobic." *Colorado Libraries* 14 (June 1988): 23.

Offers a unique view of user instruction from a library user who sees a pressing need for such instruction.

Spinella, G.M., and J.A. Hicks. "Cooperative Bibliographic Instruction: A Program between Wilmot Junior High School and Deerfield Public Library." *Illinois Libraries* 70 (December 1988): 656-659.

Sullivan, Sarah. "The Docents Program at St. Louis Public Library's Central Library." *Show-Me Libraries* 39 (Summer 1988): 23-25.

Describes a unique tour program for the St. Louis central library, sponsored and implemented by volunteers under the guidance of the Friends. The docents are continually trained to do this job.

SCHOOL LIBRARIES

Aaron, Shirley L. "The Role of Professional Development Activities in Promoting Improved Instructional Services in the Library Media Program." *School Library Media Quarterly* 16 (Winter 1988): 84-87.

The instructional role of the library media specialist is examined in the light of a new set of library standards and is seen to be everchanging. Instructional activities should be shaped by the mission of the library program and geared to the access to and use of information and ideas.

Beasley, Augie E., and Carolyn G. Palmer. "The Teaching Role of the Secondary Media Coordinator: Making It Work." *North Carolina Libraries* 45 (Spring 1988): 22-26.

Discusses the importance of media specialists in secondary schools, especially in relationship to teaching library skills in a curriculum-integrated manner. Provides ideas for such endeavors.

Grubbs, Frank. "Nine Points for Writing Social Studies Research Papers for History Day and Other Competitions." *North Carolina Journal for the Social Studies* 24 (1988): 31-33.

Presents nine points that should be considered by teachers and students when writing social studies research papers for History Day and other competitions. Discusses themes, footnotes, annotated bibliographies, sources, proofing, introductions, conclusions, the use of school libraries, and the typing of papers.

Hazell, Anne. "The National Information Policy and Schools." *Australian Library Journal* 37 (February 1988): 26-33.

Focuses on the role of school library resource services and teacher-librarians in preparing young people to become effective users of information. Links current trends in education toward teacher-librarians and teachers working cooperatively to teach information skills within the context of existing curricula rather than in isolation as "library skills," toward the development of a National Information Policy.

Hiland, Leah. "Information and Thinking Skills and Processes to Prepare Young Adults for the Information Age." *Library Trends* 37 (Summer 1988): 56-62.

Provides a thoughtful discussion of the meaning of information and thinking skills and how to incorporate them into curricula for children and young adults.

"How Do You and Your Librarian Work Together?"

English Journal 77 (January 1988): 79-82.

Summarizes forty responses from English teachers in secondary schools on how they work with their librarians. The responses are from all over the United States and describe a variety of cooperative teaching programs.

Kegley, Freda, and Julie Bobay. "Librarian/Teacher Partnerships for Better Library Instruction: Two Views." *Indiana Libraries* 7 (1988): 19-23.

Kemp, Barbara E., and Mary M. Nofsinger. "Library Research Skills for College-Bound Students: Articulation in Washington State." *Journal of Academic Librarianship* 14 (May 1988): 78-79.

Describes a program at Washington State University to work with K-12 media specialists toward the teaching of library and research skills on all levels.

Kinney, Elaine M. "Thirty Minutes and Counting: A Bibliographic Instruction Program." *Illinois Libraries* (January 1988): 36-37.

Describes a library instruction program for junior high students, done jointly by an English teacher and a public librarian in Deerfield, Illinois.

Kline, Susan B. "Taping Their Time." *School Library Journal* 34 (August 1988): 52.

Describes a high school project in which seniors use reference materials and videotaping to produce a short video program, rather than a paper on a given topic.

Krapp, JoAnn V. "Teaching Research Skills: A Critical Thinking Approach." *School Library Journal* 34 (January 1988): 32-35.

Describes a library skills program for high school students using a problem-solving approach. Provides activities and outlines specific steps.

Kuhlthau, Carol C. "Developing a Model of the Library Search Process: Cognitive and Affective Aspects." *RQ* 28 (Winter 1988): 232-233.

Reports on a study that investigates the library search process of college-bound seniors, resulting in the formulation of a theory of the search process.

"Library and Information Skills Curriculum: Scope and Sequence: The Big Six Skills." In *Curriculum Initiative: An Agenda and Strategy for Library Media Programs*, ed. by Michael B. Eisenberg and R.E. Berkowitz, 99-120. Norwood, NJ: Ablex Publishing, Co., 1988.

Provides school library media specialists a library media and information skills curriculum designed around an information problem-solving process and Bloom's Taxonomy of cognitive objectives.

The six skills discussed are task definition, information-seeking strategies, location and access to information, use of information synthesis, and evaluation.

Rankin, Virginia. "One Route to Critical Thinking." *School Library Journal* 34 (January 1988): 28-31.

The author describes a program in which she taught students to think about their own research using a daily journal.

Rawcliffe, Renee D. "Bibliographic Instruction and the Media Specialist." *Colorado Libraries* 14 (June 1988): 27-28.

Provides nine guidelines for library skills instruction in school libraries.

Sampson, Anne. *Good Book Lookers; A 3-Week Introductory Module in the Language Arts to Further Independent Reading Among Third Graders.* ERIC Reproduction Center, 1988. ED 292056.

Describes a reading module for third graders to further library and other skills. Includes a sample library skills quiz.

Scarsbrook, Paul. "GCSE and the School Library." *School Librarian* 36 (August 1988): 92-94.

Describes a school library skills program in London, England. Gives videos on how to promote and sell the library to teachers and students.

Schiffman, Shirl S. "Influencing Public Education: A 'Window of Opportunity' through School Library Media Centers." *Journal of Instructional Development* 10 (1988): 41-44.

Suggests that instructional technology theory and practice can be introduced into public schools through school library media centers. The media specialist as change agent is described, and information literacy is discussed.

Sheppard, S. "Shaping Teacher-Librarian Teams for Library Use Instruction." *Illinois Librarian* 70 (December 1988): 664-669.

Shoham, Snunith. "Patterns of Bibliographic Searching among Israeli High School Students." *Library and Information Science Research* 10 (January 1988): 57-75.

Summarizes a study with Israeli high school students to discover their search process in bibliographic searching while looking at their comprehensive behavior. Relationship between search pattern and student characteristics was studied. Findings were varied.

Stripling, Barbara K., and Judy M. Pitts. *Brain-*

storms and Blueprints. *Teaching Library Research as a Thinking Process.* Englewood, CO: Libraries Unlimited, Inc., 1988.

This book focuses on library research skills in secondary education. It provides creative strategies and processes for teachers and media specialists to teach library research as a thinking process. A ten-step research process is outlined with skills, strategies, and activities to teach life long information skills.

Voran, Judith, et al. "Using Science Topics and Concepts to Teach Library Media Skills." *School Library Media Quarterly* 16 (September 1988): 182-186.

Discusses how library media specialists can teach a variety of library skills, help to raise intellectual curiosity, and provide satisfaction using science topics.

SPECIAL LIBRARIES

Bingham, K.H., and Abigail A. Loomis. "Library Instruction for Special User Groups." *Illinois Libraries* 70 (December 1988): 627-676.

Broering, Naomi C., et al. "Implementing RECONSIDER, a Diagnostic Prompting Computer System, at the Georgetown University Medical Center." *Bulletin of the Medical Library Association* 76 (April 1988): 155-158.

RECONSIDER, a computer program for diagnostic prompting developed at the University of California, San Francisco, has been implemented at the Georgetown University Medical Center. Instruction on use of the computer system is provided by the library and instruction on medical use of the knowledge base is directed by the faculty.

Burrell, Peggy. "Online Updates: A Column for Search Analysts." *Medical Reference Services Quarterly* 7 (1988): 55-59.

Describes a successful end-user program for MEDLINE at Providence Medical Center.

Chesley, T. "Library Instruction in Illinois Correctional Institutions." *Illinois Libraries* 70 (December 1988): 659-663.

Fick, Gary R. "Integrating Bibliographic Instruction into an Undergraduate Nursing Curriculum." *Bulletin of the Media Library Association* 6 (July 1988): 269-271.

Describes the library instruction program for nursing students at Seattle Pacific University in three increments.

Hubbard, Abigail. "Training Trainers." *Medical*

Reference Services Quarterly 7 (1988): 63-67.

Discusses, within the confines of medical libraries, who should be trainers and, once selected, how they should be trained.

Loomis, Abigail A., and K.H. Bingham. "Reaching Out: Library Instruction for Special User Groups; A Bibliography." *Illinois Libraries* 70 (December 1988): 670-676.

Reidelbach, Marie A., et al. "An Introduction to Independent Learning Skills for Incoming Medical Students." *Bulletin of the Medical Library Association* 76 (April 1988): 159-163.

Describes a fresh approach to educating medical students for independent information-seeking skills at the University of Nebraska.

Strube, Kathleen. "Teaching End Users How to Search the National Library of Medicine's Toxicology Databases." *Medical Reference Services Quarterly* 7 (1988): 31-37.

Describes an experiment at the Medical College of Wisconsin libraries to teach end-users searching the NLM's toxicology database. Fewer users were interested in this database compared to MEDLINE.

Villar, Susanne. "Survey of Map Library Outreach and User Education." *WASSN Map Library Information Bulletin* 19 (June 1988): 137-149.

Summarizes a survey of map collections in the United States to assess local map library outreach and user education.

Waddle, Linda. "School Media Matters." *Wilson Library Bulletin* 62 (January 1988): 67-78.

Describes a revision of a library instruction program for high school students to teach research paper and information skills for lifelong learning.

Welborn, Victoria. "End-User Programs in Medical School Libraries: A Survey." *Bulletin of the Medical Library Association* 76 (April 1988): 137-140.

Summarizes a survey to all medical school libraries to describe their end-user program and related instruction. The need for more equipment was identified.

Wesley Patton, William. "How Shepard's Citations Lost Its Flock: Or, Can the Police Smell Probable Cause? A Substantive Lesson Plan." *Law Library Journal* 80 (Winter 1988): 131-138.

Notes the difficulties involved in teaching law students the intricacies of research tools such as Shepard's Citations. Proposes a teaching exercise that illustrates how Shepard's works and the dangers of relying too much on the tool's editorial

devices.

Wren, Christopher G. "The Teaching of Legal Research." *Law Library Journal* 80 (Winter 1988): 7-61.

Asserts that the typical legal bibliography course is a curricular anomaly not designed to teach legal research. Analyzes the flaws of conventional legal bibliography instruction. Describes the structure of a course for teaching legal research and explains how the course benefits law students and teachers.

ALL TYPES

Cheny, Paul H., and R. Ryan Nelson. "A Tool for Measuring and Analysing User Computing Abilities." *Information Processing & Management* 24 (1988): 199-203.

Reports on the need for an instrument to measure computer user abilities and discusses an attempt to develop and evaluate one such instrument. The instrument was successfully tested for reliability using the Cronbach alpha test applied to inter-item scores.

Fatzer, Jill B. "The Future of Library Literacy." *RQ* 27 (Summer 1988): 484-486.

Discusses the future of library literacy in a traditional and an innovative library setting, particularly in terms of new technology.

Fatzer, Jill B., et al. "Toward Information Literacy in Ohio." *Journal of Academic Librarianship* 14 (May 1988): 76-78.

Summarizes librarians' efforts in Ohio since 1984 in addressing the issues discussed in *A Nation at Risk*. A report was issued in 1986 called "Promised for Success" that articulates information literacy needs in the educational community in Ohio.

Hammond, Nancy. "Interactive Video for User Education and Staff Training--Less Expensive Than You Think." *Audio Visual Librarian* 14 (February 1988): 36-37.

Discusses the use of interactive video and micros for library instruction.

Howden, Norman, and Bert R. Boyce. "The Use of CAI in the Education on Online Searchers." *Journal of Education for Library and Information Science* 28 (Winter 1988): 201-206.

The education of online searchers, while universal in library schools, appears to be in transition. A considerable shift to the use of microcomputer equipment has taken place, and software for computer-assisted instruction (CAI) and for supplementing access to vendor's systems is rapidly becoming part of the instructional scene.

Mellon, Constance. "Attitudes: The Forgotten Dimension in Library Instruction." *Library Journal* 113 (1 September 1988): 137-139.

Discusses two issues related to library instruction: people's feelings in trying to find information in libraries, and the gap between library instruction in K-12 and academic library use.

Rader, Hannelore B. "Library Orientation and Instruction--1987." *Reference Services Review* 16, no. 3 (1988): 57-68.

Rader presents the fourteenth annual review of library instruction literature.

Wittkopf, Barbara. "Bibliographic Instruction." In *ALA Yearbook of Library and Information Services*, ed. by Roger Parent, 68-69. Chicago: ALA, 1988.

Summarizes the 1987 ALA activities related to bibliographic instruction.

Participants

Roster of 1989 LOEX Conference Participants

Jean Alexander
Assistant Librarian
Schaffner Library
Northwestern University
339 E. Chicago Ave.
Chicago, IL 60611

Gail C. Anderson
Education Coordinator
Greenblatt Library
Medical College of Georgia
Augusta, GA 30912-4400

William Baker
King Library
Miami University
Oxford, OH 45056

Lois Beaty
Director, Library
Johnson State College
Johnson, VT 05656

Donna Bentley
Instructional Services
University Library
University of Nevada
Reno, NV 89557

Patricia Berge
Assistant Librarian
Science Library
Marquette University
560 N. 16th Street
Milwaukee, WI 53233

Karen Susan Bergin
Bibliographic Instruction
Woodhouse LRC
Aquinas College
1607 Robinson Rd, S.E.
Grand Rapids, MI 49506

Marilee Birchfield
User Education Librarian
University Library
Ohio State University
1858 Neil Avenue Mall
Columbus, OH 43210

Sherri Bisogno
Reference Librarian
Mansfield Campus Library
Ohio State University
1660 University Drive
Mansfield, OH 44906

Cheryl Blackwell
Bibliographic Instruction
Stockwell-Mudd Libraries
Albion College
602 E. Cass Street
Albion, MI 49224

Jean Bloodworth
Reference Librarian
Olin Library
Rollins College
1000 Holt Avenue
Winter Park, FL 32789

Dana Boden
Coord, Library Instruction
Helm-Craven Library
Western Kentucky University
Bowling Green, KY 42101

Carlene Bogle
BI Coordinator
University Library
Cal Poly-Pomona
3801 West Temple Avenue
Pomona, CA 91768

Morell D. Boone
Dean, Learning Resources
& Technologies
Eastern Michigan University
Ypsilanti, MI 48197

Mary Ellen Braafladt
BI Coordinator
College Library
College of St. Scholastica
1200 Kenwood Avenue
Duluth, MN 55811

Keitha Breault
University Library
Ferris State University
Big Rapids, MI 49307

Patricia Senn Breivik
Director, Auraria Libraries
Lawrence at 11th St.
Denver, CO 80204

Libbie Brooks
Coord, User Education
Main Library
University of Georgia
Athens, GA 30602

Nancy Broughton
Information Services
IMC
University of Wisconsin
225 N. Mills
Madison, WI 53706

Lucille Brown
BI Coordinator
Sojourner Truth Library
SUNY College of New Paltz
New Paltz, NY 12561

Renee Bush
Head, Reference
Science/Engineering Library
SUNY-Buffalo
Buffalo, NY 14260

Raymond Calvert
Reference Librarian
College Library
Manatee Community College
P.O. Box 1849
Bradenton, FL 34206

Doug Campbell
Director, Library
Northwestern Michigan College
Traverse City, MI 49684

Helen Carr
Reference Librarian
College Library
Montgomery College
Takoma Park & Fenton St.
Takoma Park, MD 20912

Sandra Cary
Public Service Librarian
Engelbrecht Library
Wartburg College
P.O. Box 1003
Waverly, IA 50677

Michele Cash
BI Coordinator
Schurz Library
Indiana Univ at South Bend
P.O. Box 7111
South Bend, IN 46635

Thomas Cashore
Online Search Coordinator
Love Library
University of Nebraska
Lincoln, NE 68588-0410

Jan Colter
Reference Librarian
Coutts Library
University of Alberta
Edmonton, Alberta T6G 2G5

Williams Coons
Information Literacy Spec.
Mann Library
Cornell University
Ithaca, NY 14853-4301

Jacquelyn Coughlin
Assistant Librarian
College Library
SUNY College of Technology
P.O. Box 3051
Utica, NY 13504

Carole Cragg
Reference Librarian
Bethel College LRC
3900 Bethel Drive
St. Paul, MN 55112

Peter Cupery
Science Reference Librarian
Univ of Wisconsin-Parkside
PO Box 2000
Kenosha, WI 53141

Donna Davidoff
Sr Assistant Librarian
Butler Library
Buffalo State College
1300 Elmwood Avenue
Buffalo, NY 14222

Bob Diaz
Assistant Librarian
Undergraduate Library
University of Michigan
Ann Arbor, MI 48109

Maria Dittman
Instruction Librarian
Memorial Library
Marquette University
1415 W. Wisconsin Avenue
Milwaukee, WI 53233

Jon Drabenstott
Assoc. Dean, Learning
Resources & Technologies
Eastern Michigan University
Ypsilanti, MI 48197

Linnea Dudley
Reference Librarian
Marygrove College Library
8425 W. McNichols Rd
Detroit, MI 48121

Carolyn Dusenbury
Director, Public Services
Meriam Library
California State University
Chico, CA 95929

Karen Dyson
Coord, Library Instruction
Paley Library
Temple University
Philadelphia, PA 19122

Phyllis Eisenberg
College Library
Piedmont Virginia Comm Coll
Route 6, Box 1A
Charlottesville, VA 22901

Susan Falgner
Head, Public Services
Archbishop Alter Library
College of Mt. St. Joseph
Mt. St. Joseph, OH 45051

Richard Feinberg
Coord, Library Instruction
Main Library
SUNY-Stony Brook
Stony Brook, NY 11794-3331

Lynne Fox
Instruction Librarian
Michener Library
University of Northern Colorado
Greeley, CO 80631

Polly Frank
BI Librarian
Memorial Library
Mankato State University
Box 19
Mankato, MN 56001

Paul Frantz
Coord, Library Instruction
University Library
University of Oregon
Eugene, OR 97403

Elaine Gawrych
Instruction Librarian
University Library
Northeastern Illinois Univ.
5500 N. St. Louis
Chicago, IL 60625

Barbara Geisey
Director
Wayne College LRC
University of Akron
10470 Smucker Rd
Orrville, OH 44667

Monica Ghosh
Coord, Library Instruction
University Library
Michigan State University
East Lansing, MI 48824

Kate Gibbons
Medical Reference Librarian
Virginia Commonwealth Univ
Richmond, VA 23284

Craig Gibson
Head, User Education
Holland Library
Washington State University
Pullman, WA 99164-5610

Deb Gilchrist
Bibliographic Instruction
Mortvedt Library
Pacific Lutheran University
Tacoma, WA 98447

Jan Glover
Medical Library
Yale University
333 Cedar Street
New Haven, CT 06510

Linda Goff
Library Instruction
University Library
California State University
2000 Jed Smith Drive
Sacramento, CA 95819-2696

Adrienne Granitz
Circulation Supervisor
College Library
Piedmont Virginia Comm Coll
Route 6, Box 1A
Charlottesville, VA 22901

Bonnie Gratch
Director, Information Services
University Libraries
Bowling Green State University
Bowling Green, OH 43403

Denise Green
Public Services
Beeghly Library
Ohio Wesleyan University
Delaware, OH 43015

Deborah Harris
Reference Librarian
College Library
Lansing Community College
419 N. Capitol Avenue
Lansing, MI 48911

Timothy Hartnett
Reference Librarian
Feinberg Library
SUNY-Plattsburgh
Plattsburgh, NY 12901

Rae Haws
BI Coordinator
Parks Library
Iowa State University
Ames, IA 50011

A. Heins
Jordan College Library
360 W. Pine
Cedar Springs, MI 49319

Judith Hesp
BI Coordinator
England Library
Philadelphia College of
Pharmacy & Science
42nd & Woodland Avenue
Philadelphia, PA 19104

Christy Hightower
Science Reference Librarian
University Library
Univ. of California-San Diego
La Jolla, CA 92093-0175

Levirn Hill
Assistant Librarian
Butler Library
Buffalo State College
1300 Elmwood Avenue
Buffalo, NY 14222

Beth Hoffer
Reference Librarian
Bradford College Library
S. Main Street
Bradford, MA 01833

Pat Hogan
BI Coordinator
Moellering Library
Valparaiso University
Valparaiso, IN 46383

Barbara Inglis
Assistant Librarian
Voskuyl Library
Westmont College
955 La Paz Road
Santa Barbara, CA 93108

Rebecca Jackson
BI Coordinator
Hornbake Library
University of Maryland
College Park, MD 20742

Raymond Jansen
University Library
Bradley University
1501 W. Bradley Avenue
Peoria, IL 61625

Louis Jeffries
Reference Librarian
University Library
Memphis State University
Memphis, TN 38152

Kathleen Jennings
Kirtley Library
Columbia College
Columbia, MO 65201

Miriam Joseph
Reference Librarian
Pius XII Memorial Library
Saint Louis University
3650 Lindell Blvd.
St. Louis, MO 63108

William Kane
Purdy Library
Wayne State University
Detroit, MI 48202

Linda Karch
Sr. Assistant Librarian
Health Sciences Library
SUNY-Buffalo
Abbott Hall
Buffalo, NY 14214

Kathy Kauffman
Associate Librarian
Good Library
Goshen College
Goshen, IN 46526

Jan Kennedy Olsen
Director
Mann Library
Cornell University
Itthaca, NY 13504

Jackie Kenyon
Director, Library
Jordan College
360 W. Pine
Cedar Springs, MI 49319

Kathryn Kerns
Reference Librarian
Meyer Memorial Library
Stanford University
Stanford, CA 94305-3093

Carolyn Kirkendall
IMC Librarian
University Library
Eastern Michigan University
Ypsilanti, MI 48197

Gary Klein
Business Specialist
Carlson Library
University of Toledo
2801 West Bancroft
Toledo, OH 43606-3390

Elen Knott
Reference Librarian
Reynolds Library
Wake Forest University
PO Box 7777, Reynolds Sta.
Winston-Salem, NC 27109

Lois Komai
Associate Librarian
Steenbock Library
University of Wisconsin
550 Babcock Drive
Madison, WI 53706

Michael Kruzich
BI Coordinator
Mardigian Library
Univ. of Michigan-Dearborn
Dearborn, MI 48128-1491

Judy Larson
Reference Librarian
Our Lady of the Lake Univ.
411 S.W. 24th St.
San Antonio, TX 78207

Gloria Lebowitz
Off-Campus Librarian
Central Michigan University
8550 Lee Hwy, Suite 125
Fairfax, VA 22031

Abigail Loomis
Coord, User Education
Memorial Library
University of Wisconsin
Madison, WI 53706

Frank McBride
Reference Librarian
Herrick Library
Alfred University
Alfred, NY 14802

P.J. McGinnis
Dulany Library
Williams Woods College
Fulton, MO 65251

William McHugh
Reference Librarian
Northwestern University
Evanston, IL 60208

Alice Mackov
User Education Librarian
Scott Memorial Library
Thomas Jefferson University
1020 Walnut Street
Philadelphia, PA 19107

Linda Makonnen
BI Coordinator
University Library
Ferris State University
Big Rapids, MI 49307

Patricia Mardeusz
Reference Librarian
Bailey/Howe Library
University of Vermont
Burlington, VT 05405

Gail Marredeth
Reference Librarian
University Library
Cleveland State University
1860 E. 22nd St.
Cleveland, OH 44115

Shirley Maul
BI Coordinator
Vassar College Library
Poughkeepsie, NY 12601

Sandy Maxfield
Information Services
Engineering & Science Library
Mass. Inst. of Technology
Cambridge, MA 02139

Glenn Mensching
Access Services Librarian
University Library
Eastern Michigan University
Ypsilanti, MI 48197

Teresa Mensching
Director, LOEX Clearinghouse
University Library
Eastern Michigan University
Ypsilanti, MI 48197

Wayne Meyer
Coord, Computer Search Serv.
Bracken Library
Ball State University
Muncie, IN 47306

Marguerite Mitchel
Director, Library
Stephens College
Columbia, MO 65202

Sylvia Newman
Reference Librarian
Science & Medicine Library
University of Toronto
7 King's College Circle
Toronto, Ontario M5S 1A5

Darlene Nichols
Undergraduate Library
University of Michigan
Ann Arbor, MI 48109

Nancy Niles
Bibliographic Instruction
Learning Resources Center
SUNY-Cobleskill
Cobleskill, NY 12043

Marsha Nolf
Bibliographic Instruction
Manderino Library
California University of Penn.
California, PA 15419

Pamela Pasak
BI Coordinator
University Libraries
University of Florida
Gainesville, FL 32611

Natalie Pelster
Reference Librarian
University Library
Northwestern University
Evanston, IL 60208

Martha Perry
Reader Services Librarian
Xavier University Library
3800 Victory Parkway
Cincinnati, OH 45207

Mary Jane Petrowski
Assistant Librarian
Undergraduate Library
University of Illinois
1407 W. Gregory Dr.
Urbana, IL 61801

Roger Phillips
Reference Librarian
University Library
Taylor University
Upland, IN 46989

Rosario Poli
Coord, User Education
University Library
Case Western Reserve Univ
11161 East Blvd.
Cleveland, OH 44106

Mary Popp
Head, Library Instruction
University Library
Indiana University
Bloomington, IN 47405

Bonnie Preston
BI Coordinator
College Library
Catonsville Community College
800 S. Rolling Rd
Baltimore, MD 21228

Dan Ream
Head, Reference Services
University Library
Virginia Commonwealth Univ
Richmond, VA 23284

Carol Reed
Bibligraphic Instruction
Carlson Library
University of Toledo
2801 West Bancroft
Toledo, OH 43606

Billie Joy Reinhart
Information Services
University Library
Cleveland State University
1860 E. 22nd St.
Cleveland, OH 44115

Kathryn Reynolds
Coord, Library Instruction
University Library
Wright State University
Dayton, OH 45435

Lori Ricigliano
Head, Reference
Univ. of Puget Sound Library
1500 N. Warner
Tacoma, WA 98416

Patricia Ridgeway
BI Coordinator
Van Pelt Library
University of Pennsylvania
3420 Walnut Street
Philadelphia, PA 19104-6206

Loretta Rielly
Coord, Library Instruction
University Libraries
Northern Illinois University
DeKalb, IL 60115

Ann Chamberlain Roseberry
Bibliographic Instruction
Millar Library
Portland State University
P.O. Box 1151
Portland, OR 97207

Sandra Rosenstock
Reference Librarian
Firestone Library
Princeton University
Princeton, NJ 08540

Phyllis Ruscella
BI Coordinator
University Library
University of Central Florida
Orlando, FL 32816-0666

Carole Schildhauer
Assistant Librarian for CE
Mass. Inst. of Technology
Bldg. 10-500
Cambridge, MA 02139

Marty Schlabach
Information Literacy Spec.
Mann Library
Cornell University
Ithaca, NY 14853-4301

Wesley Schram
Purdy/Kresge Library
Wayne State University
Detroit, MI 48202

D. Ross Sherwin
Bibliographic Instruction
Cameron Library
University of Alberta
Edmonton, Alberta T6G 2E1

Elizabeth Sibley
Curator, CCLI-North
University Library
University of California
Berkeley, CA 94720

Judith Sikora
Reference/Systems Librarian
College Library
Genesee Community College
Batavia, NY 14020

Timothy Smith
Instruction Librarian
Alden Library
Ohio University
Athens, OH 45701

William Snyder
User Education Librarian
Newark Campus Library
Ohio State University
Founders Hall
Newark, OH 43055

Judy Solberg
Library Instruction Liaison
Hornbake Library
University of Maryland
College Park, MD 20742

Keith Stanger
Access Services Librarian
University Library
Eastern Michigan University
Ypsilanti, MI 48197

Mary Stanley
Bibliographic Instruction
University Library
Indiana U-Purdue University
815 W. Michigan Street
Indianapolis, IN 46202

Jeanne Stevens
Reference Librarian
Macalester College Library
1600 Grand Avenue
St. Paul, MN 55105

Paula Storm
Science Librarian
Mardigian Library
Univ. of Michigan-Dearborn
Dearborn, MI 48128-1491

William Strickland
Reference Librarian
Howard-Tilton Memorial Library
Tulane University
New Orleans, LA 70118

Elizabeth Strother
Head, Dental Librarian
School of Dentistry Library
Louisiana State University
1100 Florida Avenue, Box 229
New Orleans, LA 70119

Dorothy Tao
BI Coordinator
Lockwood Library
SUNY-Buffalo
Buffalo, NY 14260

Hubert Thompson
Bibliographic Instruction
Library
Illinois Institute of Technology
3300 S. Federal Street
Chicago, IL 60616

Jean Thompson
Assistant Director
College Library
Middlesex Community College
100 Training Hill Rd.
Middletown, CT 06457

Theresa Tobin
Assistant Librarian
University Library
Mass. Inst. of Technology
Cambridge, MA 02139

Thomas Tollman
BI Coordinator
University Library
University of Nebraska
Omaha, NE 68182

Harold Tuckett
Coord, Automated Serv.
Undergraduate Library
University of Michigan
Ann Arbor, MI 48109

Barbara Valentine
User Education
Main Library
University of Georgia
Athens, GA 30605

Michael Van Houten
Head, Public Services
Stockwell-Mudd Libraries
Albion College
602 E. Cass Street
Albion, MI 49224

Alan Wallace
Bibliographic Instruction
University Library
University of Tennessee
Knoxville, TN 37996-1000

Angelo Wallace
Assistant Director
University Library
University of Toledo
Toledo, OH 43606

Mary Jane Walsh
BI Coordinator
Colgate University Library
Hamilton, NY 13346

James Ward
Director, Library
David Lipscomb College
Nashville, TN 37204-3951

Davin Weber
Instruction Librarian
University Library
Southern Alberta Inst.
of Technology
1301-16 Avenue, N.W.
Calgary, Alberta T2M 0L4

Janet Pursel Welch
Coord, User Education
Jerome Library
Bowling Green State Univ.
Bowling Green, OH 43403

Margaret Wells
Head, Bibliographic Instruction
Undergraduate Library
SUNY-Buffalo
Buffalo, NY 14260

Emily Werrell
Instructional Services
Steely Library
Northern Kentucky University
Highland Heights, KY 41076

Threasa Wesley
Coord, Instructional Services
Steeley Library
Northern Kentucky University
Highland Heights, KY 41076

Sharon West
Head, Information Access Serv.
Rasmuson Library
University of Alaska
Fairbanks, AK 99775

Marvin Wiggins
BI Coordinator
1124 Harold Lee Library
Brigham Young University
Provo, UT 84602

Cathleen Wild
Instructional Services
Lycoming College Library
Box 17
Williamsport, PA 17701

Karen Williams
Reference Librarian
University Library
University of Arizona
Tucson, AZ 85721

Linda Wilson
BI Coordinator
Virginia Tech Library
Blacksburg, VA 24061

Elaine Wright
Head, Information Services
Science & Medicine Library
University of Toronto
7 King's College Circle
Toronto, Ontario M5S 1A5

Kris Wycisk
Reference Librarian
Zimmerman Library
University of New Mexico
Albuquerque, NM 87131

Sandra Yee
Assistant Dean, Media &
Instructional Services
Eastern Michigan University
Ypsilanti, MI 48197

Victoria Young
Head, Readers Services
University Library
Xavier University
3800 Victory Parkway
Cincinnati, OH 45207

Mark Zussman
Reference Librarian
College Library
Lansing Community College
419 N. Capitol Avenue
Lansing, MI 48901

Diane Zwemer
Instruction Librarian
College Library
UCLA
Los Angeles, CA 90024